# Chicken Soup for the Soul®

# Tough Times for Teens

Chicken Soup for the Soul: Tough Times for Teens
*101 Stories about the Hardest Parts of Being a Teenager*
Jack Canfield, Mark Victor Hansen, Amy Newmark.
Published by Chicken Soup for the Soul Publishing, LLC    www.chickensoup.com

Front cover photo courtesy of Photos.com. Interior photo courtesy of iStockphoto.
com/Pixel_Pig (© Colleen Butler). Back cover photo courtesy of Thinkstock.

*Cover and Interior Design & Layout by Pneuma Books, LLC*
For more info on Pneuma Books, visit www.pneumabooks.com
Distributed to the booktrade by Simon & Schuster. SAN: 200-2442

### Publisher's Cataloging-in-Publication Data
*(Prepared by The Donohue Group)*

Chicken soup for the soul : tough times for teens : 101 stories about the
  hardest parts of being a teenager / [compiled by] Jack Canfield, Mark Victor
  Hansen, [and] Amy Newmark.

      p. ; cm.

  Summary: A collection of 101 true personal stories meant for older teenagers, written by teenagers and adults about tough times during their teenage years, including
substance abuse, sexual abuse, self-destructive behaviors, eating disorders, love gone
wrong, family problems, illness, and death of loved ones.
   Interest age group: 014-019.
   ISBN: 978-1-935096-80-1

   1. Teenagers--Conduct of life--Literary collections.  2. Teenagers--Conduct of life--
Anecdotes. I. Canfield, Jack, 1944- II. Hansen, Mark Victor. III. Newmark, Amy. IV.
Title: Tough times for teens

PN6071.T34 C48 2012
810.8/02/09283                              2011941746

PRINTED IN THE UNITED STATES OF AMERICA
on acid∞free paper
21 20 19 18 17 16 15 14 13 12          01 02 03 04 05 06 07 08 09 10

# Chicken Soup for the Soul®

# Tough Times fr Teers

101 Stories about the
Hardest Parts of Being a Teenage

Jack Canfield
Mark Victor Hansen
Amy Newmark

Chicken Soup for the Soul Publishing, LLC
Cos Cob, CT

Chicken Soup

www.chickensoup.com

for the Soul

# Contents

**❸**

# ~Friendship in a Time of Need~

**❹**

# ~My Own Worst Enemy~

**❺**

# ~Sticks and Stones~

**❻**

# ~Grieving~

**❼**

# ~Silver Linings~

**8**

## ~Family~

**9**

## ~Love Gone Wrong~

**⑩**
## ~Second Chances~

# introduction

Let's start with a warning. This book contains material for older teenagers. A book about tough times for teens inevitably will contain stories about mature subjects that may not be suitable for younger teens. The stories in this book may upset young readers, as teens just like them recount their tales of mental illness, sexual abuse, gender identity issues, eating disorders, untimely deaths, and other difficult events in their lives.

For older teens, this book may be just what you need. If you are going through a difficult time, perhaps you will feel less alone, or see a solution, in this book. Perhaps it will encourage you to seek help or comfort, as did so many of the teens who contributed their personal stories to help other kids. Or it will help you understand what a sibling is going through, or what might be going on with that quiet kid who sits alone at lunch or that popular girl you heard sobbing quietly in the bathroom one morning. Maybe you are that quiet kid who sits alone at lunch and this book will give you the little push you need to turn things around, or at least to feel like you're not the only one.

Being a teenager is exciting but it is also hard. Everyone has ups and downs during these years. The kids in this book have had it worse than most teens, and they are unselfishly sharing their stories with you to comfort you, and give you some useful advice too. These stories should help you understand yourselves, understand your peers and family members, and help all of you through these challenging but potentially gratifying years as you mature into adults.

~Amy Newmark

# Tough Times for Teens

**Chapter 1**

## Bravery

# Winning Life Back

*Who will tell whether one happy moment of love or the joy of breathing or*
*walking on a bright morning and smelling the fresh air,*
*is not worth all the suffering and effort which life implies.*
*~Erich Fromm*

While the majority of my senior class was getting ready for prom—which I was told was the biggest, most important moment of one's high school life—I was preparing for a much different event. A bigger and more important moment in my life than prom would ever be.

I was about to undergo a second back surgery.

From the time I was fourteen, I sort of felt like Benjamin Button, except that my elderliness was internal rather than external. Whenever I went to see the spine doctor I was always sitting amongst exclusively silver and gray-haired patients. I think the closest patient to my age was at least forty years older than me. Yeah, you can say I felt out of place.

When it came to school, life was beyond excruciating. High school was an incredibly self-conscious period and having to wear a hard plastic back brace that highly resembled a corset and made you look as though you possessed a duck tail whenever you bent over didn't make it any easier. It sounds weird when I put it this way, but drugs made my school life miserable as well. I was on the hard-core stuff that most addicts wished they had, stuff like vicodin, percocet, oxycontin, oxycodone, etc. I had to choose between dealing with sheer agony or feeling as though there were a million cotton balls stuffed into my brain after I took the medication. There was no happy medium. Life was awful and I never thought my suffering would end.

At age seventeen, only a year and a half after my first back surgery, I was already heading for number two. My first one failed because the fusion did not take place in my L4 and L5, which subsequently caused two of my four titanium screws to crack completely in half. Apparently, only one percent of all patients who get the surgery crack one screw and I cracked two! Of course this was happening to me. With these odds you'd think I'd have had a good shot at winning the lottery!

I had my surgery in May, during the home stretch of my senior year. It was a brutal race to get all my credits done before graduation, especially since this was a much more invasive surgery; the surgeon went through my stomach and replaced my disc with a cadaver bone and then replaced all four of the screws in my back. He also extracted some bone marrow from my right hip. The other challenge was that the only credit I really needed was math because I skipped out on it the previous year while I was out of school for three months after my first surgery. Let me tell you something, trying to complete your pre-calculus homework after surgery on oxycodone sucks! In all honesty, I don't remember much about that hectic month other than it was incredibly stressful.

My goal at the beginning of my freshman year was to graduate as Valedictorian, and nothing less. I used to judge myself so hard when I didn't meet my own expectations. I felt like the world's biggest failure. I was failing my doctors because I could never seem to will my body into healing itself and I was failing myself because I wasn't attaining the grades that I so desperately wanted. I was forced to take a hard look at my life and reevaluate my expectations.

Life is about winning, but who said there was only one definition for the term? My stubborn and misguided fourteen-year-old freshman self would have told you that "winning," meant getting straight A's no matter what. It meant being the absolute best. I'll have to admit that I agree with one part of that statement—you should strive to be the absolute best, strive for *your* absolute best. When life throws you a curveball don't shrink from it. Sure the bat may tremble in your hands, but you swing that bat full and hard, and show the world you are a force to be reckoned with.

When I stepped off that stage at the end of senior year—taking my diploma with me—I didn't think about the fact that I wasn't Valedictorian. I thought about what I had accomplished and how proud I was that despite my challenges I put my best foot forward. I was definitely a winner in that moment and couldn't wait to see what came next in my already incredible life.

~Amanda Yancey

# The Survivor

*The soul would have no rainbow had the eyes no tears.*
~John Vance Cheney

I sunk down a little deeper into the bathtub, pushing my head under the red water. I held myself there for as long as I could stand before sitting up, gasping for breath. I sighed as I grabbed the sharpest thing close to me; this time, it was a razor. I pressed it against my skin and took a deep breath as I slid it against the outside of my arm. I watched as the deep crimson blood came to the surface and I let loose the tears that I had held for such a long time. This became my nightly ritual.

Each night, I cut myself countless times in that same old, white bathtub. Each night I prayed for the memories to go away as I scrubbed my body clean of him.

I was raised inside a very emotional family. When my little sister died, my older sister and I became the rocks of the family. My dad provided the money, while my sister and I provided the love and support both of us so desperately needed ourselves. Even to this day, I can't express emotions correctly for fear that I will be seen as "weak." Blow after blow came to the family, but I tried not to cry as everything crumbled around me.

Around the time of my little sister's death, my Aunt Pat and Uncle Greg stepped up to the plate, acting as second parents. They took us wakeboarding, cooked for us, and generally acted like the best parents I could ask for. My uncle was a second-degree black belt and taught me self-defense. They supported us and loved us when our parents weren't able to. I created a very close bond with my aunt and uncle. They were our protectors.

Everything changed after I moved to Indiana.

In Indiana, I became a young teenager, but I was anything but bright eyed and bushy tailed. In fact, around the time I became a teenager, I developed severe anxiety and depression. I felt alone in my new environment and I had few friends. I was angry and mean to nearly everyone. I was soon diagnosed with depression and placed on antidepressants.

And soon after that, my entire world was wrecked again.

I traveled to Virginia for my new little cousin's baby shower, the daughter of my only aunt and uncle, my beloved second parents. That night, I couldn't sleep. I barely thought about it as I climbed into bed between my aunt and uncle because, even as a troubled preteen, I would crawl into their extra large bed to rest until I could fall asleep. It was an odd behavior, but it gave me comfort. That night, however, went all wrong.

I woke up to something horrible. I was instantly alert but lay there, absolutely frozen, not willing to believe what was happening.

My uncle was clearly awake and he was touching me all over my body. I could've screamed, but stayed completely silent. I was terrified as he continued to molest me. I had heard stories of people being threatened or hurt if their molesters knew they were awake, so I kept my eyes shut, praying for it to go away, to stop. Wishing to myself that this was just a dream, a nightmare I couldn't wake up from. My uncle touched me everywhere as my skin crawled and I wanted to scream and cry. He kept going exactly where he pleased, only stopping when he heard my mother, an insomniac, climbing the stairs. I was so terrified that I inched closer to my aunt's side of the bed and prayed that he wouldn't come closer. I couldn't leave the bed for such intense fear that he would know I was awake during what he did, so I stayed absolutely still next to my aunt, waiting for the morning to come.

I left for home the very next day, alone. My mom had no clue what had gone on, and I begged my sister to come get me in the car at 6 a.m. instead of letting my uncle drive me to the airport. She agreed and I felt the greatest relief as I left my uncle behind.

I got home and fell apart. I started a dangerous habit of cutting and burning myself to forget. My dad was always working, so he didn't notice how depressed I was becoming. When my mom came home, she noticed almost immediately, but I was too ashamed to tell her what happened. I felt like the molestation was my fault and that she wouldn't believe me or understand. I finally told my counselor, who helped me break it to my mom. Telling someone was the hardest thing I ever had to do.

I'm not going to say that things became easy after I told my secret, because they didn't. I continue to go to a therapist weekly to deal with my Post Traumatic Stress Disorder (PTSD) and I still have nightmares and flashbacks. But now, I have the support I need. My family surrounded me with love and help. My mother is also a sexual assault survivor, and she believed me instantly, as did the rest of my family. It took a lot of adjustment. I still had trouble with friends who didn't understand and I had a lot of trouble with relationships. I had a lot of boyfriends who didn't last very long, and I was very sensitive to their advances. I couldn't handle much affection.

Needless to say, I was needy and sensitive to almost everything, but I survived. My family and friends gave me the support I needed to make it through. While I felt constantly battered, I was never alone. I always had someone to listen to me cry and, some day, I will get past this.

~Abby Moriarty

# Reflections in an Empty Pool

*If you can find a path with no obstacles, it probably doesn't lead anywhere.*
~Frank A. Clark

For the first time in my life I felt as though I wanted to jump out of my body. It was useless and I was helpless. The roar of the crowd had somehow faded into a dissonant hum swirling over my head. I was lost in my own mind, a very lonely and unforgiving place.

Less than a year ago, everything had changed. I was in a terrible car accident. Although barely breathing, I was told I was lucky to be alive after the crash.

Alive? Maybe. Living? I'm not so sure.

After the accident, I was forced to become a spectator of the thing I loved most: swimming. Less than a year before, I had made the varsity squad for the third consecutive season and I had set my sights for the big State meet. However, someone else had other plans for me.

I knew I had come a long way from that bloody pavement and that I had survived for a reason, but it was torture. As my teammates swam, I looked longingly at my legs as though they were a pair of friends who had betrayed me.

The accident had left me paralyzed, with no use of my legs, my hips, or most of my trunk. I felt more lifeless and flaccid each day. As I watched I tried not to pay attention to who was swimming or what her time was. I knew that I could have beaten many of them and that left me sinking deeper and deeper into my shiny new wheelchair.

As the meet ended, I gave high-fives and hugs to my almost-forgotten teammates. They were exhausted, hungry, and complaining. Oh, how I longed to be them. Any of them—even Beth with the zits and Lauren with the bad grades. Those things you could fix. What could you do with a paralyzed sixteen-year-old wannabe swimmer in a wheelchair?

Call it naïveté, call it adolescence, or call it just plain stupidity. Whatever the case, there was no question in my mind as the swim season was being posted in the school halls that I was going to swim too, just as I had every year before. I hadn't really been back in the water much since my accident, but I wasn't really willing to look at what my life might look like without it. So, I signed up and made an open-ended, conscious decision to ignore the fact that I wasn't totally sure how my new body would fare as a swimmer, not to mention a regular high school student.

Surprisingly, I found out right away that my body could float. Much like my spirit, I wasn't going to be brought down easily or without a fight.

I had spent dozens of weeks lying in a hospital bed, counting dents in the ceiling and peeling away scabs on my knuckles. Those weeks, although important to my overall healing, led to a complete deterioration of my muscles. I couldn't even lift my own head off the starched and bleached synthetic pillow to request more morphine. By the time I was well enough to sit up in a wheelchair, I could barely flex my leftover muscles enough to push myself in a wheelchair.

However, in a matter of only a few months, I was stronger simply from activities like showering and getting into a car, and with that, I decided I was strong enough to swim.

That first day of practice was wretched. Being named a member of the lowest level swim group for the first time in my life was the least of my worries. I peered from my chair at the water and realized I didn't even know how to get in.

With a lot of help and a lot of pride-swallowing, I was lifted into the pool by my coaches and teammates. The icy chill of the chlorinated pool felt like magic. My legs looked alive and dancing as I gazed down into the lap lane. I was in the water, and nothing in the entire universe was going to stop me from swimming—not the cold, nor my own body.

From that day forward, I pushed myself farther and farther each day. Going from fifteen-minute practice sessions, to almost the entire allotted hour, I wasn't going to let my newly challenged exterior get in my way.

I didn't realize it then, but the moment I had my teammates lower me into that pool was a catalyst for my journey, and the instant when I found myself. I recognized the battle I faced and decided I needed to fight for my life, and to make it something great.

Without the accident, without the struggle, without the fear of having it all snatched away from me, I would have truly never found myself and found what everything means to me today. Through this experience, and others like it, I have found the world, and it is mine to keep.

~Ryan Rae McLean

# The Beauty of imperfection

*Our strengths grow out of our weaknesses.*
*~Ralph Waldo Emerson*

I was born healthy, with fingers and toes intact. At two weeks of age, I began to develop a type of vascular birthmark called a hemangioma, a benign tumor made up of rapidly growing blood vessels. Mine became very extensive, and covered my entire lower lip, much of the left side of my neck and both sides of my face.

If I were to submit a résumé of medical procedures, beginning at thirteen months and extending to the present, the list would be quite lengthy: Nine months of daily injections of interferon as a baby, eleven surgeries, and seven laser treatments to date. Needless to say, the cycle of surgery and recovery has been strenuous, but the most difficult part has been enduring the insensitive comments of others, and learning to accept myself in spite of them. People often ask, "Did you burn yourself?" or "What is that ugly purple stuff on your face?" Others would point and whisper, "Oh, look, it's the girl with the birthmark." A lump would form in my throat each time I heard comments like these from adults and children alike. And each time, I died a little inside.

I began to realize that I had two options: I could either withdraw into myself, or I could summon the courage to open myself up—to demystify and educate others about vascular birthmarks. I chose the second path. I became involved with the Vascular Birthmarks Foundation, "an international charitable organization that provides support and information to people affected by hemangiomas, port wine stains, and other vascular birthmarks...." By age thirteen, I began moderating a teen discussion forum on their website at www. birthmark.org. In this way, I was able to connect with and give advice to other teens struggling with vascular birthmarks.

I finally realized that I could use my vascular birthmark as a strength by reaching out to others. And in helping others, I was healing myself as well. As a freshman in high school, in order to increase awareness about vascular birthmarks, I designed turquoise silicone bracelets inscribed with the message I coined, "Courage—Confidence—VBF" and sold them in my local community as well as worldwide on their website. I personally raised over $5,000, which was used towards research. This fundraiser inspired a subsequent campaign, called "Kids Who Care," in which children across the country sell bracelets in their communities during the month of May to support "National Birthmark Awareness Day" on May 15th. I was later nominated and elected by the VBF board to serve as the youngest board member in their history. I am their Student Representative.

Today, I like to think of myself as a typical seventeen-year-old girl even though getting to this stage in my life has been anything but typical. Though I would not have chosen my vascular birthmark, it has implanted in me a responsibility to make the world more accepting and tolerant, and in this way, it has become my greatest strength. Although my journey was a rough one at times, I believe that it has made me a strong, sensitive, and compassionate person—it has allowed me the ability to truly empathize with others, and to create hope for those who have not yet realized the beauty of their imperfections.

~Saige Falyn Cavayero

# i Can Be Happy

*You have to leave the city of your comfort and go
into the wilderness of your intuition. What you'll discover will be wonderful.
What you'll discover is yourself.*
~Alan Alda

"So, I'm a guy, like, 100% dude. But... I was born in a girl's body. I'm an FTM, female to male transgender." These are the words of Adam, the first scripted transgender teen television character, my favorite character on the teen drama *Degrassi*.

You might be wondering why that was my first line to open this up. You may understand it already. But that line, that poorly worded, very scripted line, describes me. Yes, me.

Hi, my name is Jonah Daniel. I am fifteen years old. I am transgender.

•••

On May 17th, a happy, bubbly, cute little baby girl is born. Liza Deanna, her parents call her. The little girl seems as normal as any other baby girl. Seemingly content with life. And she is, until a few years later, when she realizes there has been a horrible mistake.

Later on, the girl sometimes wears pink and dresses. But her favorite color varies from blue, to black, to green, almost never straying into the pinks or purples. She plays with dolls alone, pretending to be the daddy. She finds her mind often wandering, drifting away to a land where she is no longer she, but he. Where he wears baggy T-shirts and long shorts, plays with trucks, and plays sports. But then he realizes, this is not reality. And she sits there, hoping that God decides to listen in: "I want to be a boy. I want to wake up tomorrow and be a boy."

Two years later, the girl is taking a walk with her sister, discussing her best friend, Michelle.

"Is it normal to tell her I love her?" she asks, confused about the feelings she has towards her.

"It's normal to say you love her like a sister," her sister replies.

But it doesn't feel like that kind of love.

A year later, the girl starts overnight camp. There, she meets a girl named Julia. Julia is the coolest person the girl has ever met. Julia is funny, smart, nice, good at sports... and Julia wears boys' clothes.

The girl didn't know this was even possible. If you're a girl, you wear girl clothes, and if you're a boy, you wear boy clothes. So when the girl gets home, she asks her mom to shop in the boys department. Her mom agrees without hesitation, but the girl feels awkward about it. Most girls don't do this, she's sure. And then she realizes that she really and truly feels like she is a boy.

Two years later, the girl is at a new private school. She wears her boys' clothes and hangs out with her friends. She is absolutely obsessed with a girl in her grade. She starts to get curious. The girl knows that it's possible to like someone the same sex as you, proven to her by her two aunts. But this girl likes guys, she's sure. She looks on the Internet, and finds that it's possible to be something called bisexual, which is where you like both boys and girls. Finally, the girl thinks to herself, I know what I am.

The girl is incredibly depressed. She hates herself; she hates her life. She hates everything. The girl is put into a psychiatric hospital where she is put on medications and made to go in groups that make her feel better for short periods of time. The girl goes in and out of the hospital for years.

Two years later, the girl comes out as bisexual to her family and close friends. But that doesn't feel quite right. So she thinks about it some more, considering her options of what to come out as, and decides that she's not bisexual, that she is gay.

The girl comes out to the world.

On a website where people ask you questions, multiple people ask her if she is transgendered.

"What does that mean?" she answers. "I've always been a girl, if that's what you're asking..." But the girl starts to get more and more confused. What does transgender mean? She looks into it more and finds out—you are one sex, but you feel like the other. Finally, she thinks. This is the right one. This is me.

She lives in pain for a while longer. She is so uncomfortable with her body. Showers and baths are painful experiences, until she starts taking her baths in a bra and underwear.

That summer, the girl heads off to her overnight camp for her last summer there. Being around the boys so much, she gets jealous that they have the life she wants. Being around the girls so much, she gets depressed, wanting to be happy in her body. She wants to be anyone but herself.

Then the girl makes a decision. I am going to transition, she says to herself. When I get home, I'm going to be a boy. The girl calls her mom and tells her this decision. Her mom doesn't seem to like the idea, but she's not protesting. She says she has to do some research, and learn more about this. Over time, she becomes more and more supportive and accepting of the idea.

A week later, the girl needs to leave camp. There is too much going on in her head, and she needs help with it. The transgender stuff is too much. She needs help.

• • •

Fast forward a few months to the present. The girl is no longer a girl named Liza, but a boy named Jonah—me. I go to a public school where they make accommodations for my bathroom use, make sure the teachers use the correct name and male pronouns, and have many supports put in place for when I need them. Everyone knows I am transgender, and I am the talk of the school for a short amount of time. I don't hide my identity. I am what I am, and I am strong to show and embrace it.

But I'm still not happy. I may be living the life of a boy, but I'm still not a boy. Not biologically. No matter what surgery I undergo, I will still be a transgender person. I will never be just a boy.

This lands me in the psychiatric hospital, where I have already been numerous times. In the hospital, I spend a week and a half repeating the same statements over and over again.

"I don't want to be happy. I want to be dead."

"There's nothing you can do for me."

"I don't want help, so why are you wasting your time trying?"

And so on and so forth.

Through some combination of medications and positive thinking, though, something changes in me. I am happy again. I am not happy with the brain and body that God gave me—I never will be. But I can be a happy person, I realize. I have so much going for me—the most supportive family and friends I could ask for. I'm a funny person, nice and caring about others. I have so many positive traits, and so many people who care. And so, with the support of all of these people, I share my story.

~Jonah Miller

# Light at the End of the Tunnel

*Even our misfortunes are a part of our belongings.*
~*Antoine de Saint-Exupéry,* Night Flight

When I was five years old, my older cousin James molested me. Today, I can roll this word—molested, molested, molested—around in my head, and accept the fact that this is what happened to me. Before I met my delightful counselor, Bethany, we never used this word. My parents always referred to the incident as "that awful thing that happened when I was five."

For years, like most victims, I thought what had happened to me was my fault. Five isn't that young, I'd think to myself. I could have prevented what happened; I should have been stronger. The stress of these feelings had consequences, and I developed habits such as tearing out my eyelashes and eyebrow hair.

I began plucking my eyelashes near the end of second grade—around the time that I confessed the molestation to my mother—and then slowly stopped at the end of eighth grade. But the first time I ever went to a psychologist was when I was eight years old. The therapist's name was Barbara, and I never found her to be very helpful. I saw her Tuesday of every week for two years, and my stomach coiled like a spring, hard and tight each time, before I walked into her office. I always felt as though I was in trouble when I went to see her. Barbara would scrutinize me as she sat, legs crossed, on her brown leather chair, asking if I'd finally stopped picking my eyelashes. I hadn't. Eventually, I told my mother that seeing this psychologist was doing nothing for me and so we left Barbara.

Years later I was able to stop pulling out my hair and thought that I had finally healed, but around age eighteen I started noticing that I had abnormal behavior toward men. The clues began to click into place after I took a psychology class in high school. I learned that everything that happened to a person during their childhood was critical to how they developed as an adult. My mind flashed from one image to the next: a kaleidoscope of sight, sound, and smell, as I unraveled the Band-Aid over the thirteen-year-old wound. I realized that anytime I was alone with an older man, my pulse quickened and I immediately felt nauseous; this included uncles or my friends' dads, people I trusted.

It all led back to James.

It occurred to me that I needed help, and that was the first major step in my recovery. My mom took me to Bethany for the first time, and she had a maternal quality that put me at ease. Instead of telling her my problems on the first day, Bethany and I discussed my entire life story, so that she could get a clear picture of who I was. By the time we got caught up to my current situation and how I felt about James now, I learned what I still felt after all these years was guilt. I broke down into tears, and Bethany gave me advice: "Write a letter to James, explaining to him how he has hurt you, but don't send it."

The following day I made a goal to write that dreaded letter. I'll admit that at first I was scared to write to James, even though I knew I'd never send it, but once I sat down and pressed the red pen to the crumpled pages of my notebook, I was stunned by how easily the words flowed. By the conclusion of the letter, I discovered I was no longer guilty. Instead I was angry—angry because this one horrible event seemed to dictate my entire life. James had messed everything up! Because of him, I resorted to picking out my eyelashes to relieve the stress I felt day to day and I was terrified of men older than me. I was furious. How could I trust someone to be my boyfriend, if my own cousin—a person I idolized—had turned out to be so untrustworthy?

When I finished writing down how I felt, I sobbed into my pillow and then screamed at the top of my lungs. It felt good to let all that bottled emotion out.

A few weeks later, something amazing happened. I was a quarter of the way through my fall term in college and I met this really wonderful guy named William in my English class. We were placed in a reading group together—which I was very pleased about because I found him exceptionally charming during our class discussions—and we got along right away. Not only did we joke, but we also engaged in some deep conversations, and the best part about it all was that I wasn't having any anxiety issues. For the first time I was able to function like a normal human being!

I will never forget the day when I finally saw the light at the end of the tunnel, and knew deep down in my heart that things were going to change for the better. I had a habit of hanging out near my classroom thirty minutes before it began, and as I rounded the corner on this particular day, I saw Will. Three chairs lined the wall near the classroom door and he sat in the one on the far left. My heart gave a jolt, but not from fear. I took a seat in the right one, leaving a chair in between us, because I was still cautious. We easily struck up a conversation and began joking around once again. Then he did something that would put my anxiety issues to the test. He grabbed his backpack and jacket, stood up from his chair, and sat in the middle one, right next to me! I was stunned by how relaxed I felt about this situation. I wanted to talk to him for hours. It was like nothing I'd ever experienced before and I was secretly reveling in it.

The next time I saw Bethany I was glowing with elation. For the first time in my life, tears of happiness coursed down my face when I told her the news. It was a great moment.

I want other girls out there to know that being molested is hard, and no doubt changes one's life forever, but it does not have to dictate your life. You are responsible for creating your life the way you want it to be, and once you know this, you can overcome any obstacle life throws at you.

~Schuyler Newberg

# Chicken Soup for the Soul

# Ginger Beer

*Nobody can make you feel inferior without your consent.*
*~Eleanor Roosevelt*

My teacher, Miss Wallace, stood beside the bench in the science lab. She held a beaker in one hand as she explained the procedures of a chemistry experiment to a small group of students. I leaned against the bench and focused my attention on her hand as it moved towards another beaker filled with an acidic liquid.

But instead of continuing the experiment, her hand paused in midair and she glanced at me.

"I heard you were in the cross-country race yesterday," she said.

I nodded and smiled. I hadn't come in first, but I was proud of my efforts.

Her mouth twisted into a sneer. "So how did you do? Did you actually manage to finish the race?"

Sarcasm laced her voice. And then she sniggered as if she had made an amusing joke.

I frowned in bewilderment. Then my cheeks flushed with warmth as I stared at her in shock. I knew what she referred to—it was my weight. My figure was chubby, not athletic. I enjoyed running, but she obviously didn't think I could run three miles. Her words were like the acid in the beaker: they burned.

"Of course I finished the race," I said softly. I swallowed several times and pushed back my tears. Why was she humiliating me?

After the chemistry lesson, my friend Kate took me aside. She had overheard the teacher's comments, and she shook her head in disbelief. "Yesterday in class, when you weren't there, Miss Wallace asked where you were. I told her you were in the cross-country race." She stopped and looked at me with sympathetic eyes. "Miss Wallace also laughed about you then—in front of the whole class, and she said you wouldn't ever be able to finish the race."

A blanket of shame crept over me in that moment; I felt ashamed of my body and ashamed that I'd attempted that race. What had I been thinking?

Kate squeezed my arm. "I told Miss Wallace that you were a good runner—of course you would finish. She should never have said that yesterday... or today."

I smiled with appreciation at my friend, but battled even harder to keep my emotions locked down.

It wasn't the first time people had made rude comments in reference to my weight. I was only about one stone (fourteen pounds) overweight, but it didn't stop some people from looking my way and occasionally spitting out names such as, "Fat Pig! Lump of fat!" or saying, "You're nothing but a fatty!" My nature was to be shy and gentle, and those words stung. I never provoked anyone and didn't deserve those cruel remarks.

Added to this were difficulties at home: my father was in the midst of a nervous breakdown, my older brother behaved like a wild maniac due to a drug problem, and my mother was constantly exhausted from full-time work to support our family. She was the glue that held the family together and I didn't want to burden her with any more problems. And anyway, the thought of even speaking my troubles aloud caused me to cringe with embarrassment.

Several years before, when I was a child, my mother attempted to concoct homemade ginger beer. Yeast was the vital ingredient, of which she added a little extra—she thought it would help. The bottles were placed in the basement of the house, to give them time to brew, until one night our sleep was shattered by an almighty BANG! And another BANG! And yet another BANG! Were we under attack?

No, we weren't. The ginger beer bottles were exploding from the overdose of yeast.

I felt like one of those bottles: full to the brim with emotions, and about to explode. And written across the label of my bottle was one word: Worthless.

Later, when I was nineteen years old, somebody handed me a teaching tape on the topic of forgiveness. "Forgiveness doesn't justify the actions of the person who wronged you," the voice on the tape said. "Forgiveness releases you from bitterness and helps you to move on with your life. It brings freedom."

Miss Wallace's face appeared in my mind. I remembered sad blue eyes peering at the class while she taught. Her figure was plump and soft curves jiggled as she moved around the science lab—she was double my size. I suddenly sensed that Miss Wallace was also like a bottle of ginger beer; emotional pain was stuffed deep inside her, and some of it leaked out the day she ridiculed me in public. Her mockery was wrong, but instead of anger, I now felt pity.

"I choose to forgive her," I whispered in the silence of my bedroom. I made it my prayer.

After I made my choice to forgive, I began to collect affirming words from friends, whether written by them on cards, scraps of paper, e-mails, or scribbled down in my own hand so I wouldn't forget what they said. These encouragements were bound with a rubber band inside a shoebox and sometimes scrapbooked. On days when discouragement came knocking, I'd pull out these words and remind myself that, yes, I am valued. One day, I hope Miss Wallace discovers this too.

~Louise Johnstone

# A Lonely Astronaut

*Always be a first-rate version of yourself,*
*instead of a second-rate version of somebody else.*
~Judy Garland

Here's the formula for being young and gay as portrayed by TV, books, and movies: Take an extremely troubled gay teenager, alone with nobody to talk to about his/her feelings. Eventually, s/he comes out by either 1) Confiding in someone who ends up blabbing to the entire school or 2) Kissing someone of the same sex, which is seen by someone who then blabs to the entire school. In both cases, everyone knows the poor kid's sexuality but it's all good in the end because (mostly) everyone is all right with it and s/he ends up meeting a whole bunch of other gay kids and nabbing a boyfriend/girlfriend in the process as some sort of reward. The end.

True to life, right?

Not quite. I first came out to my friends when I was fourteen. Like any other coming out, it was difficult. While we were hanging out one summer day, I told my two friends (both girls) I had something really important to tell them but couldn't say the words myself. I ended up making my friends guess my secret, and one of them eventually did.

Once I knew I had the support of my friends and felt more

comfortable with myself, I took to exploring the life of gay youth everywhere—I read page after page about Nelson and Kyle's strong friendship in Alex Sanchez's novel, *Rainbow Boys*, wondering when my spontaneous friendship with a guy at school was going to happen. I waited for someone to come up to me and say, "I know you're gay. Let's be friends!" I watched the *Degrassi* character Marco get together with his über-crush Dylan and dreamed of the day the boy I was infatuated with would even notice me (it never happened). These books and TV shows were all I ever knew of being young and gay in the world, and they were the only source I saw as truth.

So I waited patiently for all of that to happen to me. Or maybe just some of it.

Over the next few years, I would slowly come out to siblings, other friends, and finally, parents. But still, I had no gay friends, and no crush asking me out. I live in Vancouver, Canada, a fairly open and diverse city, but I didn't know a single other "out" student in my grade. My friend Chelsea would ask what I wanted for my birthday, and I used to tell her, "a boyfriend." But all I really wanted was someone—a gay boy like myself—with whom I could talk about all this stuff. I didn't feel like it was too much to ask for.

Don't get me wrong. Having supportive friends who were girls was fantastic, and I couldn't have asked for better friends, but I felt as though they could only relate and offer so much sympathy. To talk to someone who was going through the same things I was going through—that was what I wanted. Genuine empathy.

I would soon discover that the idea that all gay people got along and were friends was a myth. I helped form the Gay-Straight Alliance at my high school, and attended a couple of drop-ins at a gay youth centre downtown. However, in both cases, I felt out of place either sitting silently and uncomfortably in a room with straight girls and (I think) lesbians, or among the teens who chatted like longtime friends. I felt like a different kind of gay species altogether.

Once I opened the closet door, I expected it to be like walking into a party and meeting others just like myself—that through the act of coming out, people would be able to hear my call somehow.

But when you make the enormous effort to reveal such a big part of yourself to others and nothing really changes and no one seems to be out there, what do you do? All of a sudden, the TV shows, books, and movies I had read and watched with dreamy eyes were almost mocking me: "Normal gay people can find each other, but you're just a loser and you'll always be alone."

I felt like an astronaut, calling out into space, the words falling into black silence. I searched for life, and even when I found it, I felt as alien as ever. It's a catch-22. If you don't look for people, you may not find them. But if you do call out and find nothing, you may feel even lonelier. So I continued searching, trying to ignore the ache that lingered.

It wouldn't be right to end this story on a bleak note. In the words of Dan Savage, it gets better. After high school, I did meet a lot of gay people — through volunteering and mutual friends — and I eventually did have a couple of relationships. My calls were answered, despite the long time it took to do so. And although I'll probably never have as many close gay friends as the guys on *Queer As Folk*, if gay youth today can find community and avoid loneliness, I'm glad. Having in real life the kinds of friendships and relationships that I had read about and seen in the media all those years is an astronaut's dream.

~Aaron Chan

# Not Your Typical Senior Year

*He who has a why to live can bear almost any how.*
~Friedrich Nietzsche

Senior year of high school is supposed to be about three things: friends, picking a college, and graduation. My senior year wasn't like that... not at all.

Brian and I met when I was a freshman and he was a sophomore and dated throughout high school. He enlisted in the United States Army the summer before my senior year, the year he graduated. When he first enlisted, we didn't think that he would be shipped off right away, but we were wrong. He enlisted in May and was sent to Fort Benning, Georgia two months later, three days after my senior year began.

On top of the usual voices saying, "This is your last year of high school, make the best of it," and, "You need to pick your top choice school," I also had to worry about Brian. The mailman and I became very good friends during the time Brian was in basic training. I remember when I got that very first little green envelope. My school's theater department was putting on one of our biggest musical productions yet: *Peter Pan*. My mom and I had been texting sporadically throughout rehearsal, with me mainly asking if anything had shown up in the mail yet. When she brought me my fast food dinner, she also handed me that little green envelope. I tore it open as quickly as I could, trying to save as much of the envelope as possible.

Reading that short letter, I knew that he made it to Georgia and they were getting him processed. I lived off that feeling until the next letter showed up. The letters kept coming until December, and then my soldier himself made an appearance at the airport. We were just supposed to pick him up, but I had to run out of the truck and attack hug him. It had been four months since I'd seen him, the longest we'd ever been apart. Christmas was fantastic, despite coming down with the stomach flu. No present in the world could compete with the man in the digital camouflage ACUs sitting beside me.

Sending Brian back to Georgia to complete basic training was nearly impossible. But, much like I did before Christmas, I lived week to week off letters.

Until that one night. Who knew a person's whole world could change with one simple phone call? I was at a basketball game playing in the pep band when Brian called. Naturally, I lied to my band director and told him my mom was calling and I had to take it. In the period of a fifteen-minute phone call, Brian told me that he would have three days off after basic training graduation, and then he would have to get on a plane and go to his base station... in Germany. After he told me he was going to be stationed in Germany, he gave me the worst news I had ever received.

"There are rumors going around that the company I'm going to is getting deployed in about two months." And in that moment, I felt my whole world crashing down. I wasn't strong enough to do this. There was no way on earth I was going to make it through deployment, no way, no how! With the news of his shortened vacation time and his possible deployment, I gathered up the resources I could and found a way to Georgia. Which, I came to find out, was a good thing.

Seeing Brian graduate basic training was one of the happiest days in both of our lives. But what happened the next day was even better. Brian's mom and two little sisters joined us in Georgia after the friends who brought me to see him had to return to Indiana. Little did I know that Brian's mom was carrying a very important package. On the way to dinner with his mom and his sisters, Brian seemed really nervous. He kept telling me that it was the traffic, but I knew him too well. Something else was going on.

After we got to the restaurant and ordered our food, Brian's mom asked if she could borrow my camera. Confused, I handed it to her and she started taking mindless pictures of Brian and me. Well, that is... until he turned to me and asked me something that went like this:

"Hey baby."

"Yeah?"

"Will you marr—"

"OH, MY GOD!"

That was the gist of my proposal on March 6th, in Columbus, Georgia. Now, on top of finishing my senior year, Brian being stationed in Germany, and the possibility of a deployment on the horizon, I had a wedding to plan. I left Brian in Georgia that weekend, and my heart sank. It sank even lower when I found out that the rumors of the deployment were true. My fiancé was being deployed to Afghanistan.

My story isn't very common among teenagers, but I know that there are more than a few of us out there who are dealing with something like this on a daily basis. Brian just returned home from his deployment in June of this year, and we were married eight days later. After my first semester of my sophomore year at a local college, I plan on packing my bags and making my way to spend a year or two in Germany with my now husband. You see stories of girls becoming teen moms out there all of the time, but it's very rare you find a story of a teen military wife.

I am not a very strong person, or at least I wasn't before Brian joined the Army. Now, I am an army wife, so I have to be Army Strong. For any girl, or boy for that matter, dating a man or a woman in the United States Military, this one is for you. I know that you are strong, and I have faith in you. Hold on to those letters and those ten-second phone calls. They may be all you have right now, but at least they're something.

I made it... you can, too.

~Paula Perkins Hoffman

# Tough Times for Teens

## Chapter 2

## Loving and Losing

# Summer Without Whitney

*Unselfish and noble actions are the most radiant pages*
*in the biography of souls.*
~David Thomas

As I stood reading the plaque, newly engraved and shiny, I felt a lump form in my throat. I could feel the tears collecting on the inside of my eyelids. I slowly read the message: "This tree was planted in memory of Whitney Dawn Riegle."

For as long as I could remember, my cousin Whitney and I spent every summer together at our grandparents' house. As soon as the weather got warm, my uncle, my aunt, my cousin, and I could be found embracing and laughing in the doorway of the house. We were all so glad to see each other. Among the many things Whitney and I did over the two months we had together, we mainly argued. We were usually either comparing who was better or smarter, or just doing it to irritate our grandmother. Even though Whitney was two years older and a grade ahead of me, I still challenged her.

I was always jealous of Whitney—her long, beautiful brown hair and her gleaming green eyes that could touch your heart from across the room. I also envied her ability to hide her weaknesses, because she always appeared so strong. I envied her likeable personality and her generosity to everyone, even people she didn't know. I admired everything about her.

Every summer ended as the one before, with us going home and going back to our everyday lives, and school. We called each other every holiday and birthday. As we got older, we would fall behind and just call whenever to catch up. One year, around Christmas and New Year's, I called Whitney and we talked for a little bit. She said she'd call me back later because she was on her way to a friend's house. Before I knew it, school was back in session and I didn't second-guess her being busy.

Then, one night while doing homework, my phone rang. I glanced at the caller ID. It said Dad. I reached for the phone and answered. We said our hellos and then he demanded to talk to my mom. He never really wanted to talk to my mom—it was always "Tell your mom this and that..." Walking downstairs to get my mom, I was curious as to what his problem was. When I got downstairs, I saw that her door was closed and the lights were off.

"She's asleep. What's up?" I asked

"Have you talked to Whitney lately?"

"A few days ago, and I called today and no one answered. Why? What's wrong?" He paused and the milliseconds felt like minutes.

He finally just said it. "Whitney tried to kill herself today."

My heart stopped. I didn't want to believe it. "They got her heart started again, and they took her to the hospital. Everything is going to be okay. I'm at work. I have to go kid. I love you." I hung up the phone and let it roll out of my hand, hitting the floor. I ran downstairs and burst through my mom's door and struggled to tell her the heart-wrenching news.

"Whitney..." Tears rolled down my face uncontrollably, and somehow through the tears and sniffling I got out the rest of the news. She grabbed me and pulled me close. All I could do was cry; I couldn't stop the tears.

Before I knew it, the week was over and my uncle had decided to pull the plug. The wake and the funeral were the following week. Over two hundred people came to the wake. The church was packed.

At the funeral, there was a slideshow with slow, sad music. My uncle made his speech, reading quotes and Bible passages. He also told stories that caused a little laughter in the room. One particular story he told inspired me to want to follow in Whitney's footsteps even more, and also put tears in everyone's eyes.

"Yesterday, a woman I had never met came up to me and shook my hand." Tears started to fill his eyes. "She apologized for our loss and told me Whitney had played with her kids at the pool." A few tears rolled down his cheeks, and he quickly wiped them away. "I never knew Whitney did stuff like that, that impacted people so much." It made me think about how much one little thing could impact someone.

By the next week I was back home and catching up on school-work. The rest of the school year went by, and I was just as excited for school to be over and summer to start. As I always did, I went to my grandmother's house. It was quiet, still, and empty. It was strange but the days passed anyway.

A few days after the Fourth of July, my uncle invited us over for dinner. No one talked and all we could hear were scraping forks and the grumbles of everybody's digestive systems. I was relieved when everyone was done eating. We all walked outside; my uncle went straight to the garage and pulled out his Harley, and he convinced me to go for a ride with him. I hesitantly climbed on the back and we rode away down the street with the nippy summer evening breeze in our faces.

We rode down random streets for what seemed like a while, but was actually less than ten minutes. My uncle pulled into some play-ing fields. I was a little curious as to why we'd come here, of all places. Although I knew my dad, my uncle, and Whitney all had a great love for softball. For as long as I could remember, Whitney had played second base and my uncle had coached her.

We walked up to what looked to be the concession stand dur-ing game time, but the fields were silent and the stands were empty, probably because it was a weeknight. On one wall of the building was a locked plastic box; to one side of it there were tiny remains of papers and staples, where rosters had been hung. The other side was paperless and looked empty. But then it caught my eye—in the corner was a gleaming gold-plated plaque. As I stood reading the plaque, newly engraved and shiny, I felt a lump form in my throat and tears start to form. I read it slowly: "This tree was planted in memory of Whitney Dawn Riegle by the Cary Youth Softball Foundation." We walked over to the tree, planted almost in the middle of the fields she had once played on. All in a blink, looking at the tree, tears rolled down my face one by one. I tried to be strong and wipe them away before my uncle could see.

As we drove away, many thoughts filled my head. But the one that overpowered them was the story my uncle told at the funeral. I thought that if I was kind to everyone, then I could make an impact—just like Whitney.

~Delayne Jo

# She Was Full of Dreams

*A friend knows the song in my heart and sings it to me when my memory fails.*
~Donna Roberts

Have you ever felt so close to someone, it's as if she has a piece of you? A person who takes up half of your scrapbooks and possesses half of your wardrobe. You know her as well as you know yourself, or better. Put simply, you have her memorized. Every crease on her face, the wide spectrum of colors in her eyes, the sound of her laugh, the way her fingers feel enlaced with your own—it's all second nature.

Rubie was my person.

We met in our first grade class at Carlton Hills. We quickly became friends and filled our days with picnics, girl scouts, catching bugs, dressing up like princesses, and swimming in the neighborhood pool. As we got older, more of our time was invested in concerts, boy watching, shopping, make-up, and formals. Regardless of the activity, our only objective was to be together.

This girl was more than special to me—she inspired me. She was full of dreams to ride horses, become a rodeo queen, and conquer the world. I had never met anyone with such a free spirit.

It was in the middle of eighth grade when Rubie's incident occurred. She had suddenly become very quiet, which I found

e it made me question the stability of our

gret the words I said that evening for the rest of my life. furious that she had been ignoring me, so I contemplated g ties with her for good. When I called her to inform her of decision, she hung up on me. Every time I called, she would hang up, except for one time when she muttered a few words I couldn't hear.

Little did I know that prior to my call she had taken dozens of pills. Her mumbles were due to her lack of consciousness or ability to breathe.

When I first heard the news from her mother several days later, a piece of me died inside. When I went to visit her, I had to pretend to be her sister. I stuck the bright orange identification sticker on my shirt, took a deep breath, and stepped into the elevator.

It was day outside, but once I entered that section of the hospital, time blurred. The halls were narrow and most rooms only had curtains for doors. The air was stale. Everything seemed dead quiet except for the hurried tapping of fingers on keyboards, beeping monitors, and the occasional quick-paced footsteps of a frantic nurse. I followed solemnly as I was led to Rubie's room. The nurse warned me to brace myself.

As I entered her room my eyes teared up. I saw her lying in that hospital bed, hooked up to all those machines and IVs, and I was hit with the reality of it all. The best friend of my life was lying in front of me, hanging on to life by a thread, alive only because of a miracle and a group of fast-working paramedics.

Her long brown hair was ragged from lack of bathing, her eyes were sunken and her wrists were torn up with scars. She did not resemble the Rubie I was accustomed to. I spent countless hours in that room gripping my chair, reminiscing, pacing, dabbing her mouth with watery cotton swabs, and praying. I prayed until my heart throbbed and my eyes were sore that she would make it through.

As hours turned into days, she found the strength to open her eyes and communicate nonverbally. Aside from that, there never seemed to be any sign of improvement. Whenever she would get well enough to move out of the ICU, there would be another episode which usually involved screaming, flailing, biting the nurses, strait-jackets, or Rubie pulling out her own hair.

There was a wave of panic that swept the floor every time her monitor made an unsteady movement. The nurses informed me her recovery would not be an easy one. While vomiting on her kitchen floor, she had inhaled and contracted a very bad infection in her lungs. I stayed by her side all day, every day, until they forced me to leave.

The most painful sight was catching her off guard, staring into empty space. There was no hope in her eyes.

It made me wonder. Whatever happened to that beautiful, spir-ited, fourteen-year-old girl who was so full of life? What could cause someone so talented, lovely, and ambitious to want to end it all? I made it my mission to remind her — of all the good times, of how she was beautiful and loved, and how truly precious her existence was.

I began by bringing her pictures every day. They made her smile for the first time in weeks, even though she no longer had any memory of them. Most importantly, I elaborated on the countless stories and inside jokes behind them. I pinned them up on a clipboard beside her bed so they were always in sight.

One particular photo that struck me was one I had taken the previous summer on a sunny afternoon in a field behind my back-yard. We were having one of our many pretend photo shoots in which I was the photographer, and she was my model. She wore a white flowing dress with a backdrop of green bushes and leafy trees. Her long wavy hair shone like an angel's. She had one foot balanced on a small boulder, and was focused on her footing. Her porcelain skin glowed and freckles danced on her soft cheeks. There was more beauty in that snapshot than any camera lens could fully capture. When the nurse saw it, she was taken aback. Rubie hadn't always been a disaster.

One afternoon, I was half asleep on the chair next to Rubie's bed when I got a call from Ilya, our older friend who was in a local band called A Dull Science, telling me that he wanted to visit. When I informed Rubie, she got so excited she demanded that we do her make-up, after which she smeared black eye shadow all over her lids and globbed on lip gloss, oblivious to the fact that she looked absurd.

He brought her the best surprise she'd ever received—his old electric guitar. Written in Sharpie next to a scribbled sun and cloud, the guitar read,

"Dear Rubie,

You have always been there for us, and so we will always be there for you. We could not imagine not having you around and so, for us, please don't go anywhere. You are so loving and caring, how could anyone not be so in return? Just so you know, we love you, and no matter what happens you're the best."

She was delighted for the first time in far too long, and I could tell she believed the words that were written.

That night Rubie urged me to cuddle with her on the hospital bed. Despite the nurse's admonishments, I couldn't decline her begging. Before she fell asleep in my arms she gave me a peck on my cheek and told me she loved me.

Rubie was likely going to be discharged the following day. It was then that I realized how much we had overcome together.

As I played with her hair and she dozed off, I could finally fully appreciate her for everything that she had meant to me. Most importantly what I realized was that the best way to combat hurt and neglect was through love. We have to continually remind the ones we have that we love them while we still can, because they can slip away in a heartbeat.

~Monica Maria Bess Petruzzelli

# Address
# in the Stars

*He spake well who said that graves are the footprints of angels.*
*~Henry Wadsworth Longfellow*

Lora lived her life with passion. Lora lived with bravery and strength. Lora lived with immense love and understanding for others. Lora also lived with muscular dystrophy.

Lora didn't live long enough. My friend Lora died when she was only seventeen years old, and although we all knew the end would come sooner than any of us wanted, her death was still a shock. We were in high school, and suddenly she was not.

It took such a long time after she was gone for me to really understand how fast life can come and go. It took even longer for me to realize that she wouldn't ever be truly gone; that her life would always be an example to me of how I should live my life.

Although Lora was young, I always believed that she was wiser than I could understand. When Lora and I would spend time together, she was never afraid to tell it like it was, or say what was on her mind. When I listened to her talk, I always found myself trying to act as brave as she was. She faced her own death with confidence, which was something I was not mature enough to do, so she taught me.

When I first met Lora, she explained how fragile she was by listing all the things she could not do. As I solemnly understood each thing, I had an eerie feeling she could hear my thoughts. It was as if she felt my sympathy, but wanted to cast it aside. At the end of her list, she warned that I couldn't make her laugh too hard, or she wouldn't be able to get enough air because her diaphragm was too weak. I nodded in agreement, which caused her to burst out laughing at her own joke.

When she regained her composure, she looked me straight in the eye and said she would rather die than to be alive but not be able to laugh with her friends. There was a long list of things she could not do, but having fun was not on the list. She always made that clear by the way she lived her life.

At the beginning of her last summer, Lora and I were spending an afternoon together with our friends. As our carefree conversation came to a lull, Lora started a very different one. She promised us that when she died, she would be a guardian angel to each of us. She said we shouldn't be scared, because she wasn't. Lora said that we'd better not sit around and cry when she was our angel, or she would get very bored watching over us. She asked us to live our lives big, so that she would be kept busy trying to keep up with all of us.

Two days before she died, Lora and our friends had come over to my house. I was in the kitchen, pulling some food out of the oven and Lora was around the corner in the living room. Lora shouted around the wall for me to check my cell phone. When I did, I had a text from her that said, "I miss you." I laughed, and responded, "I'll see you soon." I listened for her phone to alert her of the text, and then I popped around the corner to find her beaming at me.

Life with Lora was a hundred blessings. She had an incredible amount of wisdom and was a valuable example of living with strength, intention, and hope. As little as Lora was in stature, she left deep footprints wherever she went in this world. In her death, she grows stronger, and her imprints grow deeper because we grow wiser as we remember the things she told us along the way. I will be forever thankful for her true friendship on Earth, and the messages she left us and still sends while she's in heaven.

When I got a call on her last morning asking me to come to the hospital to say goodbye, I saw the text message Lora had sent me a few days earlier and I saved it so that it would never slip away. "I miss you too Lora, and I'll see you soon."

~Lauren Thoma

# 4:08

*We understand death for the first time*
*when he puts his hand upon one whom we love.*
*~Madame de Stael*

It's 4:08 p.m.
The room is silent
Except for her breathing;
Steady,
Slow,
And slightly forced.
The window is open
And outside the sky is
Blue
And the sun is
Golden
And everything is peaceful
Out there,
But in here,
It's cold
And with every breath
Comes a tangible dread.
The trees blow with a gentle wind
And everything
Looks its most vibrant color
Except for her face,

Her white, white face,
With that odd yellow undertone.
My eyes are red and raw,
And she takes her last breath,
And every living thing
Holds still,
Because it's 4:08,
And nothing's living when my mom's gone.

~Allison Sulouff

# Gone Too Fast

*Where you used to be, there is a hole in the world, which I find myself*
*constantly walking around in the daytime, and falling in at night.*
*~Edna St. Vincent Millay*

was sixteen years old the day he died. I was too shocked to cry.
He was my best friend's oldest brother, my favorite of the four
she had. Even just thinking about him now makes my heart
race. Like he's sitting next to me, reading what I am writing about
him.

Nate was the most interesting person I had ever met in my life.
His speech was captivating, his looks took my breath away, his antics
made my sides hurt, and his excited energy always kept my undi-
vided attention. His sister made him out to be a big pest, but I knew
better.

I had known the Davis family since I was six years old, when
Lenore Davis and I became best friends on the first day of first grade.
Since that day, the two of us were inseparable. I was at the Davis's
house constantly from that point on. We went through everything
together, from our obsession with Bratz dolls to the Avril Lavigne
"punk" phase. Because he was two years older, Nate never hung out
with us; he was always doing his own thing.

The first time I saw Nate as the statuesque being that he was, he
had just walked in the front door on a Friday afternoon. His fawn-
colored hair was windblown, and he had a backpack thrown over
his shoulder. I was coming down the stairs looking for my jacket,

when he passed by me saying, "Hey, Christi." I lost all words. For the first time in my nine years of life, I had been stumped by someone's unimaginable beauty. I ran back up stairs, slammed Lenore's door shut, and leaned against it breathing hard with a sigh of relief and thrill. I never actually told Lenore that I had fallen in love with her brother, but she guessed it over the years. From that point on, going to Lenore's house was my favorite thing to do. Even if Nate wasn't home, just knowing that he would be soon warmed every fiber of my being.

Our seventh grade year was a big year overall, especially around Christmastime. That was the year that the fourth Harry Potter movie came out. Lenore and I went crazy; we must have seen it at least half a dozen times. I remember feeling bad for her mom who had to ferry us from her house to the AMC and back. Naturally, when the movie came out on DVD, Lenore and I bought it right away. We had movie nights with some of our other friends and somehow, some way, we always ended up watching our Harry Potter. One afternoon, I was over at the Davis house and Lenore and I had nothing planned for the day, so we ended up in her family room watching Harry Potter. Nate had just turned fifteen and was always out with his friends so I hardly ever saw him. However, on this particular day, he was home.

So there Lenore and I were, sitting on the squishy blue couch in her family room. Nate had just come down the stairs to grab a snack but took a detour to see what Lenore and I were watching.

"This movie again?" he asked with utter disbelief, but sat down on the couch next to me anyway. Lenore rolled her eyes and stood up to grab the remote to turn up the volume. Nate, thinking she was going into another room, asked, "While you're up, can you get me some food?" Lenore pointedly rolled her eyes again, yet agreed to get all three of us something. With each step she took, my heart beat faster and faster. Sure, I'd gotten used to being around Nate, but something felt radically different.

The scene in the movie had just changed to Hagrid, the half-giant, and his French love interest admiringly viewing dragons late at night. I, of course, knew all the words and was slightly embarrassed by the romantic scene that was about to unfold.

"'Agrid!" Madame Olympe Maxime called.

Call it instinct, just a feeling, or the connection between two like hearts, but I turned to look at Nate and was unsurprised to see him gazing back at me.

"Oh, 'Agrid. I thought you weren't coming. I thought perhaps you 'ad forgotten me..."

I had no idea how it happened exactly, but it was as if it was the most natural thing in the world. As if this was what we were supposed to be doing all along. I wasn't even as nervous anymore. I just knew this was how it was supposed to be. This realization came as he slowly leaned down to put his lips to mine, closing his eyes as if he wanted to hold my face in his memory forever.

"I could never forget you, Olympe."

As we drew apart, he looked me in the eye and smiled brightly, completely unabashed. I turned pink but managed to smile at him too.

"What is it that you wanted to show me? When we spoke earlier, you sounded so... exhilarated."

I looked at him, taking a breath, exercising my newfound courage and whispered,

"Can we get closer?"

I'll never forget the day he died. It was a Monday, sometime around the middle of March. I called Lenore straight away and used every ounce of self-control not to cry over the phone. She told me he was leaving a friend's house late the night before when his car was hit head-on by another. The driver was drunk. The paramedics said that Nate probably died instantly from the impact alone. I felt the blood drain from my face and forced my legs to move so I could sit down. I could barely breathe. We sat on the phone in pure silence for what felt like hours, but was really just a few minutes. The world around me kept going; people were leaving campus, going to the lockers, running to detention. I wanted to yell at all of them to stop and sit in silence with me, to stop and hear the sound of my heart breaking. To stop and make sure that I was still there.

At the funeral, in a chapel packed with teary eyes, I didn't cry. At her house, afterwards, with people sharing memories of him, I didn't cry. When Lenore broke down and cried on my shoulder, I didn't cry. It wasn't until I was all alone and sat down on that squishy blue couch to turn on our Harry Potter, fully expecting him to be sitting right there next to me, that I let the tears roll down my cheeks and wash over my heart.

~Christi Grewohl

# Choices

*Drinking and driving: there are stupider things, but it's a very short list.*
~Author Unknown

I grew up in a small town outside Savannah, Georgia where no one locked their doors at night and the main entertainment was Friday night high school football. The only crime to speak of was the occasional speeding ticket and maybe every once in a while a fight would break out at the one and only bar in town on a Saturday night. It's just a sleepy little town where parents want to raise their children away from the crime and danger of a big city, and where teenagers dream of leaving to find something bigger and better.

All that changed for me on one muggy summer night in July. It was my eighteenth birthday. My best friend Lisa's parents were going to be out of town for the week, so Lisa and my other two best friends, Kim and Jewel, decided to throw me a party at Lisa's house. My parents thought I was going out to dinner with Tyler, my boyfriend, then going over to Kim's to stay the rest of the weekend. Tyler came by to pick me up at six. My parents always said the same thing to Tyler before every date: "Drive carefully. You are driving around with precious cargo in your passenger seat." My mom gave us hugs and sent us out the door.

When Tyler and I arrived at Lisa's, the party was already in full swing—Lisa's house was packed. We had always liked going to parties and hanging out with our friends, although nether of us drank alcohol or did drugs. However, a few days before, Tyler and I had decided to maybe have a few drinks at the party. As soon as Kim and Jewel found out I was drinking, they both joined in. After about three margaritas and some other random drinks people just kept handing to me, I was pretty drunk, so I quit to look for Tyler. By the time I found Tyler, I was feeling sick and I wanted to go home. But we had a problem: Tyler was just as drunk as I was, if not more. When I told Tyler I needed to go home because I wasn't feeling good, he said he was fine and he'd take me home. Even as drunk as I was I still knew better, we both knew better then to drink and drive. At that point I just didn't care—all I could think of was how much I wanted to go home.

With some difficulty, Tyler and I made it out to his car. I don't remember getting home or much after, for that matter. I do remember my parents running outside in their pajamas and how scared they both looked. My mom helped me to my bed and my dad put Tyler to bed on the couch.

That night, after puking up my guts, I finally fell asleep and had a bad dream:

It's early morning. I wake up to my parents crying. Kim, my friend since we were five years old, has been killed in a car accident. After Tyler and I left, Kim, who had more to drink than me, got into her car. She didn't put her seatbelt on, didn't turn her headlights on, and headed towards the highway to go home. She was going about ninety miles per hour and driving on the wrong side of the road. Kim never saw the truck coming. The driver, who also wasn't wearing a seatbelt, didn't see her in time to swerve. They hit head on. Kim died immediately, and the driver was thrown through the truck windshield and was in a coma.

I woke in the late afternoon, screaming out Kim's name in a cold sweat with tears running down my face. My mother rushed into my room and held me until I stopped crying.

It's been eleven years since that night, and I haven't touched alcohol again. Every year around my birthday I have the same nightmare over and over again. I see my parents crying while they come into my room to tell me what happened to Kim. The only difference is that now my mother isn't around to hold me until the tears stop and tell me it really is a nightmare, not just the alcohol fogging my brain. Because Kim really did hit that truck. I later learned the driver's name was David, and he was in a coma for a week before he died. He left behind a three-year-old son, who was named after him, and a wife seven months pregnant with a little girl.

Whenever I look back on that day, I wonder if Kim would have been drinking if I hadn't. I wonder if she would have driven home if she hadn't seen me do it first. What would have happened if I hadn't made the choice to drink that night? Would Kim still be alive? Would David? I know Kim made the choice to drink and drive that night, but a part of me will always feel responsible for what happened.

I may not have changed the world with my story, but I do hope that by sharing it I make people realize the responsibility they have to themselves and to everyone else out there. Don't ever think that your choices are yours alone. Every choice, whether good or bad, is like a pebble dropped into still water—each ripple represents someone your choice affects. That's quite an impact, isn't it?

~Makaila Fenwick

# Thank You Laura

*When you are sorrowful look again in your heart, and you shall see that in truth you are weeping for that which has been your delight.*
*~Kahlil Gibran*

"Alex, I'm here!" I hear a strong but innocent voice. Excited feet thunder down the stairs, and a girl with a big smile appears, ready to have an amazing day. My best friend Laura and I are spending our last day together before she goes on vacation.

The air is moist and our legs stick to the seats in her mom's car while we drive to Malibu. We are two thirteen-year-old girls in a car, blasting music and giggling. Two girls whose hearts have yet to be broken, with just the thought of summer in our minds. Life is simple at this point and there are no worries.

• • •

I look at my mom, and I am in the middle of saying something I think is important. My mom is clinging to the telephone as if trying to cling to the person she has just lost. I check the caller ID and see that Laura's mom called at two in the morning. I know right then that Laura is gone.

"Is it Laura?" I say, really not wanting the answer.

My mom's eyes look like she wants to say no, but the words come out: "Yes."

When I hear the word "yes," everything clicks. My best friend that I have grown up with and have spent every moment with has passed away. I don't want to believe it.

Laura was on vacation in Italy when she fell off a banana boat and hit heads with another girl. Laura was hit in the wrong spot, causing bleeding in her head. She was fine for several hours—she just thought she was getting sick—but when she went to sleep she never woke up.

It took me a year and a half to realize she was gone. From time to time I would call her cell phone and text her that I missed her, but I received no response.

While most girls were straightening their hair for some boy or thinking about their first year in high school, I was lost in the fear of losing everyone around me. I had to learn that things in life will never stay the same, and that not everyone gets the chance to live till they're old. One summer, one day, changed my life forever. I thought at the moment it would only change my life in a horrible way, but Laura's death also taught me many beautiful things.

I learned to appreciate the day and the people you are with all the time. I learned that life isn't fair, and it's not a bad thing. I had to realize some people's time comes faster than others, and in a way, I think Laura was more special because she finished what she needed to do on this Earth much faster than most people.

I am only nineteen, but Laura has made me want to do the biggest things with my life. I am hoping to travel the world and take care of children and help people in any way I can.

I know Laura will be waiting for me on the other side. That same smile will be there. And when I see her I will thank her, for lending me a bit of her magic.

~Alexandra Cooper

# In My Memories

*Pleasure is the flower that passes; remembrance, the lasting perfume.*
*~Jean de Boufflers*

I'll remember your laugh,
The happiness within
You made everyone smile,
You would always listen.

I'll remember the times
We went down by the creek,
Started a fire,
That you could make last a week.

I'll remember when you
Rode your bike everywhere,
And the smile on your face,
When you leaped in the air.

I'll remember the time
You carved names in the tree—
My sister's, yours,
And your precious dog Maggie.

I'll remember your voice,
Deep down in my heart,

It'll always be there,
No matter how far apart.

And now I look back,
And I see just why,
God wanted you,
And not them or I.

Because you were an angel,
With every action and sound,
And tell God I give him credit,
He picked the best friend around.

I'll remember everything,
The good and the bad,
I will cherish the happy,
And cry for the sad.

I know deep down,
You are looking after me,
The same way that I now
Look after your tree.

And there's one thing I promise,
No matter what I do,
I promise you this,
I'll remember you.

In memory of Dakota Galusha

~Kierra Burda

**18**

# Thirty Minutes of Wonderful

*I would rather have thirty minutes of wonderful
than a lifetime of nothing special.*
~Shelby in Steel Magnolias

I can still envision her long blond hair blowing in the wind like a flag catching the breeze. I can still picture her big smile and see her bright blue eyes dazzling through her oversized white sunglasses when the sun would hit them just right. I can still hear her laughter echoing down a hallway or weaving its way through a room. She was the friend who I invited over and my mom would ask, "Are you sure you don't want to invite someone else?" not because she didn't like her, but because Brenda possessed an overenthusiastic energy and a big voice. My mom just didn't quite appreciate Brenda's spirit like I did. More than anyone, I understood her uniqueness. Little did I know that this vibrant girl, my friend since second grade, would be such a big part of my life, even after her death.

It's a Friday in March, and I'm sitting in Coach Harmon's English class hanging on her every word as she reads to us from her worn copy of *To Kill a Mockingbird*. Just as Scout is about to endure her second uncomfortable moment with her first grade teacher, Miss Caroline, a knock interrupts the steady stream of words. A young man, wearing jeans, a white T-shirt, and ragged Converse tennis shoes, is slouching in the doorway holding a note in his hand. Of course, I know he is here for me. We are traveling out of town for spring break, and my mom promised to get me out of school early today. However, I do wish that Coach had been a bit further into the story, because I wanted to know just how much trouble poor Scout was about to be in. Nonetheless, excitement shoots through me as I think of all the time I will be spending with my best friend, Brenda.

I went to school with Brenda in Oklahoma City for most of my elementary and middle school years. Then, my freshman year of high school, my dad received a promotion at work that required us to move to Texas. Even though miles of highway separated us, Brenda and I remained close. We spent holidays going back and forth to one another's homes, and we met at Lake Murray Camp for a couple of summers after I moved. Now, rounding the corner at the top of the stairs that lead to the school's main office area, I see my mom and dad. All the joy on my face disappears as I quickly observe that both of my parents have been crying. My dad puts his arm around me and carefully guides me out of the school's main door. My mom's face is wet from the giant tears that are rolling down her cheeks as she tries to speak. She looks to my dad for help. His eyes, red and swollen, are beginning to water. After what feels like an eternity, I finally shout, "What? What happened?" My mom gently reaches out, tucks my hair behind my ear and says, "Brenda died last night, honey. A drunk driver jumped the median on the highway and hit her car; she died instantly."

Hearing this, I am speechless. I just talked to her last night. She was fine. Suddenly, I feel sick. My knees are buckling, and I can no longer stand. Just before I hit the ground, my dad scoops me up and holds me tight as I sob in his arms. Then, the rest of the afternoon flickers past. Things begin to happen quickly and somehow, in my blurred state, I arrive at Brenda's home.

Mrs. Berringer, Brenda's mom, hugs me so tight that breathing is a struggle and my ribs hurt. Then Mr. Berringer and Brenda's two sisters take turns hugging me. I keep saying how sorry I am; it is all I can get out. We cry and reminisce for a couple of hours and all I can think is how odd it is to be in Brenda's house, knowing that she isn't, and will never be here again. As I prepare to leave, Mrs. Berringer asks if I want anything from Brenda's room. Hesitation sweeps over me because, inside, I am thinking there is no way I can go into her room, the very room that we once had sleepovers in, staying up all night and talking. Even though inside I'm saying no, my head must be nodding yes, because Mrs. Berringer, extending her arm, replies, "Go ahead sweetie, I'll wait here for you."

Slowly, I trudge to the back of the house, down a long hallway leading to Brenda's door. Arriving at the door, I pause and take a deep breath before stepping in. Her room is exactly as she left it. Clothes strewn on the floor, her bed un-made, and her closet door open with things spilling into the bedroom. I know exactly what I want, and after a few minutes of looking, I see it—her navy blue baseball cap with white embroidered letters that say NY. Her Yankees cap, worn in because it was her favorite, is resting at the foot of her bed. I pick it up and as I pull it close, tears stream down my face and my heart begins to ache. It still smells like her. I carry my treasure out of her room, hug everyone once again, and head for the front door. Just as I am about to depart, Mrs. Berringer asks me if I will speak at Brenda's funeral. She says that it will mean a lot to her, and she knows this is what Brenda would have wanted. Once again fighting back tears, I smile and say, "I'd be honored."

Sitting in the church, I am numb and still in shock from the few days preceding. The whole thing is surreal to me; I just can't believe this is my reality. As I go over the speech I prepared in my head, my mom nudges me and tells me to look around. She wants me to notice how many people are packed in the church. I realize that every pew is filled from left to right. People are standing along the sides of the church, and the back doors are open for people to stand in the foyer. Any stranger or onlooker would think this was an Easter Sunday mass.

What I say that day at Brenda's funeral is not important. What is important is what happens after. Sitting and reflecting on the things that had been said about Brenda, I gain a certain amount of clarity.

Everyone who spoke about Brenda shared the different ways in which she had positively affected their lives. They all mentioned her big heart, her selfless nature, and her knack for looking out for the downtrodden. I knew these things about her already, but as I scan the room, a thought occurs to me. God took Brenda home because she had done more with her life in seventeen years than most achieve in a lifetime. She had touched each and every life in that room.

Today, whenever I see goodness, kindness, sensitivity, bravery, or selflessness, thoughts of my sweet friend come to mind. I named my little girl after Brenda Marie, and I always have some part of her with me.

~Jamie Rinehart

# Tough Times for Teens

## Chapter 3

## Friendship
## in a Time of Need

# Putting Together the Pieces

*Hope begins in the dark, the stubborn hope that if you just show up and try to do the right thing, the dawn will come.*
~Anne Lamott

The first thing I notice about the waiting room is that my chair has no corners. The cold, green plastic has been moulded into the shape of a beanbag chair with none of the comfort. I feel like I am that chair, stuck in a world where everything comes in cycles that never really begin or finish.

I don't know what to expect when I see her. Is she going to cry? Is she going to hate me for making her come here? Maybe she won't even come out of her room at all. I pick at my nail polish, watching the little red flakes land on the dark carpet and disappear. The room smells like cleaning products and emptiness. Just being here is depressing me. I look out the window, but all I can see is the grey winter sky and the wooden fence that I could never climb over, even if I was on the other side of that scraped up pane of glass and had a reason to want to escape.

I hear muffled footsteps from socked feet because she isn't allowed shoelaces. Coming towards me is a ghost. Her hair is strikingly dark against the whitewashed walls and pastiness of her delicate skin. It covers her face like a curtain. She looks different dressed in a grey oversized sweat suit that proudly proclaims "GRAD 2010." I wonder if we will even make it there. It feels so far away and unlikely now.

She won't look at me. I see the redness of her eyes, and how tired her body looks as it labours to make it down the empty, narrow hall. She dumps herself into a chair across from me and looks away, subconsciously pulling her sweatshirt tighter around her wrists. Even now it's like she's still trying to protect me, as if what I don't know can't hurt me. If only she knew the truth—what I don't know only hurts me more, because she feels she can't talk about it with me.

I ask if she wants to play a game or something. She stands up, and drops herself into another chair by the bookshelf, next to a 5,000-piece puzzle. Silently we try to put the puzzle together, one piece at a time. We start at the edges before realizing we can't start to piece things together until we turn all the pieces face up. The box shows three happy kittens sitting in a beautiful field of flowers. I look at the scattered bits of colour in front of me and find it strange that we are sitting here trying to put these kittens back together when I never even knew that she was falling apart. I wonder how many pieces she is in right now.

I awkwardly try to make conversation, asking about how therapy is going, how often her parents come to see her, and if she's feeling any better. All of these are answered by a noncommittal shrug, her eyes not leaving the puzzle. I feel like I'm suffocating as I hold back tears, trying to stay strong for her.

Once again I fail her, and a tear slides down my cheek. I turn away from her, not wanting her to see how broken I am inside. I look at my watch; we have been sitting here for hours, and pretending not to be upset has worn me out. I tell her I have to go, but will try to be back tomorrow. I casually wipe my eyes with my hand as I stand up, but she knows. She grabs my hand, forcing me to turn and face her. Her big brown eyes look into mine, and I see that she, too, is failing to hold back tears.

"Thank you for coming to see me," she says, her voice cracking slightly, "and I'm sorry about this...."

I squeeze her as tight as I can, and tell her everything is going to be okay. I don't even know that hope is all I have to hold on to as I turn and wal metal door, praying that tomorrow will be a little bit easier the long road to recovery.

~Janine Russell

# ssitudes

> *In everyone's life, at some time, our inner fire goes out. It is then burst into flame by an encounter with another human being. We should all be thankful for those people who rekindle the inner spirit.*
>
> ~Albert Schweitzer

When I was in seventh grade, we were told to find a word we didn't know and put it in a sentence. Perusing the dictionary, I looked at the endless possibilities, all spelled out neatly in black ink. I could've used shul, incite, or algorithmic, but I wanted something unique. On a whim, I turned to the "V" section. And there, running my finger down the row, I found it. Vicissitude. It meant change, particularly a negative or unpleasant change.

It was perfect. Since I'd moved the summer before, I'd had to go through tons of changes. But the friends I'd left behind had remained constant. Immediately, I knew what I wanted to say.

"Friends," I scrawled on my paper, "are the people that hold your hand through the vicissitudes of forever." Underline. Exclamation point.

Two years later, I sat staring at my eighth grade scrapbook. In honor of the unique word, I'd used it as the title for my collection of memories. At the end, I'd put the finished product of our seventh grade project on a page of its own: an orange and pink heart surrounding the sentence. I remembered how confident I'd felt then, sure that my friends wouldn't abandon me.

But sitting there, I was alone. It was February of freshman year, and I couldn't remember the last time I'd laughed or smiled. Those days, I was more secluded, more tired. I dragged myself through each school day like a sloth, the time trickling past as slow as molasses. When I got home, all I wanted to do was sleep. Even though my friends invited me places, I declined. I had no time for friends.

Looking at the glossy pages of my past, I felt like a completely different person. The girl in the picture was strong, healthy, and full of life. Now, my very reflection was a stranger in the mirror, with shadowed eyes and a pale complexion. Just looking at myself made me feel disgusted. I wished I could go back to the person I'd been, but didn't know how I'd changed, or when it began. It was like I'd emerged from a coma, only to find that I'd lost what had made me "me" after such a long sleep.

Ten months later, I found out how it had happened. I sat in a deceivingly comfortable chair at Children's Mercy Hospital, waiting for the verdict. I'd been weighed, tested, and inspected. They'd taken everything from my blood pressure to my temperature, asked me countless personal questions, and written it all down neatly on official-looking paper.

My new doctor came in and closed the door. I glanced at my mom, who sat beside me. The concern on her face mirrored the doctor's.

"You're severely underweight," he announced, folding his hands on the desk. "Your blood pressure's very low, and it skyrockets when you stand up. Your body temperature is also low. What you've described is depression, which is common among patients with eating disorders."

I choked at his words.

"The good news is we can turn this around. I'd like to get a few blood samples today and see if your heart has suffered from trying to maintain your body's vital functions. I'd also like to set up an appointment for next week."

To a point, I was relieved. "I don't have to stay in a hospital?" It had been my biggest fear. My dad had threatened me with it since my aunt, who was a doctor herself, had voiced her concern at Thanksgiving.

"We'll have to keep a close eye on your weight, but no, Jessica. If we can turn this around, then you won't have to."

And so my fight began. At first, it was hard. The voice of the eating disorder told me not to eat, and to cheat if I did. As I struggled with it at home, I pretended everything was okay at school. My friends didn't say anything, but more than once I saw their sad expressions, or heard them wondering why I disappeared once a week, for appointments.

My pride kept me from telling them the truth. I didn't want pity, and I didn't want tears. Mom had already cried enough, blaming herself for teaching me about healthy eating and watching me go overboard. I'd never thought I was fat; I'd only wanted to be healthy.

The following February, though, the truth had to come out. My doctor, the eating disorder specialist at Children's Mercy, put me in the hospital. My weight was still dangerously low, and my life was draining fast. After a week of getting the nutrition I needed, I was released. It was then that I knew I had to come clean.

That night, I called one of my close friends, who I'd known since seventh grade and had been suspicious for a while. I told her about the hospital, about everything, and, amazingly, she understood. I told another friend, too, who was in a volunteer group with me. They both offered help, and even though I didn't confide in everyone, just knowing I had their support boosted my confidence.

Several months after I was released from the hospital, I had to explain again while on a retreat. The volunteer group leader had remarked on my diet, lamenting that I'd brought most of my own food. My friend, who'd been the second to know in February, encouraged me to explain. As hard as it was, I managed to tell our group leader, and was amazed again that someone understood. The rest of the retreat passed in a blur, without incident. On the way back, I couldn't help but smile. For two days, no one had said anything. No one had remarked how painfully thin I was, or asked me how my meal plan was. I looked at my friend. "Thanks," I said.

She glanced away from the road, her hands firm on the wheel. "For what?"

"Everything," I said. And it was true. She'd known me before the eating disorder freshman year, and after I'd started to recover. She'd stayed a friend even in my darkest moments, when I'd pushed people away. Unlike I'd thought then, in my depression, she'd never abandoned me. She understood that I was getting treatment now, but didn't treat me like I was different or fragile. She'd held my hand through all the minor and major changes, and because of her, I once again believed my seventh grade statement to be true. "Friends are the people that hold your hand through the vicissitudes of forever." She had done just that, and because of her and several other steadfast friends, not to mention my family, I knew it was possible. One day, I would be the same laughing, vibrant girl I'd been in my scrapbook. Even better.

~Jessica M. Ball

# 21

# A Love You Never Have to Question

*A friend is the one who comes in when the whole world has gone out.*
*~Grace Pulpit*

couldn't help but relax as I sat listening to my closest friends talk. The three of us had been best friends since we were toddlers — I felt safe around them. We had shared everything: bubble baths, ice cream, smiles, tears, jokes, anger, secrets and childhood adventures. We had done it all.

"Guys I have to tell you something," Marie stammered, a smile spreading across her face. She was thirteen, the youngest of the three of us. It was rare for her to have news, so we leaned in with excitement.

"Well, um... it's kind of hard to say...." she stumbled over the syllables.

"Go for it! Come on, you know you can tell us anything," I urged her.

"Well, uh... it's my dad. He moved out." She finally spat out the words and broke into laughter. I sat stunned for a moment then finally managed to mumble, "Sweetie, why are you laughing?"

"I'm not sure really; I know I shouldn't. I don't think it's a laughing matter, but well... I just don't know." That was typical of Marie. She was admirably strong, and only those closest to her knew that she was laughing because she was too hurt to cry.

"Are you okay? When did this happen? I don't understand!" Christie and I questioned our friend. All three of us had always lived in a sort of fairy tale with perfect homes and happy families. The idea that our bubble had been popped was terrifying; my stomach twisted into knots as we waited for Marie to answer.

"Well, it happened a month ago; I was too nervous to tell you guys right away. I guess I thought that maybe he would move back in," she whispered, growing solemn and sad.

"I can't believe it," I whispered. I was oblivious to the fact that Marie's parents hadn't been getting along. "But Marie, we are here for you, okay?" I continued. "Any time you want to talk or escape, you know where I am." I wanted to do more for her. More than anything I wanted to piece together the puzzle that her parents couldn't solve, but all I could do was offer my support.

On the twenty-minute drive home, I threw a handful of questions at my mom. She revealed to me that she had known the entire time, but that our moms had agreed to let Marie tell us in her own time. She could sense the anger and confusion bubbling inside me.

"I don't get it!" I barked. "Why are they doing this to poor Marie? They are adults. Why can't they just figure it out?"

My mom told me that it was more complicated than I could understand. She was right; my parents had been happily married for eighteen years. I had no concept of divorce, and no answers for why the love between two people could evaporate.

Two weeks later, the three of us gathered in Christie's bedroom again with popcorn and movies. I was determined to make Marie's night as fun and lighthearted as possible, but my plan was quickly forced to take a disturbing detour.

"Should I tell her?" Marie asked, her eyes falling on Christie.

"Tell me what guys? What's going on?" I sensed that Marie had more bad news, but I wasn't at all prepared for what was coming.

Marie took a deep breath, and stared at the floor: "The other day

I was surfing around on my brother's MySpace, and I found a conversation he was having with a friend. He was discussing our family and he revealed that my mom had become an alcoholic."

"Oh my gosh! Do you think that's why your dad moved out?" I asked, again taken by surprise. I never imagined that her mother would succumb to something like that.

"Well, I thought for a second that was it, but then I read..." her voice trailed off and she began taking deeper breaths.

"He said that my dad had an affair. I didn't have to question it because the other day he said he was going to the movies with his friend Paul; an hour later Paul called the house and asked me if my dad was busy."

After a minute of silence she made eye contact with us, and that was it. Tears began rolling down her cheeks, and before they could hit the floor I was holding her. The three of us sat on the carpet bawling in each other's arms. This time there were no words to be said; Marie's life wasn't just falling apart, it was shattered. I tried to share her pain, but I knew that no one could feel exactly what she felt. No one was there to catch her tears as she glared out her bedroom window, watching her dad pull out of the driveway for the last time. No one was there to hold her tight while she cried herself to sleep. Nobody held her hand in the hallway at school as a hundred smiling faces passed her, unaware of the tear in her heart.

Marie's situation made me think about the word divorce. Whenever I heard someone say that their parents weren't together, I never really thought twice about it. It wasn't until I witnessed the devastation in Marie's life that I recognized how painful and traumatic it really is. Her parents fought a war over custody for the children, and dragged them through a nasty separation. Anyone could see that the entire family was dealing with animosity and depression. However, there were tiny changes in Marie that only her best friends could notice.

For as long as I had known Marie, she was obsessed with the idea of having a family. She loved children and couldn't wait to be married and become a mother. When she lost her family, she also lost her trust and faith. She no longer wanted to fall in love, afraid of the chance it could fall apart. She scratched children off her list as well, not wanting to bring anyone into a world so cold and cruel. Marie always loved a delicious meal, but now she went months eating hardly at all. However, after everything she lost—happiness, love, trust, hope, respect, and even a few pounds—nothing disturbed me more than the light we watched fade from her eyes. She was always a bubbly, optimistic kid; now she wore a catatonic expression and harbored a deep resentment for the world.

As months passed by, and seasons changed, Marie's life stayed the same, and we realized that it could take years for Marie to truly smile again. The three of us learned a lot that year, but the most important lesson we took away from it all was the importance of friendship. Christie and I were more than just good listeners for Marie—we were her safe haven from all the drama in her world. We got so much closer, and saw that it was our childhood that made us best friends, but it was these life changes that would make us inseparable.

~Hannah B. Leadley

# 22

# Being There

*Unable are the loved to die. For love is immortality.*
*~Emily Dickinson*

Ally was my best friend, and she was there for me through everything. I remember lying in a field together watching the horses run within the borders of their fenced-in playground, talking for hours about anything that crossed our minds. When ninth grade ended, this kind of day became just a memory.

Ally was a horseback rider; it was her passion. When summer came, her father took her down to South Carolina to their second house to horseback ride in a competition. She would be gone for three months and I knew I'd miss her over the summer. The day that she left we took a picture. I still have it framed in my room.

The day I got the news I was home sick from school. I got a phone call from my friends at school. They were crying. I couldn't make out a word of what they were saying. Then, as one of the girls took a deep breath, I made out a name: Ally.

Ally had fallen off her horse. She hit her head. She was in a coma.

Tears started to stream down my face. I sat down to take a minute to breathe, but breathing was harder then it seemed.

How can life go from wonderful to unbearable in a matter of seconds? I didn't understand. Ally didn't deserve this. No one did.

The days went by so slowly and every one of them was filled

with tears. There was a Facebook ƥ
could update us on everything that

It was late afternoon when I ƴ

"Alexandra has been slowly ƈ
coma for the last two days," h
night last night. She has not w
She is almost breathing on h
off the respirator very soon

After I read that pos
going to survive and be fine. I wʊ
friend—so that's what I did.

When Ally was transferred to the Montreal Ϲ
I went up right away. Sometimes when I visited she wouɭ
hand out to grab mine. She would smile even though her eyes weɾ
closed. When I left, a tear would seep out of her closed eyelid. I knew
Ally felt that I was there. Maybe she wasn't conscious, but she knew
that her best friend was there.

Ally progressed day by day. I spent my summer going to see her
at the hospital; some days were good and some days were bad but
that didn't stop me.

Ally is now recovered. We have since parted ways—she had to
repeat a grade—but we both know somewhere in our hearts that
no matter when, our shoulders are always there for the other to lean
on.

This experience has taught me many life lessons. The one that
is the most important is not to take anything for granted. No one
knows what kind of obstacles they will have thrown at them. Tell
your family and your best friends how much they mean to you. You
never know when they will be taken from you. I'm just one of the
lucky ones.

~Katherine Randall-Mallinson

## 23

# Remember Me in the Sunset

*The most beautiful discovery true friends make is that they can grow separately without growing apart.*
~Elisabeth Foley

I stood on the front porch blinking back tears I refused to cry, watching Olivia's pretty face glance sadly back from the window as they pulled away. Kentucky... practically a country away from where I stood and, as Anne of Green Gables would say, my "bosom friend" was moving there. All I could choke out after her was, "Don't forget to remember me."

Olivia isn't just a friend; she is my "kindred spirit," sister in Christ, writing pal and all-around best friend. We share more than interests; we share faith, dreams, and real passions. Why did she have to leave me?

I went inside feeling like God had let me down. Olivia's moving was hard, but I knew He brought us together and would hold us together through time and distance because He is greater and stronger than both, but what bothered me was that just after finding out her family planned to move, Chicken Soup for the Soul had chosen one of my poems for publication. It was my first published piece and, being a fellow aspiring writer, Olivia was more ecstatic than I was. And best of all, especially with her pending move, it was a poem I had written for her. God has a way of making beautiful memories out of heartbreaking experiences.

I wanted so much to give Olivia a copy of the book with her special poem in it in person, as a parting gift, but this was our last visit and the books hadn't come yet. I kept asking God why He couldn't have made them come in time. I failed to remember that His timing is always on time.

After watching her go I slipped upstairs to my room, my chest feeling both heavy and empty, took my cedar wood box from its place on a shelf, lifted the lid and took out the small pile of envelopes that were held safely in its keep. One by one I opened the cards and letters, smelling of sweet cedar like a peaceful forest, and read the notes my "bosom friend" had written me over time. They made me smile, laugh and cry all at once. The secret names we'd given each other, our "top secret" alphabet, cards, letters of sisterly love, etc. They all meant so much to me, but one card stood out among the rest. It was the Valentine's Day card Olivia had made me when I was away for a long while and getting lonesome and homesick. It had a wonderful poem on the front that brought tears to my eyes the first time I read it, and now tears filled my eyes again. I hadn't lost her. This wasn't goodbye. I closed the card, breathing in another wisp of that forest fragrance, clutched it to my chest and whispered, "Thank you God, I'm sorry for thinking you let me down. Your perfect timing is always right. I still trust you."

The next afternoon the box of *Chicken Soup for the Soul: Just for Preteens* books arrived, each holding my poem, "Heart to Heart," under the chapter name, "Friendships to Last a Lifetime." A perfect name to describe our friendship, a perfect chapter to promise this wasn't the end... and it was one day too late. Or so I thought. But, as usual, God had a plan that was better than my own. "It will give you an excuse to see her again!" Mom said. "Call and see if she can swing by and get it on their way through." I hugged my wonderful mom and dashed upstairs to call Olivia. "I have something I have to give you before you go. Will you be coming through town on your way to Kentucky?" She didn't know for sure but promised to let me know when she did. It was Thursday night and they'd be leaving Saturday.

I hung up the phone with peace in my heart. This was why the books had come a day later. If they had come when I thought, the day before would have been our last "see you soon" (we had decided not to say "goodbye"). But instead, angels carried them here just one day "too late" and God gave me the gift of seeing her off on the long road ahead and getting that one last hug in the memorable parting I had so badly wanted.

I wrote a note on the inside cover of her book, tucked another telling her what page held the poem and how much I was going to miss her inside, and set it on the counter, knowing she would come by.

Saturday afternoon, she did. I ushered her in the door and took the book from its place on the counter, handing it to her without a word. I was afraid if I said anything I'd burst into tears. She held it in her hands for a moment, saying, "Oh my gosh, I can't believe it's here! I can't believe it's here!" Her beautiful blue eyes filled with tears, and that was it for me. I hugged her tight and squeaked out, "I love you, Liv."

"I love you too," she squeaked back. Mom grabbed the camera and snapped a couple of shots of us, teary-eyed and smiling, and Chicken Soup for the Soul actually ran one of those shots with a story on Liv and me in their contributor newsletter a couple of months later.

After one more big hug, Olivia clutched the book and headed back to the truck. I stood in the driveway, still crying, and waved "see you soon" as they pulled away. Olivia's pretty face glanced back, wet with tears, but that contagious smile of hers was shining through this time. I'll never forget that look. It was the kind of goodbye I had prayed for, the kind that is treasured and remembered.

When the truck was out of sight I turned to find Mom's open arms. She was crying too. Mom, my little brother and I had a tearful group hug and headed in. I took one more look over my shoulder. The road was empty, but my heart was full again.

The Bible verse on the last card I sent Olivia read:

"Love never gives up, never loses faith, is always hopeful, and endures through every circumstance." (1 Corinthians 13:7)

That must be what had filled my heart because I was hopeful, I had faith, and I knew this friendship would endure through the circumstances.

Moments later, Olivia texted me (she doesn't like texting, but I was out of minutes and I guess I'm special enough for her to make an exception). It read: "Crying. Thank you. It's more beautiful than you know." It was just a simple poem, but it was written from one heart to another.

I gazed out at the hills to the east where my "kindred spirit" was heading, and whispered what was written inside the cover of the book she was holding somewhere on the road right then....

"Until soon again,

My dear friend,

I will remember you in the sunrise.

Remember me in the sunset...

The poem says the rest."

~Rae Starr

# 24

# Letting it All Out

*Smooth seas do not make skillful sailors.*
*~African Proverb*

"**W**anna come over to my house for lunch tomorrow?" Rich Carson asked me with a grin. He was gorgeous, a senior, and a big fish in our little pond of a high school. I'd had a crush on him since middle school.

"Um, sure," I stuttered. "Your mom's going to be there, right?"

"Yeah, of course," he answered with a shrug. "I'll meet you at your locker and we can walk over to my house together."

"Sounds great," I said, trying to appear casual, even though my insides were a mess. Rich Carson had invited me to his house for lunch. That was practically a date!

I was so excited that I could barely sleep that night. I dressed carefully the next morning and floated to school. My morning classes dragged by. I saw Rich in the hallway once. My heart skipped a few beats when he waved at me.

Lunchtime finally arrived. I dashed to my locker, where Rich was waiting for me. We walked the two blocks to his house, chatting and laughing the whole way. We got inside and I immediately looked around for his mother. The house was totally quiet and I knew we were alone. Although the thought made me nervous, I didn't say a word. I couldn't mess this up. Guys like Rich Carson didn't give girls like me a second chance.

Before I could worry any further, an adorable Cocker Spaniel jumped up on my leg. I plopped down on the living room floor and began playing with the dog. Rich sat down on the couch and watched us with a strange look on his face.

"Shouldn't you make us a sandwich or something? I only have forty minutes," I reminded him.

Before I knew what was happening, Rich had pushed me down on my back and was lying on top of me.

"You know you didn't come here for lunch," he murmured, as he began kissing me.

I tried to protest and push him away, but he was too strong. I felt his hands slide up the front of my shirt and I really panicked. I told him repeatedly to stop, but he ignored me. I was terrified.

In one last desperate effort, I lifted my knee and managed to hit Rich between the legs. He rolled off of me and started swearing. I jumped up and ran toward the door. I banged my foot on the coffee table and nearly fell, but somehow I escaped from the house. I could hear Rich cursing at me as I fled.

I ran all the way back to school at full speed. I headed straight for the nearest restroom and got sick. My whole body shook as I realized what could have happened.

I somehow made it through the remainder of the school day. I went home, grateful that it was Friday. My mom knew something was wrong with me the moment I walked through the door. I sobbed as I told her what I'd done. I expected her to lecture me for being so stupid, but she was wonderful. She didn't make me feel stupid or naïve. She said she was just glad that I'd escaped before any real damage was done.

The problem was, I disagreed. I felt very damaged.

For the next few days, I was a basket case. I cried almost constantly. Getting through each day was a struggle. Luckily, I had only one more week of school before summer break. Rich was a senior and was not required to attend the last week of school. Thankfully, I never saw him again.

I had already made plans to be a counselor at an out-of-state

Christian camp that summer. I couldn't imagine being nearly 500 miles from home when I was hurting the way I was.

My mom and I talked it over. I insisted that I needed to cancel my plans.

"I'm just not strong enough, Mom. I can't go," I said tearfully.

"I know it seems difficult right now, but you'll be fine once you get there. You'll be too busy to worry about all of this," she said. "Besides, if you get there and realize it's too much for you, just call and we'll come get you."

I agreed to give it a try.

During my first few days at camp, I tried to act normal and pretend that nothing had happened, but one night, the pretending was just too much. I locked myself in a bathroom stall and just let it all out. I thought I was alone, until I heard a voice say, "Are you okay over there?"

Startled, I sniffled and wiped my eyes. "Yeah, I'm fine."

"You don't sound fine," the voice said. "You sound like you could use a friend. You wanna talk about it?"

So right there in the bathroom, I told my story to the girl in the other stall. I wasn't sure who I was talking to, but telling the story seemed easier that way. When I was finished, I waited for her to blame me for what had happened.

But she never did.

And neither did the other girls I told that summer. Every one of them hugged me and told me that I wasn't to blame. One girl even shared that something similar had happened to her, and she'd never told anyone until I came forward with my story.

Talking about it brought healing to both of us.

Rich Carson had tried to hurt me that day. He tried to take something important from me, but he didn't succeed. That experience, although scary and painful, gave me so much more than it took from me.

It taught me to trust other people and believe that they will accept the real me. It taught me not to hide painful feelings, but to share them with someone else because they're so much easier to carry when you're not doing it alone.

And best of all, that summer, which was both the best and the hardest season of my life, brought me four lifelong friends who I can count on, no matter what.

~Diane Stark

# 25

# One Act of Kindness

*Today, give a stranger one of your smiles.*
*It might be the only sunshine he sees all day.*
*~Quoted in P.S. I Love You, compiled by H. Jackson Brown, Jr.*

It was a warm, humid Fourth of July. It was early and the house was already empty, much to my dismay. All my housemates had left for the holiday and I was alone. The feelings of guilt and shame washed over me. I hated being alone. There was no way to hide from the pain that I felt about my best friend's death that previous winter. At least when I was working, I could bury myself in the task at hand. Having five other roommates in a small house also provided many distractions from what was going on inside my head.

It should have been the best summer of my young life. I had achieved my dream of landing an internship at one of the most beautiful environmental centers in the mountains of Appalachia. I could fall out the back door of the house and hike down to a beautiful lake, follow trails through the forest, or even mountain bike. I got to teach environmental education to young campers, work with wild animals, and learn many fascinating things about nature.

Yet, I was empty inside. My heart was heavy with guilt. I blamed myself for not stopping my best friend, Michael, from taking his life. I kept beating myself up for not recognizing his deep pain or seeing the signs before his suicide. Michael and I spent the summer before hiking or biking in the mountains. We were best friends for over two years. He taught me a lot about courage and loyalty. We always laughed when we were together, making bad jokes or pulling pranks on each other. Michael was fearless. He was never afraid to tell me how he was feeling or thinking.

After Michael died, I changed from being outgoing and friendly to withdrawn and shy. I felt so odd compared to my classmates in college. My friends and family didn't know how to deal with me. They tried to listen when they could, but it seemed they just didn't know what to do. They wanted me to return to the way I was before. When I watched my peers, I saw many happy young people who were excited to learn new things, and on occasion struggling with school and relationships, while I was isolated by my pain. As I sat in my bedroom that Fourth of July, I cried out to God: "God, I'm really lonely. I wish I was dead. Why did you have to take Michael away from me and from his family? I never wanted to live this long. Why didn't you take my life instead?" I wrote a letter that day asking God to take my life.

I was so anxious when I read the letter that I rushed upstairs. I realized I was dangerously close to developing a plan to take my own life. I was afraid what I might do if left on my own. The house phone rang suddenly.

When I went to pick it up, I recognized the gruff voice of the director on the other line. "Hi. Is this Lisa?"

I answered yes, but was somewhat surprised. I didn't expect Tony to know me, much less care about a lowly intern. We ran into each other at the nature center and played ultimate Frisbee on occasion, but that was it. Tony asked me if I wanted to go biking on the Rails to Trails path that day. I immediately said yes, knowing I needed to get out of house immediately.

Tony was a big guy with a thick white moustache and a mop of white hair. I barely reached his shoulder. He easily tossed my mountain bike into the back of the pick-up truck. As we headed to the trail, he told me that his kids were tied up for the day and he didn't want to waste a beautiful summer day sitting at home. One of the things I really liked about Tony was that he didn't push for a lot of conversation. We lapsed into a comfortable silence as he drove to the trail.

Once we unloaded the bikes, we just started pedaling down the trail in the warm sunlight. Tony told me stories of growing up and adventures from his younger days. He would occasionally ask questions and I would try to answer them as best I could. For the first time in seven months, I felt the ice thawing around my heart. I knew Tony wasn't going to judge me or think I was weird if I didn't feel like talking. It was nice to be accepted for who I was.

We ate lunch and pedaled on the trail for hours. Many times, we just rode along in a companionable silence watching the world go by. The sunlight danced through the trees and occasionally we heard the cascade of water flowing over rocks in the stream. As I learned over the years, nature had a way of soothing my soul in a way few other things could. I don't think Tony knew it, but his presence drove away many of the fears haunting me that day. There was a wisdom and steadiness to him that helped to calm me. For the first time, I saw there might be hope in spite of my pain.

Tony asked on our way home if I had plans for dinner. I shook my head shyly and said not really, but I didn't want to bother him. He looked me square in the eye and said, "I would like to share dinner with you and don't think you should be alone." At that moment, I felt tears of gratitude fill my eyes and nodded yes. I looked away quickly, embarrassed by my emotions. Tony gave me time to pull myself together. That night, we shared a great dinner of barbecue and watched the baseball game on TV.

That day, two strangers connected on a spiritual level. One simple act of kindness can go a long way in changing someone's life — maybe even save it. I don't know if he ever realized that he helped a young lady realize that life just might be worth living after all. That young lady went on to become a social worker who tries to show others that there is hope, even in the midst of tragedy.

Thank you, Tony, for taking the time to reach out to a stranger.

~Lisa Meadows

**26**

# Following the Beat of a Fallen Marcher

*Could we change our attitude, we should not only see life differently,*
*but life itself would come to be different.*
*~Katherine Mansfield*

The lights came up, blinding me while I turned to the crowd to make my customary salute. I glanced down at my uniform, my eyes glued for what seemed like minutes on the silver ribbon pinned there on the left side of my shirt. I looked up momentarily to get my bearings, only to realize that all eyes were on me, waiting for me to make the first move. I was frozen.

"This is it," I had announced in my normal pre-show speech earlier that day. "Tonight we do this for Cody. March well. Play your best. Make it his show."

It was the accident that woke me up. As a senior, I was the drum major of my high school marching band. The position comes with a lot of built-in prestige and responsibility. I had always looked up to my high school drum major, and so when I got the role, I wanted people to look up to me, too. I wanted to make a difference in their lives, to help them in band, but to also inspire them for life. I was a little arrogant, though, and impersonal. I learned the names of my band mates but I didn't really get to know the people behind the names.

Cody was one of those names. I honestly paid little attention to him. He was a freshman, so I felt I had little in common with him.

I would say, "Band, you are dismissed," and the freshmen were always quick to respond with "Thank you, ma'am." They, who stood at attention nearly one hundred percent, were the quickest to respond to instructions and were also the ones who looked lost and insecure.

Cody fit this description. He was an intense marcher—always at attention, first at practice, never late, and first to memorize music. I had always wondered why, out of all of the freshmen, he was the most concerned with doing it all "right."

It was his love of music.

I learned later that, as a child, he would sit on his front porch listening to the marching band practice, secretly longing for the day he would join them. He started bassoon lessons early in life and hoped to continue throughout high school. But Cody had hopes and dreams that were cut short.

It happened on a Friday—one of those wet and dreary September ones. The football game was that evening, and we were required to slosh our way through the muddy field to perform for halftime.

"Hey guys!" I shouted over the noise in the band room. It eventually quieted down. "Because it's so nasty outside, Mr. Brown has decided that we will not be wearing full uniforms tonight, just the band shirt and black bibs." I could hear the whines begin immediately.

"Those of you," I plunged ahead, "who forgot to wear your shirts today, as we asked, need to find a way to get them to school. No exceptions. Call a parent, sister, friend, boyfriend, or whatever it takes for you to have it in your hand in two hours when we leave."

During this break, I left the room and returned, an hour later, to find chaos in our band room.

"Did you hear about Cody?"

"Do you think he's okay?"

"I heard they've called an ambulance!"

"They say there's blood everywhere."

Rumors were flying around the room, and I felt disoriented, like my body was there but my brain was soaring above. Conversations clouded the air around me, and faces full of shock and confusion flooded the room. Moments later Mr. Brown walked in the room, only to confirm our fears.

"I have some bad news, folks. While Cody was walking home to get his band shirt, a car lost control on the wet roads and hit him from behind. He's been taken to the Community South Hospital and is in intensive care. We don't know anything else," he finished.

Cody was pronounced brain dead the next day and passed away peacefully as the weekend finished.

This was a tragedy that hit me very deeply. I remember feeling like it hadn't happened, that Cody would show up for practice on Monday. I regretted the way I had ignored him. I felt guilty and ashamed of myself. I was supposed to be the key to unlock musical doors, to expand his horizons and understanding of the world of music and all it could offer. Yet I hadn't, and all Cody's musical dreams were washed away with the rain.

That weekend after the accident was one of the hardest of my life. I began to look at an in-depth analysis of how I had acted as drum major. I came to the realization that I wasn't doing enough for my band. I learned about myself; I rediscovered myself. I wasn't serving with all of my heart.

I then began what I would like to think of as my "real" time as drum major. I took time to get to know my band.

During breaks, I sat with different people each day and slowly learned more about my band. I sat in sectionals, listened to each member play, and was able to help teach and correct mistakes. When I was in charge of Marching Fundamentals, I was personal, pointing out all the improvements my newfound friends were making. I let my genuine love and passion for all music shine through in all that I said and did for my band. They became my band, and I became their drum major.

And then, standing there on my podium, seconds away from our memorial performance for Cody, I was struck with the thought that this simple desire to be a better drum major had more far-reaching consequences than I had ever imagined. I could be that person to inspire my friends, like that long ago drum major of my freshman year inspired me, to continue playing through all of life's stormy paths.

With that realization, I summoned all my courage and faith in myself, lifted my arms, looked all of my expectant friends in the eye, and began the simple beats that would allow me to step up and be the kind of role model I always hoped I could be.

~Melanie Vandenbark

# 27

# Jamie

*No one ever really dies as long as they
took the time to leave us with fond memories.*
*~Chris Sorensen*

Last September I started my freshman year of high school. I was confident and excited, ready to start a new chapter of my life. However, throughout the first few months, I struggled to find where I truly fit in and where I felt that I belonged. That is, until swim season began that November.

I had been swimming for ten years, so this was a sport I loved and knew very well. However, this was the school's first year with a swim team, so I didn't know what to expect, and neither did my teammates. Over the next few weeks, our team came together. All of those hours of swimming truly began to pay off as we improved and became a team, and more importantly, a family. We became good friends, creating handshakes and quotes that you'd see and hear every time we were together, and I finally felt like I found a place where I belonged. My teammates were like my best friends and older siblings, and one stood out in particular—Jamie Kotula.

Jamie was a junior everyone loved, filled with energy and life. He was fun to be around, and his bright smile and great sense of humor could immediately brighten your day. He was the light of the school, a truly amazing person, a wonderful friend, and the greatest teammate you could ever ask for. And to me, he was like an older brother, someone who I could always count on to be there for me, and to tease me as well.

As the season went on, Jamie became a skilled swimmer who was in love with the sport. I looked forward to seeing him practice, and watching him jump up and down as he cheered during relays, bringing a whole new level of enthusiasm to the sport for us all. One Thursday night, I remember him doing a victory dance after beating Ally, who had gotten a head start due to a recent injury We loved seeing him there, but little did we know that Thursday was the last time we ever would.

The following morning began like any other Friday morning. But soon the entire school was assembled in the auditorium. I sat down next to my best friend Erika, and everyone was still and silent, so I began to worry that something was wrong. I leaned forward to a friend who was sitting in front of us, and asked what was going on.

"Someone died," she said, and I felt my stomach drop. "You'll see."

I looked over at Erika, completely panicked, and glanced around the auditorium again. Who wasn't there? I checked off the names in my head as I saw faces... Vince, John, Chris... who was it? A teacher? Someone I didn't know?

Then our principal made his way to the front of the auditorium, and everyone fell silent. I never looked up at him, I could only stare straight ahead, but I heard his voice as he spoke slowly. "I can tell that you all sense the seriousness of the situation, by how quiet you are. I am sorry to inform you that one of our students was involved in a traffic accident this morning, and suffered fatal injuries. I am sorry to inform you... that Jamie Kotula passed away this morning."

I heard some girls scream, and I heard myself yelp as my hands flew up to cover my face. Erika put her arms around me, and pulled me into her lap as I began shaking and crying. The next hour was a blur. As we sat in the auditorium as a school, praying for Jamie and for his family and friends, I never stopped crying, nor did anyone else. He couldn't be dead. I had seen him the night before.

We would later learn that on his way to school that morning, Jamie's car hit a patch of ice, causing it to spin out and veer down a hill into the trees, killing him instantly. For the rest of that Friday, our junior class stayed in the chapel. Some returned to classes. But the majority of the school sat together in the bathrooms, walked the halls, or joined the juniors in the chapel as we tried to make sense of what had just happened.

That night a prayer service was held for Jamie at his church, and a candlelit vigil at the soccer field where he played, followed. The next day we had a swim meet, and we all met in the locker room before to dye our hair red like Jamie's. We used Sharpies to write words of remembrance on each other. Then we all gathered by the pool at the start of the meet, and stood in a circle, arm in arm, as our coach read a speech he had written about Jamie the night before.

The following day was the viewing, where we presented his parents with a pair of my swim shorts, which Jamie wore at practices to cover up the hole on the butt of his jammers, and with a dinosaur swim cap, so that he'd always have a part of our team with him. The next morning was the funeral, which we attended as a school, together saying our goodbyes to Jamie.

The next few weeks seemed to take forever. Everything reminded us of him, and the hallways of school seemed empty without his infectious laugh and smile. The pain and longing to see him again felt unreal, and the thought of getting back to anything normal seemed impossible.

However, during that hard time, I found a source of hope — my friends. From the moment we learned of the accident, we came together as a school in order to support and comfort each other. We became a family that was there for each other through every moment. And eventually, with the help of friends, things began to get better.

I only knew Jamie for a couple of months, but that was long enough for his life and death to have a huge impact on my life. I learned to value and appreciate what I had, and to enjoy every opportunity I was given. We will always keep Jamie in our hearts, knowing that we now have a beautiful guardian angel watching over us. He will never be forgotten.

~Megan Carey

# 28

# When My Teacher Saved My Life

*If nature had intended our skeletons to be visible*
*it would have put them on the outside of our bodies.*
~Elmer Rice

All it took was a tear in my geography teacher's eye to save my life.

I had been battling an eating disorder for over six months—living off a half cup of cereal for breakfast with no milk (120 calories), a small cup of low-fat yogurt for lunch (80 calories), and a half cup of pasta with tomato sauce for dinner with a half cup of milk (300 calories). I don't know how it all started. Maybe it was when my brother called my skinny body fat, maybe it was when my dad congratulated me for being more muscular than the other girls on my volleyball team, maybe it was watching my mom exercising and dieting all the time. Whatever it was, my eating disorder hit me hard. I ran on the treadmill for twenty minutes before school, I biked three miles to get to school, I went to Nordic Ski practice for two hours after school, and I biked three miles back home. Pounds melted off me and I felt strong, fit, and fast... until my symptoms began to hit me hard.

I became chronically cold—shivering in eighty-degree rooms. I became pale and weak. I was dizzy and light-headed, almost fainting when I stood up. But I loved my new body. My previous too-muscular thighs had become thin and sleek. My round facial cheeks faded into sharp angles and high cheekbones. I was addicted to improving my body.

Then, one day in May, my geography teacher pulled me out of class.

He was my favorite teacher in the world. He was funny, kind, and like a father to me. He seemed to always keep an eye out for me. He made me feel special.

When he pulled me out of class I was shivering from my eating disorder-induced chills. He shut the door behind me and looked me straight in the eye.

"Are you okay?" he asked. "You haven't seemed quite right in class."

"Yeah," I lied casually. "Just tired." I feigned a yawn and looked away.

I realized he was staring at me oddly, so I looked back in his eyes. I was shocked to see his eyes looked wet. An uncomfortable knot formed in my stomach.

"Christine, I don't know what's going on with you, but I w' you to know that everyone here cares for you. You're strong, be ful, and smart. I want you to beat whatever it is you're going thr I don't want to lose you. You understand?"

"Y-yeah," I said, awkwardly, before hastily retreating back the door to my seat.

During the rest of the class I didn't make eye contact sat in my seat with many confused thoughts going throu What was wrong with me? Why was I starving myself? know?

When I got home I almost passed out again. at my stomach like a knife, but I couldn't make couldn't. When my mom came home I averted impulsively deciding to speak.

"M-m-om?" I asked, my voice breaking. "I think I need to go to the hospital."

I expected her to break into a panic, asking me what was wrong, but to my surprise my mom looked at me calmly and replied, "I know."

That evening I was driven right to the eating disorder hospital. I was admitted into the top floor, where I was moved into a room with other identical, teenage stick figures. I didn't show up to school for the last three weeks of class. Instead I lived at the hospital in a small bedroom. I slept, ate, then ate again, then ate again. I ate six meals a day. I had lost thirty pounds in a month, had a heart rate below forty, and I was at a high risk of sudden death or cardiac arrest. I didn't want to die. Instead, I ate everything served to me.

Never had food been so delicious. I felt as if it was the best thing in the world. The sourest strawberry tasted like a piece of heaven. A piece of chicken seemed to melt in my mouth like a piece of cheese-cake. Food... food... food. My deprived brain couldn't stop thinking about it.

After three weeks I moved back home and steadily gained all my weight back over the next few months. My thighs that I had hated so much came back. My cheeks reappeared. My prominent ribs faded back from my skin. At times I cried, feeling as if all my hard work had been for nothing, but soon I began seeing myself for who I really was. I was strong, smart, athletic and... beautiful.

Now I am going in to high school. Although many of the girls I met at the eating disorder center have relapsed, I know that no matter what, I will never fall into such a terrible loop. Instead, I think of my favorite geography teacher, and the tear in his eye, and remind myself that no matter what, I have all the friends and family I need to sup-port me, without killing myself through an eating disorder.

I never got to see my favorite teacher again after going to the hospital, but I won't let him down. After all, it's not every day your geography teacher saves your life. Without him, I wouldn't be around

~Christine Catlin

# Resolution

*One's suffering disappears when one lets oneself go, when one yields—*
*even to sadness.*
*~Antoine de Saint-Exupéry*

"Wow." That was the first word out of my psychiatrist's mouth when I handed back the questionnaire. She scanned it once before she looked at me. "Did you know you were this depressed, Kate?"

The test had included questions such as, "How much motivation have you had over the past two weeks?" and, "Have you ever had thoughts of suicide or self-inflicted pain? Have you acted on them?" My answers were true, but I didn't think anything of them.

A knot started to form in my stomach. "I guess I know that I get sad a lot, but I don't know how bad it is in comparison to everyone else. Everybody gets sad, right?"

"Yes, but not like this." I had been seeing Dr. Robb for about a year, focusing on my anxiety. The appointments had gotten intense; I saw her weekly. We were trying to solve the problem of my attendance record at school.

Ever since mid-October, I refused to go to class. I couldn't even explain why. There was this inexplicable force that compelled me to stay home, chained to my bed. I was scared to leave. Something bad would happen if I left my bed. My heart would race at the thought of school and all those people staring at me. I couldn't even find a good enough reason in my mind to go to the kitchen for food. Only when it was critical that I eat would I make chocolate chip cookies and eat the entire batch myself, chasing it down with a glass of milk.

It was now the end of November. And there was finally a reason. I was sad. Not just upset about a fifty on a math test, but a heart wrenching, throat swelling, limb numbing sad. And there was nothing I could do. I was truly crushed by this. The diagnosis probably could have helped other people. It's a clear, distinct answer. But it frustrated me. I wanted to fix it.

Grade ten wasn't supposed to be like this. I wanted it to be fun and carefree. That's how it was for all my friends. There were parties every weekend and the most they worried about was who was hooking up with whom. I was stuck under my covers with no motivation to get out.

It's not like I didn't try, though. On a few occasions I felt good about the day ahead of me, but the slightest negative feeling I got from something would set me off again. This continued for five months.

By the time second semester came around, I still hadn't gotten to school. I switched out of the specialized arts high school I was attending because I wasn't able to catch up with the rest of my classmates. I ended up returning to my first school. With many of my friends there, I thought it might help, but unfortunately, I still had the same feeling of loneliness and desperation, just in a new setting. Getting to school was easier with the more relaxed environment, but my attendance still wasn't perfect.

My shyness wasn't helping either. My best friends were incredibly outgoing and friends with lots of people. Of course, I met all of these people but I never really connected with any of them. I just withdrew even more.

"You just have to put yourself out there," Jennie, Sarah and Miranda would tell me. "It's so much easier once you make the first move." But I didn't believe them. I couldn't.

One day near the end of March, I couldn't take it anymore. Nothing was going right. I was fed up with feeling sad all the time. I was totally powerless against my depression. I thought there was only one way to get rid of it. It involved getting rid of me, too.

I grabbed the ibuprofen from the medicine cabinet and poured at least fifty extra-strength tablets into a mortar and started to grind them up. Once they were powder, I poured them into a filled water bottle. My hands shook as I brought the bottle to my lips. The smell of the ibuprofen filled my nose. As the powdery water entered my mouth, I felt that it was too much. The smell, the taste... I spat it out. The tears that had been running down my cheeks went into overdrive and I couldn't see the space in front of me. Had I really just tried to do that? What would have happened if I swallowed? If I finished the whole bottle? I cried the rest of the day until dinner. I had to look happy in front of my family.

The next few months were better, only because I didn't try it again. I was still lonely, socially awkward and upset with myself. My friends invited me to more parties and I was glad to be included, but once I got to the parties, I was the same as at school—invisible.

Finally June came. One of the girls in my grade threw an end-of-exams party and invited quite a few people. I was looking forward to it, as it meant summer was approaching. At the party, everyone was drinking and smoking, so I escaped upstairs to get some air. The night hadn't been nearly as good as I had hoped and I was starting to feel really down. A boy from my drama class came upstairs.

"Are you okay, Kate?" Tye asked. I nodded and gave my usual smile and an, "I'm fine." This question was not new to me. I think I heard it more that year than the rest of my sixteen years combined.

"Okay, then," he said and walked away. When I got home, I started to think about my six-second interaction with Tye. I'm really not okay, I wanted to say. I haven't been for a while. I never was. But I'm not alone. How many other people lie about being okay? We've all got different stories and we've all got different reasons, but in the end that's what brings us together. Who knows, maybe Tye wasn't okay either. Maybe everyone at the party had something on their mind that they were trying to forget like me, and maybe if I really did open up, if I wasn't afraid to make a fool of myself, they'd open up too. My friends were right. I was just going to have to put myself out there.

~Kate Jackson

# Your Story is important

*Those who bring sunshine to the lives of others*
*cannot keep it from themselves.*
*~James Matthew Barrie*

t's December 24th, Christmas Eve. I can remember how, this time a year ago, I didn't want a Christmas. My idea of the perfect Christmas was to get a dead Christmas tree and hang things on it to represent my broken heart. I can remember that I didn't even want to celebrate my birthday days after Christmas, on January 1st.

Last year was a difficult time for me. I was suffering from depression, self-injury, and suicide. I was cutting myself because I was experiencing emotional pain inside and I couldn't deal with it. The physical pain took it away from me. It made me feel like I was alive—it made what I was feeling just go away.

I soon developed very severe depression. I wouldn't talk to people. Sometimes I wouldn't eat. The people at school would tell me that they were scared. They didn't know what was happening to me, and they didn't know how to handle it. Many times, friends from church would tell me that they didn't know what to say. Because of this, I was pushed out of that group of friends and left to fend for myself.

My parents didn't know what to do. My friends didn't know what to do. People ignored the situation, and they hoped that it would just resolve itself on its own. It didn't.

I became suicidal. I didn't see any point in living. I wanted to die and thought about it all the time. I didn't know what was wrong with me. I just lived every day thinking how much I wasn't wanted. How much people really didn't care. What purpose was there, living in a world where I wasn't wanted or cared about? I would spend hours at school failing classes, drawing pictures in my notebooks inspired by thoughts of suicide and depression.

Although I was falling apart, I kept fighting it. I had several conversations with people during times when I wanted to kill myself. They didn't understand, but they tried to talk to me, help me through these impulsive decisions. In the end, they couldn't help. They couldn't understand. I soon stopped calling people. I had written letters to friends, reached out to almost everyone around me, but nothing was working. People would say that they were there for me, and then they would just leave.

During my depression and cutting, before I even thought of suicide, I came across an organization called To Write Love On Her Arms. They are a non-profit organization dedicated to helping people who suffer from depression, addiction, self-injury and thoughts of suicide. They exist to educate, inform and invest directly into treatment and recovery from these issues. They encouraged me and told me that I was not a lost cause, that I could get help, and that these were not issues that were untreatable.

Because of To Write Love On Her Arms, I found the strength to keep pushing through my tough times. I reached out to people when I wanted to give up. I met a lot of people through the organization and when I wanted to kill myself, I would message them online and talk to them. Often, helping them with their own problems made it easier for me to keep moving, for me to keep living.

Over time, people began to see that I was suicidal, and through the help of a guidance counselor at school, I went to professional therapy. I only spent about ten sessions in therapy before my counselor convinced my mother that I was in need of medicine for depression and anxiety. I didn't believe after all this time that I would get medicine, but when I was holding the prescription in my hands, I found that hope was real. That help was real.

I've been on medicine for about six months now, and I'm loving life. It's hard to believe that a year ago I was a totally different person. It's hard to believe that life can have such meaning and purpose and that I'm fine. I've learned that although medicine can help me with my problems, I have to learn to deal with them on my own.

With the help of friends, family, and medicine that I needed so long ago, I have learned to live with my problems. My depression will always be there, and I might not always want to be alive, but I learned that if I just wait it out, it will pass. Just because I'm feeling something for the moment doesn't mean it's really what I want.

I've been free of thoughts of suicide and self-injury for over six months now. Sometimes I have an urge to cut, sometimes I have bouts of depression, but I've learned that I can deal with it.

I'm currently working online to promote To Write Love On Her Arms, and helping people get through the same issues that I have. The advice that I give to people struggling with these issues is simple. Live in a community. You need other people to help you because they understand what you are going through, but you also need people to help you get the treatment and recovery you need. Talk to the people who have the power to get you help. Talk to friends for support and encouragement. Don't give up! Keep fighting when you feel like giving up. You aren't always going to feel like fighting. You are going to feel like you can't go on. But in these times, when you feel like the world is caving, you are made stronger.

~Dylan Liebhart

# Reason to Live

*Real living is living for others.*
~Bruce Lee

Even though I hurt myself, I do not want to die. For me, cutting has become an addiction. After a few days without picking up my knife, I begin to experience withdrawal. I become agitated and irritable. My body starts to twitch and I start biting myself. Then, after once again pledging to stop cutting for good, I cave. Without thinking I unsheathe my blade and slit my arms, not realizing what I have done until it's already over. In the following hours, I am very relaxed. But as soon as I wake up in the morning and stretch my arms out before me, I remember what I did, and I wish I could wash all my scars from my arms the way we wash stains from clothes.

It was hard to come clean to others about my problem. Thankfully, I have a group of friends at my karate school who are like my family. One of the first people I told was my best friend Juan, who I see as an older brother. At first, he was angry. He didn't understand how someone as strong as myself could resort to self-harm. When I look back, I realize he was only scared for me, and wanted to protect me.

As I talked to Juan more, I told him my reasons for cutting. My biggest fear was, and still is, failing the only person who's ever truly believed in me. That person is my head instructor, Mr. Ndimby. He has seen me through some of my toughest moments. He made me laugh when I was struggling with my body image, and comforted me when my dad passed away. And even though I knew in the back of my mind that he cared for me, he was never the best at showing affection. I felt pressure to be the perfect martial artist, instructor, and student. Mr. Ndimby was the only adult I had ever really felt so much respect for, so I felt like I needed to make him proud.

It got colder, and my depression got worse. I became more anxious as the weeks drew on. Even during my winter break trip to Florida, I cried every night. When I got back home, I hit rock bottom. I started to cut every day, and the slits in my skin slowly climbed up my forearms. Afraid that other people would grow suspicious, I started to cut on my stomach as well. I wore long sleeves and hoodies whenever possible, and wouldn't change my shirt for gym. And every time I messed up at karate, another scar would appear on my arms.

It's confusing when the person you look up to the most becomes the main source of your pain. There were days when I couldn't stand to be around my instructor. I would snap at him, talk back to him, or just plain ignore him. But afterwards, I felt horrible. I knew I shouldn't blame him for something going haywire inside me. I was terrified of losing him—after all, I had already lost my father. I didn't want to lose Mr. Ndimby, too. I knew I should tell him about my cutting, but I was afraid he would get mad at me, so I stayed silent.

Eventually, Juan convinced me to confess to Mr. Ndimby. I agreed, realizing it would be in my best interest to get my problems off my chest. So I asked Mr. Ndimby to set aside a day where we could talk, and he made it happen. After work on Saturday, he took me into the back room. We sat down, and I remember him looking at me and smiling as he asked what was on my mind.

"I'm scared of how you'll react," I mumbled, looking down at my arms.

"Laura," he said firmly, "Nothing you tell me could ever make me hate you." I looked up at him, and his smile had disappeared. Feeling a bit more reassured, I took a deep breath in.

"Can I just show you, instead of telling you?" I asked, unable to find the words to explain myself. He nodded, and I showed him my forearms. He examined each cut, and I began to tear up.

"So when did this all start?" he asked, looking me in the eyes.

I told him the whole story. As we continued to talk, I couldn't hold back the tears. But he was patient with me, and tried to be as understanding as possible. When we were done, I dried my eyes, and he gave me a big hug.

That talk pretty much saved my life. If he hadn't taken the time to talk to me, I would have cut even more. After that day, I never again questioned the fact that he cared for me. I felt more confident and happy, and we continued to have talks routinely. One day, he asked me what I wanted to do when I grew up.

"I want to open my own karate school," I confessed, expecting him to laugh. He smiled.

"That's great! I'm glad you have a plan for the future."

I was in a bit of shock. When I had told my mom about my dream, she was skeptical. She told me that my love of karate wouldn't last forever, and that I should consider other career options. I was offended—karate was the only thing that made me truly happy, and I knew that I would never be satisfied if I did anything else with my life. Finally having a plan for the future gave me a little more hope.

It still amazes me that there are people in this world who love me enough to take care of me like they do. Some days I feel as if I'm absolutely worthless, but when I go to karate, I am reminded that I have a purpose in life. A hug from someone I care about can turn my whole mood around. I still cry, but now, I cry because I am happy and so overwhelmed with love.

Mr. Ndimby, especially, gave me a reason to keep going. He gave me hope when no one else could. Although I'll probably never be able to say this to his face, because I'm scared of crying in front of him, he is like a father to me, and I only want to make him proud. Someday, I will fully conquer my depression and move on with my life. And that day will come because I know that he wants the best for me. Because of him, I promise, I will get better.

~Laura Hemphill

# Tough Times for Teens

## Chapter 4

## My Own Worst Enemy

# Starved

*In order to change we must be sick and tired of being sick and tired.*
*~Author Unknown*

My parents would not let me go to school that morning.

"Why not?" I argued. "I have exams. I have work in Spanish class that I can't miss!"

My mother gave me a sad look. "You have to get some tests done," she explained, and I groaned. More tests? My father pulled me over to the couch while my mind raced.

"Alison," my father said in that calm, unruffled tone that was quiet but powerful. "You're not eating. And you know that. You can have all the money in the world, but if you don't have your health, you have nothing." For some reason, I believed him. Through these last few months, there were few times when I trusted the word of anyone but myself. But here I was, putting my faith in someone else.

I hadn't wanted it to be this way. Two years before, when I was fourteen, I started exercising and skipping snacks after school. During the summer, I did weekly weigh-ins and kept to a strict diet consisting of few foods. I memorized the calories of almost everything that was edible.

When I entered high school, a place I thought would be a dream compared to the horrors of middle school, I was surprised that things took a turn for the worse. I began to exercise in a rigid pattern, my only intention being to lose weight. Later, when it became too cold to run outside, I restricted my calories even more to make up for not being able to burn them.

I avoided parties with my friends, terrified of the food. I didn't go out to my friend's New Year's Eve party, and instead went to a movie with my parents, sipping a large diet cola while they ate popcorn. When the clock struck midnight, welcoming us into 2011, I didn't go downstairs to say hello to my brother's friends, afraid of how ugly they would think I looked.

After that, things got even worse.

I was suddenly afraid of food. At night, I would allow myself one low calorie English muffin and half a tablespoon of peanut butter. Even that was too much. One day, I ran into my room, threw the peanut butter on the ground, and broke into deep sobs. I couldn't eat that. I didn't know what it would do to my body. Carbs were bad for you at night, weren't they? And peanut butter would coat the insides of my stomach, expanding it. What about a piece of fruit? No, I couldn't have that. I wouldn't be exercising to burn off the calories, and they would stay in my body, causing me to gain weight.

Though it seems impossible, my fear of food was as potent and rational as someone's fear of heights, dogs, or fire. I really believed every food would do something horrible to my body. I finally collapsed on the floor and called out my mother's name, gulping down sobs until she came downstairs. At this point, my mother was fully aware of my eating disorder. She took me into the kitchen and gave me some carrots with light veggie dip and a piece of toast, while I counted the calories, making sure they did not exceed my limit for the day.

Not long after that day, I went to the mall with my mom. We shopped a bit, and I finally bought myself a pair of pants that didn't need to be held up with a belt or hair band.

While we waited in line to purchase our items, I swore I was going to pass out. I felt dizzy and standing was getting harder and harder. The noise in the mall felt so loud, it banged in my ears like a thousand clattering pots.

As my mom tried to figure out which exit we should go through, she noticed my pale face. "Al!" Her voice sounded alarmed, but also far away. "You look like you're going to pass out. Are you okay?" I couldn't answer with more than a mumble.

My mom was suddenly speeding things up, taking charge and locating the nearest exit. She told me to wait inside, and she would drive the car over. I was so thankful. It was January and the cold was unbearable. It seeped through my bones and nearly paralyzed me. My hands were especially dry, peeling, and wrinkled. My sister called them old people's hands. I would later find out this was a symptom of malnutrition.

Once we were in the car, my mother blasted the heat and begged me to go in the diner with her. "We can have eggs," she said. "Those are healthy." But I refused. I just wanted my piece of toast and half a tablespoon of peanut butter.

Incidents like the one at the mall were in my thoughts as my parents called me into the kitchen for a talk that morning—the morning when they wouldn't let me go to school. My mother was in tears as she told me the news. "Al, you have a heart problem. Your heart rate is so low that you can't go to Renfrew yet to be treated. You have to go to the hospital."

I wasn't really processing what they were saying; I was miles behind them, just trying to figure out how one morning could change so drastically. One minute I was preparing to ace my Spanish midterm project, the next I was gearing up to be hospitalized for anorexia.

The hospital visit turned out to be two weeks, and it was only that short because my parents were on the hospital's back, making sure I wouldn't have to endure more time there than necessary. I wasn't allowed to have a computer to do my schoolwork, a phone, binders, or gum, among many other things. It was a lockdown facility, sealed away from the rest of the units in the hospital. We were separated from the adult wing by a locked door—the adults had gray, haunted faces. Their cheeks sagged and their eyes looked dead. Their clothes hung on their depleted bodies, and they wrapped themselves in tight blankets to bear the cold, though the eating disorder wing was heated more than a normal room.

I still remember my first meal there, which I mostly picked at, and how I was shocked by its size: Lasagna, string beans, milk, water, yogurt, and an ice cream cup. On weekends, especially Sundays, there were no planned activities. The five other kids and I tried to pass time by watching a movie. After every meal, we would sit with our guilt and the seemingly massive amounts of food in our body and try to think of reasons to keep going, to keep eating, to scrounge up some bit of hope. It was the darkest two weeks of my life.

I would later go on to a residential program, a day program for several weeks, and an intensive outpatient program. I am now, several months later, at the end of my freshman year, the worst year of my life, and in an outpatient program with girls around my age or older. We talk about our struggles with various eating disorders and the problems we face on a daily basis because of this mental illness we are coping with.

My eating disorder was my blessing and my curse. It took away months and months of my life. It starved me of friendship, life, and happiness. It wanted to kill me. But, it also led me to understand that an eating disorder is not something someone can just stop. It's not something that someone has control over, or a diet used solely to become thin. It is a mental illness that ruins lives. I am now in recovery and working to free myself of it. Back then, I did not have control of my life. Back then, I was weak. Now, I am healthy and strong. Now, I don't have to be afraid. Now, I put my wants and needs above the needs of this lethal disease.

~Ali Lauro

# The Toothbrush

*Put your future in good hands — your own.*
*~Author Unknown*

I leaned over the toilet apprehensively. The floor was cold, and I only had on my cotton pajama shorts. The shallow water mocked me. I wasn't sure if it was because it knew I couldn't do this or because I had gotten myself into this awful situation. A little of both, I guess.

I tied my hair back and turned on the iPod stereo that I kept in the bathroom so that my off-key voice would have music to sing to in the shower. "Fat Bottomed Girls" by Queen blared into the small room. How appropriate, I thought grimly, as I turned up the music. The walls were very thin in our new house, and I wasn't sure how much my mom might be able to hear.

I gripped my toothbrush.

Don't think I didn't know what I was getting into. I'd read the tragic articles about girls like me in *Cosmopolitan*. I'd heard all about the disorders that girls got from the videos in health class. I'd known about the girls who almost died because they wouldn't eat.

I never tried to look like the girls plastered on magazines and dancing in music videos. I knew they weren't real. I never wanted to look airbrushed or computer generated. I never wanted to be the unrealistic girl that the media has constructed to make me feel inferior. I hated that girl.

I just didn't want to hate myself anymore.

I was tired of looking at myself in my bra and panties every night in the mirror and being disgusted. I was tired of arguing with my mother whenever she made cookies or brownies or things I would love to eat. I was tired of running for miles at the park and doing countless sit-ups only to find that I'd only worked off lunch and breakfast. I was tired of knowing exactly how many calories are in a pack of M&M's or chicken salad when all of my friends were guessing. I was tired of looking at the scale every single week and then wanting to cry. I was tired of skipping trips to the lake and swimming pool because I didn't want to be compared to the girls in bikinis. I was tired of not being able to wear tight tops because they would be considered "unflattering."

I was tired of being what I was.

I wasn't fat. Not really. I just had fat. It's like greed. Just because you have greed sometimes, you're not necessarily a greedy person. I still had boyfriends and guys who told me I was hot. I only needed to lose twenty or so pounds to be what I wanted. So why was it this hard?

I'd lost a lot of weight before. Fifteen pounds. I had been so close. My sister offended me be asking if I was bulimic, and other relatives gaped at my tighter tummy in surprise. But then my boyfriend had dumped me, and I'd developed a larger appetite. It also didn't help that my mom bought a house and didn't have the money to buy me expensive Lean Cuisines and Weight Watchers anymore.

I'd gained most of it back, leaving me in the exact same place as before: on my knees in front of the toilet.

As the water in the toilet shimmered at me, I contemplated consequences. Someone had told me that if you try a drug, it's easy to do it again because you're not so scared anymore. Would this be like that? If I stuck the toothbrush down my throat, would I become addicted to it? Would I become the next interview in magazines? Would I be the one in the health videos?

I sighed. And dropped the toothbrush onto the cold floor.

My story isn't one of overcoming a great adversary. I didn't really overcome anything, because as I write this now, I still don't always like myself. Sometimes I still drop to my knees, sometimes for God and sometimes on the bathroom floor. But I still haven't pushed the toothbrush all the way back yet, which is some sort of accomplishment, I suppose. I take it a step at a time, and I know I am doing the right thing for myself. Instead of letting all of the calories of the day fall into the bowl, I fill it with saltwater, wishing that I could lose weight by crying.

Because then I'd be thin by now.

~Kendyl Kearly

# A Pocket Full of Lies

*Even if happiness forgets you a little bit, never completely forget about it.*
*~Jacques Prévert*

The mirror is her enemy
The reflection is her fear.
She hides all her emotions
Her smile masks the tears.

Trapped inside her exterior
She's screaming to get out.
Then parallel to her reflection
She's staring herself down.

She finds every imperfection
And tears are forming in her eyes.
She hides the truth from everyone
And she's living through her lies.

So she pretends that she's happy
She smiles like she's okay.
Her happiness is but an act
And she's breaking more each day.

But she's striving for perfection
In her mind, though, she's not close.
She's working harder towards her goal
And it's hurting her the most.

Her words, they start to tremble
Then her body starts to shake.
She's crumbling under all the hurt
There's not much more she can take.

She then collapses into a heap
'Cause no matter how she tries
She's still living with a broken soul
And a pocket full of lies.

~Jessie M. Garneau

# The No-Seconds Plan

*Seize the moment.*
*Remember all those women on the Titanic who waved off the dessert cart.*
~Erma Bombeck

approached the salad bar dutifully, staring at the lettuce bin for a full minute before taking up the prongs and scooping it onto my plate.

Salad again.

It was Day Three of my academic summer program, and my seventh meal in the dining hall. I had been excited to return to the program where I had met new people last summer, where I had taken writing courses and cloud-watched with my classmates, and even danced a little at the Friday night dances. As my sophomore year of high school progressed, though, I looked forward to the summer program for another reason—I saw it as an opportunity to lose weight.

It would be the perfect new beginning. The cafeteria food wouldn't be good anyway, so it should be easy to keep a simple promise to myself. I would have only one helping of every meal, and never go back for seconds. And that one meal would be, as often as possible, salad from the salad bar.

It wasn't going well.

My good friends from last year weren't there. They'd decided to do older-sounding things instead, like getting summer jobs. I wasn't connecting with any of the people in my new classes. As for the no-seconds plan, it was getting harder and harder for me to follow. I felt faint. Why was I so weak? It wasn't as if I was starving myself; all I was doing was not getting second helpings. And I couldn't even handle that. It felt a weak ending to a whole year of failure.

I had switched from Catholic to public school that year, so being a sophomore was all about trying to break into already-established circles of friends. No one wanted to talk to me, and I figured the problem was the way I looked. I started dieting. My mom was on Weight Watchers, and the program gave her a little booklet that assigned points to each type of food—the more calories the food, the more points it got. I continually challenged myself to rack up as few points as I could each day, which amounted to a lot of cucumbers and Diet Coke. By the fourth day of such a challenge, I always thought I was losing weight, but I also felt like I was going to keel over. By the end of the week, I would cave, eating just that handful of chips or one slice of pizza, only once I started, I wouldn't be able to stop.

I bought magazines that advertised "cleansing" diets that various celebrities used, but my dieting pattern was pretty much the same: cleanse all week (usually by eating one type of food and excluding everything else), feel so dizzy that I would default to normal food, and then eat too much of that because I was so hungry.

It always came down to my lack of willpower, and I kept convincing myself that this time, I was going to beat my hunger. Once I could win the battle against my body, I would finally be able to look good, like someone that people would actually want to hang out with.

The worst time for me was when you had to turn from the food line to the tables and find a place to sit. If you didn't have a destination right away, everyone at the summer program would watch you search for someone, anyone, to sit with.

When I turned from the salad bar, I didn't see anyone from my class. Maybe they went somewhere else without me. I saw an empty table in the left corner and I had to eat. I stumbled toward it.

"Hey, Eve!"

Lenni had been in my hall last summer, but we hadn't talked much. I was kind of in awe of her. She had an eyebrow ring and her hair was dyed fire-engine red and she hung out with people who wore mostly black and studded things. She sat with them now, and they were all looking at me coolly, me with my stupid vest and flowered skirt. I must have looked like the biggest nerd in the program.

But Lenni was smiling as if it was totally normal for someone like her to talk to someone like me. "What class are you taking?"

We made small talk for a few minutes while her tablemates watched us, still silent, as if they were waiting for me to go away. Lenni didn't seem to notice. "Want to sit with us?" she asked.

I glanced at that empty corner table. It was small, unobtrusive. Safe. But then I looked at my salad, and it was so pathetic-looking with its wilted lettuce. All I wanted to do was think about something other than food. "Sure," I said.

The people at Lenni's table were not thin. Well, one of the boys was, but the girls were definitely all sorts of shapes—some built, some curvy. They didn't seem to care. The food on their trays was pretty varied. Two people were eating the chicken tenders with mountains of French fries on the side. One brave soul was sampling the casserole. Lenni and a girl named Shira had several scoops of ice cream in individual bowls on their trays, all covered with M&M's. "It's sundae sampling day," Lenni explained.

The other thing that surprised me about Lenni's table was that they were not the sullen, angry people their clothes suggested. They were all really goofy. Lenni claimed that one of her sundaes tasted like Kool-Aid and made everyone at the table try it. Shira grabbed the salt and pepper containers and narrated a conversation between them. I was fascinated. I left the table with them and we went back to the dorms together.

The more time I spent with my newfound group, the more my own reserve dropped. I cracked a few jokes of my own. I started donning the quirkier aspects of my wardrobe, including the vintage glasses I'd bought months before but never had the courage to wear.

Shira and I turned out to have the same taste in books, and we debated about our favorite storylines and characters for hours. A week into hanging out with them, I followed Shira to the ice cream cooler in the midst of one of our arguments. I took a cone back to our table before remembering my self-made rule about not getting seconds—which I had broken several times that week. Then I dug into my ice cream. It didn't seem to matter anymore.

That summer, I played tennis for the first time, performed in the talent show, won my class debate championship, and had my first kiss, but I still think the most important thing I did was sit down with the people who would show me how to be comfortable in my own body. It scares me to think about what might've happened if I hadn't met them, if I had continued down the self-destructive path I had forged my sophomore year.

On the last day of camp, I pulled Lenni aside and told her about the no-seconds plan I hadn't followed.

Her jaw hung open for a full minute before she said, "But that's so unhealthy! The plates are so small in the dining hall, and we're only in there three times a day."

"I know," I said. "You totally saved me, though. I would've been way too afraid to even approach you guys if you hadn't called me over."

"It took me three days to get up the courage to talk to you," she said. "You always seemed so smart and aloof. Like you were too busy thinking deep thoughts to talk to people like me."

Aloof.

Go figure.

~Eve Legato

# Just One Person

*A single rose can be my garden... a single friend, my world.*
~Leo Buscaglia

Six months before I turned thirteen I started pulling my hair out. I could tell you where I was. I could tell you where I was sitting. I could even tell you what I was watching on TV.

It started simply enough. Sitting in my living room, relaxing on the sofa watching a show, twirling a hair. Then, pop! Out it came, along with an odd piece of skin—a hair follicle. I was fascinated. I studied it. I played with it. I tried to find another one, and I did. I repeated this over and over, obsessed to find as many as possible.

I couldn't explain why I was doing what I was doing. It didn't feel good, it didn't look attractive constantly having my hands on my head, and it certainly wasn't constructive behavior. After one day, I had a small bald spot along my bang line. I told myself that I could hide it and no one would notice. People have thin spots along their bang line all the time. That's what I told myself. Until I discovered that I couldn't stop. "Just one more, and that's it. I won't ever do it again," I'd say. Pluck. "Okay, this is definitely the last one." Pluck. "Okay, seriously now. This is stupid." Pluck.

At first, it was easy to cover up. Make a spot, brush over my hair, make a new spot. Before I knew it, I had perfectly round, smooth patches all over my head, not a single hair in them. It got harder to cover up. It was an obsession, a compulsion, a habit I couldn't break. I tried so hard to make my hands stay at my sides, but they felt restless and twitchy, I even used gloves to make it harder to grip them. That was how I discovered tweezers.

When people started to notice, I made things up. "I have ring-worm." "I have alopecia." "Doctors don't know why; it just started falling out." Anything to take the blame off me. I even started to believe some of it. If I blamed something else, I didn't need to take responsibility. Ultimately, that led to the absence of nearly all the hair on the top of my head. I had to invest in bandannas.

School was complete torture. Being the only person allowed to wear hats and bandannas led to relentless bullying and taunting from my classmates, even people I considered friends. My grades slipped, I skipped classes, and life became a social nightmare. I remember one particular day when my bandanna was ripped from my head in the middle of a crowded lunchroom, only to have it thrown away from me and lost on the floor. It took fifteen minutes to find it. Fifteen minutes of desperation and exposed self-inflicted hideousness.

The word "freak" appeared on my locker, and girls in the gym asked me what kind of cancer I had. I started to believe that I was worthless and ugly because surely anyone who could do this to herself deserved to hear those words. It was definitely not the way I had envisioned the start of my teenage years, the beginning of my life away from childhood. I had met my new self, an unconfident nobody. I became a ghost.

On one of the days I actually dragged myself to school so that Social Services wouldn't show up on my parents' doorstep, I situated myself in my first period science class. I put my head onto my crossed arms on the table like I always did when I felt like hiding. I noticed someone had taken a seat next to me—a classmate whom I barely even knew at the time. I became a bit uneasy since she didn't typi-cally sit there; she sat in the back. Then, she did what I expected her to do. She asked me why I chose to wear bandannas every day and why I had spots on my head. I looked at her and envied her braids. I lashed out, tired of people butting into my private business, because obviously this girl was just like everyone else—there to torture a poor girl with bald spots. I yelled at her to leave me alone. I started to cry, to my horror.

Her name was Ebony. I knew that because she told me when I burst into tears. Taken aback, since I had just yelled in her face and she hadn't reacted, I stared at her.

"You know," she said, "my mom is completely bald. She hated her hair. You should just shave it, like she did. There are lots of people who think bald is beautiful."

I started to cry again, but for a different reason. Someone was showing me compassion. Someone outside of my parents. I remember thanking her and telling her she was the first person in a very long time who didn't make fun of me. I also apologized for shouting.

She said, "It's just hair. It will always grow back."

It was probably the first time in a year that I hadn't felt like a freak show act. I was relieved that someone, even though we didn't know each other, could show a person like me that sort of compassion. I don't even think she realized the impact of that moment. Just one person can make you feel worth something, make you feel like you're not a complete outcast. One person can make you feel normal.

We remained lab partners for the remainder of that year, and we spoke often. I never did shave my head, but the thought was there.

I have since graduated high school and I have amazing friends. I have also been seeing a behavioral therapist and diagnosed with a condition called trichotillomania, or obsessive hair pulling—Trich for short. Many people don't realize how common it is in teenagers, but some people, like myself, need a lot of extra guidance to beat it. Some people don't. I suppose it's like any compulsion—a roll of the dice.

Breaking the habit of hair pulling is hard work. You have to pay attention to your surroundings and what you're doing at all times. And to be honest, I didn't think I would ever be able to do it.

I'm happy to say that, as of now, it's been six months since I last pulled a hair, and recently I was able to cut it and style it. I am bandanna free. I held a party and burned my bandanna not too long after I cut my hair, at the suggestion of a friend studying photography who wanted to hold a "Girl Power" photo shoot. It was by far the most liberating feeling in the entire world to know I beat trichotillomania, and I am blessed I had someone like Ebony to remind me of what was beautiful. No matter how bleak it seems, there's someone out there who will and does care. Thanks, Ebony, wherever you are.

~Kristen Marrs

# The Good Side
# of My Reflection

*It's not who you are that holds you back, it's who you think you're not.*
*~Author Unknown*

Sometimes I look at my whole body,
And conclude that it just doesn't fit me.

I always find a problem in whatever I wear,
Or start wishing for longer, thicker, bouncier hair.

I envision my reflection with ocean blue eyes,
Or imagine myself with much slimmer thighs.

A glance in the mirror shows a blemish on my skin,
Then I wish for a fair and smooth complexion.

I'm sucking in my stomach so I can see my abs,
I'm dieting like crazy trying to get rid of baby flab.

I've spent countless hours just staring at me,
Trying desperately to find something pretty.

Then I saw something, after trying so hard to hide:
My beautiful characteristics are all on the inside.

I'm very intelligent; I can read so fast,
Though my clothing isn't the best, I wear it with class.

Man, I am funny, even if only inside my mind,
I just so happen to be quiet most of the time.

I am kind, brave, and I have a good heart,
My gigantic smile illuminates the dark.

It's awful how I wasted time pointing out my imperfections,
Never taking time to notice the good side of my reflection.

~Alandra K. Rasheed

# Nothing is impossible

*And the day came when the risk to remain tight in a bud was more painful then the risk it took to blossom.*

~Anaïs Nin

The seconds, minutes, hours, days, and months go by so fast. My freshman year at West Ranch High School is nearly over, and I think about how nervous I was at the beginning of the year. In less than three years I will apply to my dream college—CalArts—and getting in sometimes feels impossible. But I know that it's possible, because I know that everything is possible. I know this because when I was about eleven years old, I was diagnosed with a disorder called obsessive-compulsive disorder (OCD).

OCD is sometimes known as the "germaphobe" disorder. When I was ten, I would hide my clothing from my mom because I thought there were germs on it that would make her sick. But there is more to OCD than that. OCD is actually a chronic emotional and genetic disorder in which people have unwanted and repeated thoughts, feelings, ideas, and sensations known as obsessions, coupled with behaviors that make them feel compelled to do something, known as compulsions.

For example, when I thought about death, I would repeatedly say a word in my head, usually in a group of four. This was a number

I used in my "ritualizing," or repetitive actions. Often, people with OCD carry out these compulsive behaviors to rid themselves of the obsessive thoughts, but getting rid of the thoughts is only temporary. Eventually, they get in the way of your life.

At eleven, I was terrified of death and sickness more than was normal, and I ended up coping with group of four rituals. I would set out my pens and pencils on my desk in rows of four. Once, when I was working on a project, I was so obsessed with it being on exactly four pages, I couldn't focus on the assignment. In the end, I did poorly.

I also had rituals I would say in my head, depending on how stressed I was. If I was a little stressed, it was usually because I was worrying about someone I cared about. If I was worried about my sister Paris, I would say, "My sister will not die until she is in her nineties or older, and she won't die of cancer or any other illness. She will simply die of old age."

Then, I would feel guilty for not "saving" the rest of my family and friends, so I would have to say, "Every single solitary person on every single solitary side of my family, and all my friends and their families, will not die until they are in their nineties or older. And they won't get cancer, or any other illness. They will simply die of old age." Then, every time I finished saying it, for some reason the song "Best of Both Worlds" by Hannah Montana would play in my head. I had to say that ritual at least four times a day, but most of the time I said it way more than that because I was so scared. I said it at school, at home, everywhere! I got so distracted by saying it or counting to four my grades began to suffer. Everyone noticed, and started to worry.

When my sister Isabelle was born, my mom and dad would let me hold her. I thought she was adorable, but I hated holding her. I just didn't trust myself. I saw images of myself dropping her and killing her by accident. So I would avoid situations where I would have to hold her.

It's common for people with OCD to avoid situations that make them uncomfortable. A couple of weeks after Isabelle was born, we went to my Great-Grandma Yoder's house so she could meet Isabelle.

When we got there, Great-Grandma wasn't answering the door, so we grew worried. My thoughts were racing. My uncle managed to get a window opened slightly, and I was the only one who could fit. I tried arguing, but I still had to go through and unlock the door. I walked through the bedroom and saw a gruesome sight: Great-Grandma Yoder passed out on the bathroom floor, or, as far as I knew, dead. I began to scream and run around the house, eventually opening the door for my family. Great-Grandma Yoder was not dead, just unconscious. I was relieved, but only temporarily.

After that, death became so real to me, especially since my great-grandma actually did die a couple of weeks later. My ritualizing got a hundred times worse, but I was glad it did. Everyone began to notice that I wasn't okay, and my family counselor and mom decided to test me to figure out what was going on.

I was, and still am, terrified of machinery and electrical stuff. To me, it's alive. When my mom and counselor decided they were going to test me, I thought that would involve putting a machine on my head to scan my brain. I did not like that at all. So one day, I decided I had to tell my counselor everything.

I went to counseling as usual, and she casually asked how everything was. I was afraid to tell her everything I'd gone through because I was scared she'd think I was a freak. I talked about other things for most of the session until finally, at the end, I began to tell her. She seemed intrigued. My heart was racing—someone actually knew my secret. She laughed and I smiled. She told me what I had going on was simply obsessive-compulsive disorder, and that it was very common and manageable.

The next two years were eye opening. We decided I wouldn't take antidepressants because I was too young, and instead we used exposure therapy, communication, motivation, counseling, support, and even a study skills class.

Exposure therapy is basically forcing someone to do something they don't want to do. For me, exposure therapy involved touching the trashcan, which I thought was gross and full of germs. Or picking up dog droppings. Or even, most recently, washing dishes because

I was grossed out by a single dirty dish in the sink. Communication involves me telling my mom when something is bothering me. Motivation comes from knowing that if I work hard at conquering my disorder, my grades will improve and I will feel more confident.

To be honest, the best treatment is support. My family has been so amazing; my parents have kicked me in the butt when I needed it and paid for counseling and my sisters has taken the back seat so many times when I was getting all the attention. Somehow, through it all, my family got a lot closer.

While OCD is not one hundred percent curable, the symptoms are manageable, and it can get a lot better. I still do suffer from symptoms, like being afraid of the kitchen sink or obsessing over the split ends in my hair, but that's about it. I'm getting A's and B's now, I'm in the honors society, I'll be taking AP classes next year, and I even do theatre and drama club. I'm more confident, and now I believe I can do anything.

~Janessa Harris-Boom

# in the Cage

*If you don't like something change it;*
*if you can't change it,*
*change the way you think about it.*
~Mary Engelbreit

A t the age of nineteen, I had just returned home after a year of living abroad. It was difficult to adjust to living with my strict, ultra-conservative parents again after having experienced such a degree of independence.

As I was working to adapt to the situation, I met a bare-footed, long-haired guy called Luke. I was attracted to his free-spirited nature and his disregard for rules. I suppose it was part of an attempt to assert my own independence that led me to move in with him after no time at all, even though he lived far away from my friends and family.

A few months later I discovered that Luke was a drug addict. He would disappear for hours at a time, sometimes whole days. He began to steal from me and to lie about where he had been and what he was doing. I convinced myself that it was only a phase and that he would grow out of it soon. Unfortunately he didn't.

In fact, things got a lot worse. He became verbally abusive and when he wasn't shouting at me, he ignored me completely. I felt incredibly isolated and lonely and became depressed. I began to eat for comfort and stopped leaving the apartment. I lay on the couch or in the bed and just ate. Very soon I had gained sixty pounds. Luke began to tell me what an embarrassment I was and refused to be in a room with me. I lost all of my self-confidence and began to hate myself. I ate more and more, as though eating was a way of punishing myself.

One day I went out to buy food. We lived on the second floor of an apartment block and I could hardly make it back up the stairs with the bags. My heart was pounding. I grew dizzy and sweaty and had a terrible pain in my chest. When I eventually managed to reach the apartment, Luke and two of his friends were there smoking weed. One of them laughed when he saw me all red and sweating. He said, "Why do you let it out, Luke? It should be locked in a cage." Right at that moment I put down the bags of food, packed a few things in a suitcase and went home to my parents. I was twenty-three years old and had been living in a cage for four years.

I decided to start looking after myself. This involved joining the gym and registering with a weight loss club where I learned about healthy eating. I was horrified to find what I had been doing to myself with regard to the quality and quantity of food I had been eating. I was committed to the programs and began to lose weight immediately. More than that, I gained friends and a much needed feeling of self-confidence. The best part of all was realising that while I had been feeding my body for all those years, I had been starving my mind. After years of being dull and bored, barely even able to muster up the energy to read a tabloid magazine, I was desperate for something juicy to bite into mentally! I made the decision to register for a master's degree in anthropology and was amazed at my ability to think, engage with texts and to discuss important matters with my fellow students. Within a year I had lost all the weight, run my first half-marathon and almost completed my dissertation. I had come further than I had ever thought possible.

The most important thing I realised was that I had been in a cage, but it wasn't because of the relationship. It was a cage of my own making. It was me; my weight and my lack of self-esteem had trapped me. When I unlocked the cage and allowed myself to explore all the possibilities, learning about healthy, better living, I saw how much I could achieve.

~Kate Edwin

# Half Finished Novel

*The act of putting pen to paper encourages pause for thought, this in turn*
*makes us think more deeply about life, which helps us regain our equilibrium.*
*~Norbet Platt*

I t sounds clichéd, but sometimes it's true. Sometimes, music can be so powerful that it feels like you've been punched in the gut. There was a Los Campesinos! song called "This Is How You Spell," where they referred to the "trails on your skin" and how those explained a lot more than the "half finished novels" that a girl left "lying all over the place." When I first heard it playing over the speakers at my ex-boyfriend's, it felt like the entire world stopped, and there was nothing left but the suppressed recollections of one of the stranger, darker times in my life.

Starting around my eleventh birthday, I was a "cutter"—a member of a club that no one willingly admits belonging to, a club where everybody is vulnerable and anything can trigger self-destructive behaviour. In simple terms, whenever I felt overwhelmed by emotion—shame, anger, hate, sadness, whatever—I would try to physically cut that feeling out. Circles around my ankles, crosshatching on my thighs, straight lines on my wrist... they're all thin and white and faded now, but back in the day they were dark, angry marks, screaming out for something. Of course, I covered my cries for help in knee socks and long pants and two inches of bracelets, too ashamed to admit that there was something deep inside of me that I couldn't deal with.

I was, and still am to some extent, a people-pleaser. I'd put anyone's needs before my own, write an essay for my friend's drama class (a course I didn't even take) before studying for my own science test, or walk home if it meant that someone else had bus fare. It made me feel good, being able to help people the way I did, but it also inspired a lot of self-loathing. I hated myself for putting everyone else on such a pedestal, even when they really did not deserve it. I hated that I would sacrifice my own marks or wellbeing for the marks or wellbeing of others. I felt like I needed to do things for others to feel appreciated, to be liked. It was awful. I hated it.

But then I'd feel bad for hating what I saw as my only positive trait—my generosity—and I would cut, because I wouldn't have anyone to talk to about how I felt. I found it deeply ironic, the fact that the girl who talked everyone she knew through their problems couldn't think through her own, or ask anyone else for advice.

And then two things happened, and my life changed for good.

First, I started writing. At first it was just two or three quick lines here or there, words that described my conflicting feelings and how I couldn't bear them, but those two or three lines rapidly became two or three pages—stories and poems about the people I'd see on the subway, or frantically spewed "insights" that would hit me at 3 a.m. while I was busy not sleeping. As I started writing, I stopped cutting myself as much. Pens and pencils took the place of razorblades stolen from my father's toolkit, and I couldn't have been happier. By April of tenth grade, I had stopped cutting entirely, although the urge to cut still lingered.

Second, I met a boy. There isn't really much more I can say about how that evolved. I met him and he met me and I think somewhere along the line we started feeling something like what I'd assume love is. The cutting urges stopped entirely, but I stopped writing as much too. I'm not really sure why that was. Suddenly it just seemed less important to write, and more important to talk on the phone for hours, or pretend to enjoy watching 24 on his couch.

We were teenagers, so obviously there was some element of physicality to our relationship. At first, ashamed of my scars and cuts, I would insist that everything went on under darkened lights in his dad's condo, but as our relationship grew, he wanted to actually see what he was touching. Fair enough.

I'll never forget the look on his face when he first saw my scars. I expected disgust, but instead I saw a mixture of sadness and understanding as he gently traced his fingers over each and every one of them. I didn't say a word, and neither did he. It was better that way. He understood.

Throughout the course of our relationship, he taught me to appreciate that my genuine caring for others wasn't something I should hate, or be ashamed of at all. He taught me to embrace my generous side, but he also gave me lessons in saying "no," and in not feeling guilty any time I couldn't solve a problem for someone else.

We broke up this fall. It was a mutual agreement. When school resumed in September, it drove a wedge into our relationship. It could've been the fact that not being able to see each other every day put too much pressure onto our Friday and Saturday nights, or it may have been my new interest in the cocky guy in my English class, I'm not really quite sure.

In the weeks after our relationship dissolved, I started writing frequently again. I wasn't spending time watching Jack Bauer save the world and pretending to like it. I wasn't cutting at all. That actually surprised me. I had figured that I would always have two addictions, and that the boy had simply replaced one of them for a while. Apparently I was wrong, since it's been a full two years since my last cut, I'm single, and writing remains my sole addiction.

Two weeks after we broke up, the boy sent me a text message to say that I had left things at his dad's condo that I might want back. I wanted my favourite sweater back, so I went. We spoke briefly when I visited, refusing to meet each other's eye. In our awkward catch-up, desperate to fill the silence, I mentioned that I had started writing a lot again. And then, as if on cue, the song playing over his speakers changed, and I heard "This Is How You Spell" again, with its lyrics that seemed tailor-made for me.

For a split second, we met each other's gaze, and nothing more really needed to be said. I let myself out. As I sat on the subway home, reflecting, I realized something—I didn't cut anymore because I didn't need to.

The pleading screams from my cuts had found their audience, an audience that understood my story without my saying anything. The story etched onto my body had been told at long last, and it was time to start a new chapter in the half finished novel of my life.

~SS

# No Need to Be Afraid

*Nothing in life is to be feared. It is only to be understood.*
~Marie Curie

Hello, my name is Rachel. I am sixteen years old, and I am afraid of the dark.

I grew up sleeping with a light on in the bathroom a few doors down the hallway, as a lot of children do. However, I never grew out of the need to sleep with a light on. This could be because I had two younger brothers who slept with a light on, so I grew used to the faint glow coming through the crack in my doorway. But as I got older and even my brothers didn't need the light anymore, I refused to let go of it.

My nyctophobia, or fear of the dark, became even worse one night when I was twelve years old. I was dreaming that I was lying in my parents' bed, and that it was time for me to wake up. I reached over to turn the light on and a snake began uncurling itself from around the lamp. It lurched out to grab me and I woke up, sweating and absolutely terrified. I jumped up and turned on every light in my room before going back to bed and falling asleep. This began a habit that lasted well over a year.

We moved to a new house soon after this incident, and it was much larger than the ones we had lived in previously. It was also older and more noises seemed to come from the walls than what I was used to. In addition to all this, my parents, who usually slept in a room near mine, had taken the bedroom on the complete opposite side of the house. Some nights, I was fine. I would fall asleep quickly so it didn't matter. But closer to the middle of my seventh grade year I found myself unable to sleep most nights. If one were to enter my bedroom in the middle of the night, they would often find me reading a book with two lamps on and the bathroom door open. I was embarrassed to say the least.

I would spend the night at friends' houses praying for some sort of light to be on when we finally went to bed. It wasn't until one night, when I spent the night at my grandparents' house with the light completely out, that I realized how far my fear went. I was lying in bed paralyzed by fear. Finally I was able to force myself to get up, cross the room with my eyes tightly closed, and turn a lamp on. I sat down on my bed and started to cry. "This is ridiculous," I said. "I am fourteen years old and I should not be afraid of the dark." After the anger came a very pensive mood. I wondered what I was actually afraid of. I knew that nothing was going to hurt me. My dad always locked the doors and windows at night, so no one was going to break into our house. Unable to think of anything, I finally fell asleep with the light brightly shining in my room.

My fear gradually got better. By my sophomore year of high school I no longer slept with multiple lamps on, or any lamp at all. I only needed a small nightlight at the foot of my bed. I could sleep in a dark room at friends' houses if I wasn't alone, and at my grandparents' I had a small lamp on rather than the overhead light. I was improving, but it was still embarrassing to be the only fifteen-year-old I knew who slept with a nightlight.

Finally, my sophomore year Bible teacher was able to help me. For some reason, I was very drawn to her. Not only was she a great teacher, but she seemed like she really cared about her students. So one day after class, I asked her if I could come eat lunch with her. She said yes, and the next day I grabbed my lunchbox and headed for her classroom. I sat down and began to tell her my story. I told her about the fear of the dark, the lights I had to sleep with, the nightmares, and the lying in bed at night jumping at every noise.

She listened very intently and, once I was done, looked at me and bluntly asked, "Rachel, you like to be in control of things, don't you?"

The question shocked me, but I realized she was right. I had always liked to be in control of what happened, and the dark scared me because I had no control over what I couldn't see. I went home that night and, while I still slept with a light, felt better. I began reciting Bible verses my mom had shared with me, like Joshua 1:9, which says: "Have I not commanded you? Be strong and courageous. Do not be afraid; do not be discouraged, for the LORD your God will be with you wherever you go." It was strange—when I realized how irrational my fear was, I also realized that my fear had been most intense when things in my life were changing dramatically. I had never associated my phobia with the grief of losing my aunt in seventh grade, or my nightmares with the time I was told we were moving. Death, moving... those were all things that I couldn't control. And instead of trusting God with these things, or even confiding in someone like my parents about them, I let them pile up and make me scared of what was coming next.

I am still a little afraid of the dark, but in a less irrational sense than even just six months ago. Of course, things in my life have improved in the past six months, and there seem to be fewer things out of my control now, but I don't think that's it. I think now I realize I don't have to be in control of everything. Trusting God, my parents, and that everything will work out has taken the fear away. Just the other night, I decided to sleep without my nightlight on, just to see if I could. I lay in my bed and thought about all the wonderful things in my life: my family, my friends, and a whole life ahead of me, not to mention a God who watches over me, even at night. I have no need to be afraid. And the best part is, I'm not.

~Rachel Walters

# A Time to Heal

*I don't know why they call it heartbreak.*
*It feels like every other part of my body is broken too.*
*~Missy Altijd*

I was like any other teenager. I liked the summer and didn't really enjoy school. I loved watching TV and hanging out with my friends. However, as similar as I was to my peers, I was also quite different. It wasn't until I entered tenth grade that I finally become fully and completely aware of my differences.

What made me different, or at least made me feel that way, wasn't anything anyone could see. It wasn't a physical disability or disease, but a mental one. I suffered from severe depression and the moment I finally realised this, I was already too far gone.

It started to get bad when a boy I didn't know committed suicide. Why his death affected me the way it did, I'm not sure, even to this day. What I do know, though, is that I changed that day, completely and entirely. I went home early and sobbed over the boy I didn't know and the people he left behind in such agony. Never had I felt such heart-breaking sorrow before.

I hurt myself for the first time that night. The deep purple bruising on my thighs from where I dug my nails into my skin was a reminder to me of the pain I felt for everyone else. It helped me get past the grief and bury the emotions. Quickly, I turned to more drastic, harmful ways to deal with my internal struggles.

I went from using my nails to pins to knives and razors. I also moved on to cutting my arms, so I could see them every day and feel them and know that they were there. My mental state was deteriorating and I cut myself in response to strong feelings of self-hatred. Sometimes I cut just to remind myself that I was still able to feel anything. I was like a zombie, completely void of emotions except when I locked myself away to cut.

Soon, the effort of hiding my wounds from my parents became too much and eventually I told them what was going on. I was able to stop cutting for several months before it started up again, fiercer and much more severe than ever before. I was scarred from my hands to my shoulders, so I started inflicting wounds on my belly and chest.

I was completely out of control and my parents put me in counselling. I continued to cut and defy my parents and counsellors. They tried to put me on medication but I would dump the pills down the sink. I started to drink and smoke pot with friends and cut when I was alone.

Throughout the three years of high school, I wanted to die, and I toyed with the idea of overdosing on pills. I knew I was in trouble and asked my parents to send me away. But I was scared and when they actually took my pleas seriously, I refused to go.

The day that I started to heal, to finally pick up the pieces, started with my mom sitting me down for a talk. She asked what was wrong with me, why I was so broken. She asked me a single question that I will always remember: "Where did I go wrong?"

After that, I started to change again, but for the better. It was as though my mom's words sparked a need to heal. I realised how much pain I was causing other people and the overwhelming need to cut slowly started to dissipate.

That's not to say it was easy, because it was very difficult. I still cut myself, but not as often, and I still continued to drink. Even after graduating high school, I was suffering. Only after getting caught drinking did I force myself to face my problems. I started counselling again and learned new ways to cope with the emotions that I was feeling.

It's been six years since I started to cut. I'm on medication and

I'm okay with that. I know now that I'm dealing with an illness, a disease that has to be treated. I talk about my emotions with my friends and family and turn to them when I'm down, rather then bottling it up.

I will always have my scars and whether I'm okay with that or not, I haven't decided yet. But what I do know is that I fought my way to where I am now and I couldn't be happier to be alive.

~Jessica McCallum

# in the Driver's Seat

*Panic at the thought of doing a thing is a challenge to do it.*
*~Henry S. Haskins*

As a high school freshman, I looked at my older friends with envy and awe as I rode in their cars—which were cool no matter how beat up they were—and watched them drive with ease. I assumed when my late high school years arrived that I, too, would join the ranks of those who came and went to school by themselves and drove off into the weekends, having fun escapades around town.

All this came to a screeching halt (no pun intended) one night when I was a fifteen-year-old sophomore. While I was in the passenger seat, my mother rear-ended a car. For days I continued to hear the sound of the impact reverberate in my head. Worst of all, it had been my idea to go to our intended destination that night. My mother's first reaction was to scream at me to never ask her to go there again.

A female passenger from the other car launched into a tirade of obscenities, threatening to beat up my mother, while the driver tapped on our window trying to coax us out of the car. We locked the doors and dialed 911. Soon police arrived, sirens blaring and lights flashing, and the other driver told the cops we were lying about his companion acting like a lunatic. Classy.

My appetite for driving dissipated. My sixteenth birthday passed without a driver's license or even a learner's permit. The thought alone made me jittery, and I questioned my own ability to operate two tons of steel at high speeds. The road had been transformed from a place of magic and adventure into the threatening unknown.

In my junior year I finally enrolled in Driver's Ed at school. If I had come seeking reassurance about my ability to drive and the safety of the world at large, I was clearly in the wrong place. As the teacher solemnly stood in front of the class on the first day, he told us about the importance of the rules of the road, because after all, he was only trying to save our lives. Some kids had come through this very class only to wind up dead shortly after.

As the semester wore on, we watched several graphic videos of car accident victims, among them the infamous *Red Asphalt*. Even today, I can still see the images with stark clarity: a battered car turned upside down, the driver still inside, her brains spilling out onto the pavement. Another, of a girl who looked hardly older than my own sixteen years, her chin smashed into the steering wheel, her lifeless eyes vacant, her dark blood-matted hair in clumps. "Oh, no," intoned a voice-over dramatically. "She's so young!"

My trepidation only intensified when I first got behind the wheel alongside a driving instructor. I assumed practice would be calming, but I was paralyzed with fear. I began to wish I had been born in a city that ran on public transportation. Still I went through the pre-scribed driving lessons, eventually going to the DMV and passing my test on the first try. Now, I thought, perhaps with even more practice I could kick this monster out of my system.

But it was not to be. About twenty minutes before my shift ended at work, I periodically checked my watch and felt a growing panic as the minutes counted down to clock-out time. Even though I always made it home safely, I examined my car for any scratches or dings, just in case I had somehow hit a car and not noticed. If the car checked out, my fear would dissipate, letting me relax for the rest of the evening. If not, and there was some mark I hadn't seen before, I was sure the cops would show up soon. This is what is known as "phantom hit-and-run" in the world of driving phobics. Intellectually, I knew I was in little danger of being arrested for a fender-bender that had genuinely escaped my attention. But getting my brain to tell this to the rest of my nervous system was futile. I was crazy, and I knew it. Normal people didn't think like this.

The months crept on, and it became obvious to my parents and me that my terror of the road wasn't waning. My grandmother, who was as perplexed and concerned as my parents, came home excitedly one day with the book *Triumph Over Fear* by Jerilyn Ross, a psychologist who had overcome an anxiety disorder herself. In psychological terms, I had a specific phobia, and the book was littered with anecdotes of people who, like me, were terrified of driving.

Here was a welcome relief. After all, if a diagnosis existed, perhaps a cure followed. It was also comforting to know many people had suffered in silence along with me, only to be healed and go on to live normal lives. So I signed up for therapy.

Thus began the incremental bit-by-bit process of evicting the monsters of my imagination. The therapist and I compiled a list of places I wanted to drive to, progressing from the least scary (to work) to the most (to Los Angeles from my hometown of San Diego). First I knocked off one of the locations on my list with someone riding shotgun, usually one of my parents. Then I would make the big attempt alone.

But there were setbacks. Every time I heard a blaring horn meant for me. Every time I had a "close shave" that could have ended in a smash. And God forbid someone flipped me the bird or showed any kind of road rage, bringing back memories of the mentally unhinged woman I encountered at fifteen. Shockwaves of fear would hit, and I would panic. After a while, I learned to let these thoughts run their course. Partway through this process, I started taking antidepressants, which helped sooth my anxiety.

Throughout my ordeal, I never told anyone of my struggle, save the therapist and immediate family members. Instead, I made up stories as to why I couldn't drive places, saying my parents needed the car for whatever reason. At the root of this shame was the belief, however bogus, that the problem was some kind of manifestation of a fear of growing up. "Oh, that would be so embarrassing, to have your parents pick you up at college," a longtime friend of mine once said. I smiled weakly, not revealing my parents did just that. Few things in my life have been more humbling than being tethered to my parents when others my age were learning to fly.

Upon transferring from community college to the University of California San Diego, my parents announced they were buying me a new car. For most young people, a new car would be thrilling. But me? I argued. I didn't think I could afford the gas, I said. We had been getting along fine with my mom and me sharing a car. But it wasn't to be. My mother was done with me taking over her car and wanted it back. We were going to the dealership.

However, the car provided one blessing to aid my recovery. It came with a navigation system, permanently banishing one particular fear: getting lost. Yet as I drove home with my mom, she questioned why I didn't seem happier. Indeed. It's unlikely that most people receiving their first car wonder if they are seeing the inside of their coffin.

One day, I opened the door to our garage to see my baby brother grinning at me triumphantly from the driver's seat, having completed his first sojourn out on the road. Even though I was afraid my phobia would somehow have rubbed off on him, he fearlessly enrolled in Driver's Ed and passed with flying colors. Reassured he would never have to endure what I had, I also realized what I had missed.

Chipping away at my driving aversion was a process so incremental that I scarcely noticed until I looked back, and the fear had subsided. A new feeling finally emerged: freedom. On my daily journeys to school, as the expansive freeway stretched before me, instead of the usual commuter's annoyance at the long haul, I felt an incredible lightness, an empowering sense of serenity and excitement. I was going where I needed to go, on my own, and I had as much a right to be there as anyone else.

My car now takes me to and from all of my ventures, be it driving to an unfamiliar place to interview someone as a journalist or to some gig as a dancer. I have made the pilgrimage from San Diego to L.A. several times, and, yes, the GPS is there to talk me through it. That sense of worldly adventure and wonderment I envisioned as a young teenager has now arrived in full force. I hope I never take it for granted.

~Gina McGalliard

# Tough Times for Teens

Chapter 5

## Sticks and Stones

# Worth of My Soul

*Other people's opinion of you does not have to become your reality.*
~Les Brown

Every morning before the start of a new day of dreaded junior high school, I looked at myself in the mirror. I would gaze at the reflection, spotted with acne cream, wishing there was a way to get out of going to school. Those were, without question, some of the most difficult days in my life—not only because of the fact that I was completely uncomfortable in my own changing and awkward body, but also because I felt completely helpless with all the things happening around me. It was the summer before my eighth grade year that my parents' business closed and my family's house was taken due to foreclosure.

I vividly remember the day that the bankers came to inspect the prize they would win shortly in the auction. I was babysitting that day, and when three men in suits came peeping through the windows, I did not know what to do. I think, at the time, my parents were hoping to try to shield us from some of the humiliation and pain by not telling us what was happening. My two younger brothers and two younger sisters were clueless, but the reality of it all weighed heavily on my two unsteady shoulders.

After moving to a much smaller rented house, life began to feel somewhat normal again. For a while, things seemed to be looking up. I tried out for the school's dance team and made it, despite the fact that I had not had the training that the other girls had. I was so excited. Unfortunately, the cost of participating was more than my parents could afford. I was beyond devastated when I thought I might have to quit the team for lack of money. However, somehow my parents came up with just enough money to purchase the necessary items for me to participate. It felt so nice to be a part of something, to be included. It probably meant more to me than any other girl on the team.

The night of the first football game arrived. I tried my best to look as good as all the other girls. I was glittering all over in my new dance uniform. Sadly, the shoes for the dance team were considered optional, so my parents chose not to buy them. The rest of me glittered, but on my feet were plain, dingy, off-white tennis shoes. All of the other girls had purchased the optional tennis shoes in the school colors, but there I was, lacing up the same Keds knockoffs that I had been wearing in practice. It bothered me a little, but I did not dare ask for new tennis shoes when I knew how difficult it had been for my parents to pay for the rest of the uniform. Instead, I plastered on a grateful smile and went to the game with my head up.

The team had been dancing in the stands and everything was great. I was having a blast. Then the time came for us to line up to march down to the field and perform. We filed out one by one as our captain watched us. The captain of the dance team was one of those girls whose hair was always perfect and who always seemed to be able to make you feel inferior. The captain, not any older than us but much more authoritative, peered at each dancer, inspecting her every move. When she got to me, the look on her face changed. She looked me up and down. I can remember trying to be invisible, but knowing that I was more conspicuous than I had ever been in my life.

"Oh my God!" she shouted. "Where are your shoes?" All of the other girls turned immediately to stare at my feet.

I shuffled them and turned them inward as I spoke. "I didn't order the shoes," I mumbled just loud enough for her to hear.

At this point she had taken several steps toward me, and although she and I were the same height, she seemed to be glaring down at me. "Why not?" she scoffed. I did not know what to say. I surely did not want to explain that my dad literally had to pawn a gun just to pay for the uniform I was wearing.

"The coach said those shoes are optional," I managed to mutter. The words were like rocks in my throat.

"So what!" she screamed. "You are making us all look bad with those hideous shoes you are wearing. You need to get the shoes that we have."

I knew deep down that I would never get those shoes, but I just looked at her and said, "Okay."

Like a very short-lived dream, dance team soon lost its appeal. I tried hard to avoid being seen by the captain, but she always seemed to seek me out and find fault with me. I did not have the courage, confidence, or wisdom to know how to deal with problems like her, and so I did the one thing that seemed to come naturally—I ran. I told my parents I wanted to transfer to another school, and since we had moved to another rented house in another school zone, they agreed. I could have stayed at that school and faced the fears and insecurities that I had, but I moved to a new school where I could be invisible again.

Years passed and I began to realize what was important to me. It took me years to understand that my individual worth had nothing to do with the amount of money my parents had, and that running from your problems never takes you very far. There was once a time when I could not see anything good coming from the awful experience of those soiled shoes peeking from beneath that sparkling uniform. However, now that I am a high school teacher, it has been one of my personal goals to make sure that every student feels accepted and appreciated, that none of them ever feels that running is the answer, and that they all understand the worth of their soul has nothing to do with the price of their shoes.

~Courtney Rusk

# Second Lead
# Syndrome

*We find comfort among those who agree with us —*
*growth among those who don't.*
~Frank A. Clark

I have sold my first young adult novel; it's being published any
day now with a major publishing house and with any luck, I'm
going to spend the rest of my life writing books for teens. I'm
a key player in a really amazing non-profit that I think is going to
change the world one day. I've traveled the world. I've earned my
undergraduate and master degrees. I got that job, rocked that interview, earned my own money and even, briefly, went to school with
the Prince of Wales.

I've achieved personal and professional success, and there is so
much more I'm looking forward to.

And I wouldn't have done any of it if someone had actually
believed in me.

Maybe that's a little overdramatic to say, but I didn't get it. I
never got it. And not in the sense of understanding — it wasn't that
I didn't comprehend "it." What I mean is that, in a constellation of
gold stars, I was the dying light of a red dwarf planet — dim, flicker-
ing, and completely overshadowed by the glowing lovelies around

me. Whatever "it" happened to be—success, praise, extra credit—I wasn't going to get it.

That was high school for me. That was life for me. I went to an all-girls Catholic school and, despite having uniforms for equality, I somehow managed to look sloppier and less put-together than other girls. In junior year, when we all applied for the exclusive AP History course that you could take as a junior (as opposed to the more widely offered, less exclusive APs we could all take in senior year) I had the PSAT scores to qualify for the class—but since we had something like eighteen merit scholars in my grade, the class was filled by girls who had higher PSAT scores. Rather than start another class for the "extras" who qualified, we just got bumped.

I was just on the cusp of qualifying for several different honors societies in high school (which looked fabulous on college transcripts) but didn't quite make it.

When I went out for the school play... oh, well, who am I kidding? I was lucky just to be cast in the school play. I can't sing, dance or act. It was a miracle I didn't take the theater down in flames as a dancing, singing, acting turtle that was purposefully cut out of most other versions of *Alice in Wonderland*.

For my senior bioethics project, we had to design a personal manifesto—our own Code of Ethics. I agonized over the thing; I dearly loved it. I wrote these short stories about my friends and about what my ethics really meant to me, about how I saw the world working and what I could do to make it better. I wrote about how being a strong, empowered girl was important to me. I made it beautiful; I was one of those artsy kids so I knew my way around a glue stick and some quotes. And when I handed it in like a prized pony, it was returned to me with a three page note on pink notepaper in red ink (yes, I still have it, and the Code of Ethics) that accused me of demonstrating an utter lack of belief in God, and grading me accordingly.

Never mind that I do have a ludicrously strong faith in God. Never mind, even, that the project assignment hadn't even mentioned that. When it came down to it, I just wasn't the favorite. I wasn't the darling of high school.

For a long time, I had the biggest chip on my shoulder about this. I thought it was the teachers' faults: how could they not see my potential? Then I blamed my fellow students: What does she have that I don't? Can't they see she doesn't deserve any of this?

I was a grumpy teenager. I was always coming up short; I would never be the first in line, I would never be the star, I would never be appreciated. I was smart and I was driven and I wanted for one moment to be the best. I had English teachers who encouraged me and supported me and said my writing was good, and yes, I did have people who believed in me. My mom seems to be a big fan of mine, but I suspect nepotism at work.

I was never the star.

I'll tell you what; being the star is thoroughly overrated. In some of the work I've been doing lately, I've had the honor of getting back together with some of the girls from my high school, and we all sing the same song—we were never the favorites. We were never the stars. One of them is a singer and songwriter. One is a successful business lady. One founded and runs the non-profit I work with. One works for the archdiocese and rocks her Catholic for all it's worth (though we kind of disagree that she wasn't anyone's favorite). In short, they are some of the coolest people I know.

We all came out of high school with righteous anger and resentment because things weren't handed to us. We came out with the "Well I'll show them!" promise tattooed on our foreheads. We all doggedly worked harder and longer than our illustrious high school counterparts because we had something to prove.

For me, every day I was chased by the idea that someone thought I wasn't good enough—because I disagreed. I knew I wanted to be a writer from a really young age, but I kept getting told that it wasn't smart, I wouldn't make it, I couldn't succeed. I wasn't the valedictorian, I wasn't good enough for AP History, and I was a god-awful turtle. But I knew, better than anyone else, what I was capable of.

When someone tells you that you can't, the worst thing you can do is believe them. There will always be people in life and in high school that don't seem to earn the things they receive; there will be people who doubt you and don't see the passion and fire you have within and relegate you to the role of second lead.

But do you know what the most amazing thing about personal success is? Proving every single one of them wrong. Because it just so happens that in the process, when you trust your own heart, you demonstrate to the world the infinite power of believing in yourself.

~AC Gaughen

# The Fat Ballerina

*To free us from the expectations of others, to give us back to ourselves—*
*there lies the great, singular power of self-respect.*
~Joan Didion

"Suck in that afternoon snack." Miss Anne shot me a raised eyebrow stare and swatted the black leotard covering my belly button.

I sucked in my gut and held it there. "Yes, ma'am."

My snack was showing? I glanced down. I'd never noticed the round pooch below my waist before. Maybe because at thirteen I was more focused on dancing than on my protruding stomach. That sure changed fast. In one instant, I became totally aware of how unflattering pink Spandex is when it is stretched over chunky thighs. I dipped into another grand-plié.

A year after moving to Texas, the friends I'd left behind had stopped replying to my letters. I wanted, needed these new girls to like me. The way Miss Anne had singled out my pooch made it clear that to fit in here, I had to be thin.

I decided to hide my fat. I bought a wrap-around velvet ballet skirt. I sucked in my stomach during class to the point where I forgot to breathe. At the ballet bar, I stood by the one girl who was chubbier than me to appear smaller in comparison. But it was too late.

Suck in that afternoon snack. Those five words altered the way I viewed my body, giving me bionic vision that magnified every ounce of wobbly, jiggly, flabby fat. Every week I came home from ballet class deflated. The activity I once enjoyed was now a painful event, starting with the battle to squeeze my legs into the pink tights and ending when I took them off and my thighs exploded out like biscuits released from a can.

Hiding it wasn't enough. I wanted to look like the tall, lean, star pupil in my ballet class. I started eating less. I ate enough to avoid my parents' suspicion and then claimed I was full when I actually craved another slice of pizza. My secret dieting failed in epic proportions. I lasted a couple days and then some delicious, torturing smell derailed my resolve. I pigged out.

I always felt pain in my stomach afterwards. Not because I ate too much, but because I had given in and fueled my fat. Guilt clawed me inside, and I swore to make my secret diet stick this time. And the next time. And the next time. The torturing smells were too much for me to take. They always won, making me the world's biggest loser. Or, I should say, the world's fattest ballerina.

Months went by with teeter-totter dieting and hiding, but my little skirt couldn't protect me on M-Day—the day we all got our measurements taken for the ballet recital costumes, in front of everybody. On M-Day, ballet class started as usual, but we all knew what was coming. After class Miss Anne and her über-skinny assistant gathered us round the CD player. I sat Indian style on the floor behind the other girls.

Miss Anne wielded a long, white measuring tape. "Come up when I call your name."

One by one, girls went up and stood with their arms out to the side and legs apart. Miss Anne measured them without making eye contact, calling out the numbers for the assistant to write down. And for the whole class to hear. The girls waiting for their turn whispered about the current classmate on display.

"Her thighs are bigger than yours."

"Man, Julie's waist is super tiny!"

The minutes dragged by. Only two girls left to humiliate. Me and the chubbier girl.

"Lisa, your turn."

I released a breath as Lisa strode to the front. Hushed giggles bubbled on the sidelines when the measuring tape almost reached its limit to span her circumference. The whispered comments got more sarcastic and nasty. I retreated into my head, refusing to listen. Why did I have to go dead last? Now everyone could compare my measurements to the entire class. I clenched my fists. Please don't call my name. Please don't call my name.

"Angela, you're up next."

I forced myself up and shuffled toward Miss Anne. It felt as if all eyes were glued to my gigantic backside. My fingers twitched as I raised my arms and spread my legs. Just get it over with. The teacher wrapped the measuring tape around my stomach. I was tempted to suck it in, but then my costume wouldn't fit and I'd feel even more like a hippopotamus.

"Twenty-six inches." Miss Anne's voice resounded in the quiet room.

"Twenty-six inches." The perky assistant echoed.

Snickers rippled behind my back. My head spun. I wanted to shrivel up and disappear. Poof, gone! I didn't get my wish. The white tape continued to crisscross over various parts of my body. Miss Anne continued to announce my measurements out loud. I tried not to wince. Why did they have to measure us like this? Why couldn't we meet with the teacher privately? Whoever came up with this process must've been spaghetti thin.

"All done."

I nodded but didn't move. The last thing I wanted to do was turn around and face the other girls, but once again I didn't have a choice. Eyes cast down, I returned to my secluded spot in the back corner.

I left class that day wanting to die. Mom and Dad quickly noticed the dramatic change in my behavior and realized that ballet class had become toxic. They pulled me out, but the feeling that I resembled a balloon animal lingered.

For three years, I continued to believe what my ballet teacher said. For three years, I believed I was fat, ugly. No one would want to be my friend. My parents assured me that I was beautiful, but I didn't believe them. I shared their DNA. Of course they thought I was beautiful.

Without friends, I spent my time reading. I read mainly fiction, but I read the Bible some too. And you know what was weird? The Bible agreed with my parents. I found all these verses about being made in God's image and that He loved me. Nowhere could I find a verse that said God hates fat people or anyone else.

I now had two sources saying that I was beautiful, but my ballet teacher's words continued to scream in my head, drowning out every other opinion. I kept reading the Bible and with each promise of God's love, Miss Anne's voice got quieter. Every powerful scripture I read scrubbed the negative thoughts from my mind a little bit at a time.

Then, one day as I dressed in front of my full-length mirror, all the scriptures I'd read surfaced and revealed a glaring fact.

My ballet teacher was wrong.

I wasn't fat. I was healthy and beautiful just the way I was in my size eight jeans. My parents loved me, God loved me, and if I could learn to love myself, maybe people would want to be my friends. And if they didn't, so what? I already had an unconditional love that would never fade no matter what size jeans I wore.

~Angela Bell

# A Boy in a Girls' Cabin

*The value of identity of course is that so often with it comes purpose.*
~Richard Grant

When you are young, or even before you are born, many scientists believe that your brain develops a gender identity. I have a disorder called Gender Identity Disorder, or GID. My brain's gender imprint does not match my body's gender. In layman's terms, my birth certificate says I'm a girl, my body says I'm a girl, people always tell me that I'm a girl, but my mind says that I am a boy; this means that I am a female to male, or FTM, transsexual.

When somebody turns thirteen, they are excited about dating, middle school graduation, and going through puberty. I was not excited about any of these things when I turned thirteen. When you're thirteen, crushes are always a topic of discussion, and, as a trans-sexual, I knew I wouldn't be dating for a few years. My classmates were excited about middle school graduation, but the "Trans-Health Conference" (a conference where transgendered kids and adults can meet other transgendered people) was on the same weekend as graduation, so I was not quite as excited because I had to miss it. And, of course, being thirteen meant puberty. I was not excited about puberty at all! Instead of buying bras, I was going to get a chest-compressing vest or a "binder." I wouldn't be getting my period; instead, I'd be getting a small capsule of medication implanted in my arm to stop me from getting a period. The birthday I am excited about is my sixteenth, because that's when I can get a double mastectomy.

Aside from my worries about puberty, graduation, and dating, I was very happy. I had great friends both in and outside of school. I got good grades, had a new goldfish named Mikey, a brand new black bicycle, and a Wii. I was healthy, happy, and loved life. That, and I was counting the days until summer, when I could go to summer camp. I had been to camp before, and I had a great time; I made lots of friends, and had discovered that I loved rock climbing! I was so excited, but also a little nervous. I had come out as transsexual at camp the prior year. Since nobody knew me at camp that year, it was the perfect chance to come out. There was even a transsexual counselor there who I became good friends with.

This year, however, would be different. I was in the process of physically transitioning, and I was a bit less easygoing about people calling me "she" or "her." I was worried, but I kept on telling myself it would be fine.

It wasn't.

I knew that it would be an awful three weeks after the first five minutes I was there and they checked me into my cabin. "Er... Iris Preiss..." I said, hesitantly. "Uh, I'm sorry, I just have to go talk to the director for a minute," said the man at the computer.

"Why?"

"It says here that you're in a girls' cabin."

After clearing up the misunderstanding, I was settling into my cabin. My counselor walked in, looked at me, and said, "Look, the camp has a strict rule about boys being even near a girls' cabin, so you've got to leave."

"I'm sorry, ma'am," I said. "I'm a girl... sort of..."

She thought I was joking. I was glad, in a way, that she believed that I was a boy.

Later, when I took my swimming test, they told me to take my shirt off. "Uh, sorry, I have to keep it on because my skin is pale and gets burnt easily," I told them. I looked like a geek with all the other shirtless boys standing around me.

Whenever I got a package from the mailroom, I'd have to show them my slip that said Girls 8B, and they'd give me a strange look. Not to mention I had to make up an excuse for being in a girls' cabin whenever anybody asked, "Oh, what cabin are you in?"

Camp has a carnival every second session. My cabin set up a "marriage" booth for the carnival, where two people would walk down an aisle made of toilet paper, and receive Ring Pops. When I was off my shift, I was walking around the camp when I spotted my friend's boyfriend, Chuck.

"Hey, you're Jennifer's boyfriend, right?" I asked.

"Yeah," he said, "And you're the he-she, right?"

I was shocked. I knew that people talked about me behind my back; they called me a he-she and lots of names that were worse. But nobody ever said it right to me.

"Um..." I stammered.

My friend, Dana, heard and walked up to us. "How dare you say that about him!" she yelled.

"What, she's a he-she! She's in a girls' cabin!"

"So what, you jerk?"

"She's not really a boy! Her real name is Iris!"

Dana and I were incredibly annoyed at Chuck, but we quickly forgot about it.

A few days later, I saw Jennifer and Chuck walking around camp. "Hey, Chuck! Don't you owe me an apology?"

"Uh... yeah, sorry," he said.

I was pleased with myself, but Jennifer gave me a mean glare.

Back at the cabin, while our counselor was in the shower, Jennifer approached me. "Don't you EVER talk to my boyfriend again!" she yelled at me, and then she called me a "faggot."

I was shocked, and all the girls in the cabin were shocked. "What?" I retorted. "He said something awful to me, and I made him apologize."

"I don't care," said Jennifer, "if you pull something like that again, I swear I'll..." she shook her fist.

"Okay, whatever," I said, nonchalantly.

She looked at me for a minute, and I figured that she would walk away, but she didn't. Instead of walking away, she took her hand, and slapped me across the face.

I never told my counselor that she did that. I was afraid she'd do it again. She had punched me in the arm before, and hit me in the stomach. I decided I'd just stay away from her.

When I think about it today, I realize that what happened to me wasn't terrible. Hundreds of transgendered people are the victims of hate crimes every year, and I was just a victim of some teenage bullying. People get killed, abused, and abandoned because of their gender identity.

When I brought this up at my school and asked to make a speech about it after school in the auditorium for anyone who wanted to hear, my teachers said no. They said if I talked about this, they'd have to let everybody talk about something important to them. That made me furious.

"You should," I replied, looking at my feet.

"Excuse me?"

"If something's important to the students, as well as the world, you should give them a chance to talk about it," I said. And I still believe it.

~Isaac Preiss

# St. Patrick's Day

*Fill your paper with the breathings of your heart.*
~William Wordsworth

It was St. Patrick's Day, but it wasn't my lucky day. I'd avoided eye contact in the halls and kept my head tucked down during the first four periods. I was practically keeping a mental tally of how many Topsiders versus Converse I'd passed while walking on the clay tile squares of my crowded ninth grade corridor. No one even said, "Hello," which was a relief. I'd gone from being noticed as a cheerleader and beauty walk runner-up to being invisible. For someone who was grateful for earning the class vote of "Friendliest," I wasn't feeling very friendly. Pushing my long brown hair to fall forward around my face seemed like a temporary incognito solution to help conceal my latest natural facial disaster. Yes, I'd doused my complexion with astringent trying to dry up the zits. The result: Multiple layers of dead skin that resembled a frogfish.

I'd tell myself repeatedly, "You can get through this day. You're halfway there!"

I'd managed to snag a place at the end of the lunch line, as well as a faraway corner seat near the outcasts. Here, no one talked. I wasn't in the mood anyway. When I sat down, the clink of forks stopped. I resisted the urge to peek through overgrown bangs. I sensed the curious stares. A loud straw slurp seemed to signal that I'd been accepted by the outsiders, and the chorus of chewing resumed among the clatter of eating utensils. I was enjoying being lost in this remote area of the cafeteria jungle until my good friend crashed through the quiet, yanking a metal chair to sit behind me.

She whispered, "There's a photo of you circulating in a lot of classes. You're asleep in it, drooling mostly on the left side of your half open mouth, back when you had braces and you don't have any make-up on. Your face is broken out, but the only bump that looks really bad in the picture is the one on your long nose. Your zit cream makes it look more like you have a dark blotchy rash. Have you heard about it?"

Blood rushed to my blushing face and then drained, leaving a pale wash of queasiness. And just when I thought I couldn't feel sicker, she confided, "I heard the picture was taken at camp by 'You Know Who' this summer. See ya."

My friend's mention of "You Know Who" was code for letting me know the picture was taken by the same person who'd started a rumor months earlier: "You've never kissed a boy because you don't like boys and prefer girls."

Deep down, I wished I had the guts to tell her I just wanted that first kiss to be special, with fireworks, instead of during an immature game of spin the bottle. Instead I said nothing. Why didn't I stick up for myself?

Thinking back to summer camp, I vaguely remembered waking from a deep sleep, hearing muffled giggling and glimpsing a blurry flash of lightning. Maybe it had been a camera flash instead. How could I face this when I didn't have my best face on today?

So I checked out. I honestly didn't feel well. I became withdrawn for hours in my room that night and started writing in a journal to cope. I only darted out to grab a glass of water and sneak a bottle of aspirin. Behind closed doors, I counted every aspirin and wondered how many it would take to overdose. I wanted to sleep away my emotional pain forever. All because of "You Know Who."

Tap, tap, tap.

I panicked. Someone was at my bedroom door.

I startled and tossed the rattling aspirin under my pillow. I heard the insertion of a bobby pin into my doorknob and the spring release of it twisting open.

Who was it? Was Dad home?

It was my mother and her intuition. I was outnumbered. We talked a little about how I was feeling—so ugly inside and out. More than she gave advice, she just listened. She finally said, "Don't let what someone says about you define you. Always remember, every second's a new second and tomorrow's a new day. It's never too late to start all over again—no matter what."

She gave me a hug and said, "I've got a really bad headache. Have you by any chance seen the aspirin?" I didn't have the nerve to reveal it then and there, but did offer to look for it. A few minutes later, I handed it over and no questions were asked. But I always thought she knew.

If only we could rewind or fast-forward our lives to handle things better.

Years later, I got a call to pick up a book I'd ordered to give my mother for Mother's Day. However, it wasn't just any book. It was my first byline in a national anthology collection. I'd finally gotten enough nerve up to start submitting my creative writing—writing that had started with those high school journals. I'd preordered it months ahead and the book surprisingly arrived nearly eight weeks early. I dashed over to the store and as the sales lady rang me up, I asked her the date as I wrote my check. She responded, "It's March 17th. Happy St. Patrick's Day!"

For me, it was a very defining moment, as I privately recalled the St. Patrick's Day that I'd wanted to end it all. Since then, I've experienced many wonderful things, including success, marriage, and motherhood, but I have also learned to stand up for myself, even against "You Know Who," who I encountered again after high school. On that day when I stood, book in hand, I realized that my dark St. Patrick's Day had taught me that writing is healthy. Words can hurt, but they can also heal.

~Ann Dolensky

# The Church Parking Lot Attack

*Refusing to ask for help when you need it*
*is refusing someone the chance to be helpful.*
~Ric Ocasek

'd been teased before, called a few names, but nothing like what happened that night in the parking lot. That night I was scared—at church. That's not supposed to happen.

I was never one of the popular kids, but I wasn't a total loner either. I was a member of the youth group's new dance team. I'd always loved dancing, so I was super psyched when the youth pastors decided to form the team. It gave me a special place to belong. For weeks, the other girls and I practiced our hip-hop number at church. I'd been chosen to do a short solo, and I wanted to hit all my moves just right. I even practiced at home.

Finally the big night came. Our very first performance was on a Wednesday night in front of the entire youth group and a couple of adults who'd snuck in to watch. Dressed in my lipstick red pants, T-shirt, and sneakers, I found my spot on the stage and waited. With a loud thumping bass, the song bounced through the room. The girls and I stomped to the beat. As we went through the routine, I counted the steps in my head. One and two. Three and four.

The music peaked in intensity, cuing my solo bit. By now I'd gotten so lost in the music that I didn't need to count the beats. It just flowed. I kicked my right leg in the air, crossed it over my left, spun, touched the ground with my hand and popped back up as the electric guitar wailed a high note. A few people let out a whoop and clapped. I'd nailed it!

I could've danced forever except for the fact that I was losing the ability to breathe. Our song ended with the clash of drum symbols and the dance team struck a pose. The lights came on to the sound of applause. We all took a quick bow and left the stage, sweating and totally pumped.

I high-fived some of the girls. "Awesome job, guys! You rocked it!"

My heart beat to an unheard rhythm as if the music pulsed through my veins. I might not have been the most popular girl, but right then I was part of a team. That felt way more exhilarating. Together the dance team migrated to the bathroom, changed clothes, and returned to hear the pastor's message.

When service dismissed, I told the girls goodbye and went to find my mom in the smaller building across the church parking lot. Backpack tossed over my shoulder, I pushed through the sticky summer night air. I couldn't wait to tell my mom about my dancing success.

Then it happened.

A bunch of the older teens from church surrounded me, circling like a wild pack of stray dogs. My path now blocked, I froze. The group consisted mainly of guys, all taller, older, and much bigger than me. Much bigger.

"Who do you think you are?" a girl hissed.

One of the guys leered at me. "Think you're special or something?"

Insults peppered me on all sides as the group tightened their human noose around me. I turned around in search of an adult. The parking lot was vacant. No adults. Nobody. I was alone.

The buffest dude in the group lunged at me, pretending to charge. I jumped. They laughed.

"You think you can dance hip-hop?" The buff guy's eyes traveled up and down my body. "You a gangster, dancer girl?"

The circle of people squeezed me in, popping my bubble of personal space.

A male voice spoke over my shoulder. "Dance for us. Dance, dancer girl. Dance!"

I didn't move. What were they going to do? What if they tried to hurt me? Should I scream for help? How beat up would I be before someone could save me? I tried to inch toward the church doors, but they cut me off. Nausea gripped me with a firm hand.

I was at church. I should be safe, but I didn't feel safe. The bullying that infested the schools had leaked into the youth group, and I was about to be its first victim.

The sound of a creaking door caught the mob's attention. They stopped circling. Our youth group leader walked outside. My attackers must have recognized him because they backed off. I bolted through the gap in their large bodies and dashed inside the church, panting. I'd escaped.

Tears puddled in my eyes. "Thank you, God, for keeping me safe."

Voices struck up a conversation outside. The walls muffled their words, but I could tell by the causal tone that our youth pastor wasn't giving the bullies a lecture. He was joking around with them, totally clueless about what had just happened.

Later that night, I told my mom what went down. She was spitfire mad. "I'm going to speak with the youth pastor right away."

"No." I sighed. "I'll do it."

I knew the pastors needed to know, but I dreaded telling them. What would happen when those guys found out that I told? Would they return for a sequel? One with an unhappy ending? The following Wednesday, before service, I talked to my youth leader's wife and explained the whole situation. She promised to take care of it. That didn't make me feel any less afraid.

Nothing bad happened that week, but I made sure to stay with a group of friends. The next Wednesday, one of the guys from the dog pack made eye contact with me and headed my way as if on a mission. I ran in the opposite direction. Later he started walking towards me again. I ran. He stalked me all night. He was going to kill me, I just knew it! He must have found out that I told and now he wanted to silence me forever.

The next week my stomach was in knots when I arrived at church. I walked into the church foyer and there he was — waiting for me. I scurried toward the mass of people in the sanctuary, but he beat me to the door and herded me into a corner. I couldn't run this time.

The guy towered over me, but he didn't come real close. His face looked different this time. More human. His gaze didn't leave the floor and his face almost twitched as if he was in pain. "I'm really sorry. I... didn't mean to scare you."

I stood in silence. Was he trying to trick me so I'd let down my guard? No, he looked genuinely upset. Sad. Full of regret.

"It's okay," I mumbled.

He looked up at me, nodded, and walked away.

I never found out what my youth pastors said to those guys, but I know it made a difference because they never bothered me again. Not once. All I can say is that I'm glad I told someone. Who knows what they might've tried to do had I kept my mouth shut.

~Angela Bell

# An Outcast
# No More

*Do not go where the path may lead.*
*Go instead where there is no path and leave a trail.*
~Ralph Waldo Emerson

was a loner growing up, the one no one wanted around. I struggled to relate to other people my age. I was always considered by my peers to be weird. I knew I was different but I never knew why. All I knew was that most of the times I had the opportunity to connect with people and develop friendships, I'd mess it up. Then I'd hate myself for it.

School was horrible for me. I was teased and harassed no matter what I did. Even the smallest expression on my face would be questioned and criticised. I couldn't be myself. I'd walk around school trying to be invisible, trying to cover up my true feelings. And that itself was a strain on me. My classmates would throw balls of paper at me; the girl behind me would pull my hair or hit my head; a guy would hold out his foot in front of me to trip me as I walked past. In the passage on my way to class I'd be confronted with taunts like "retard" or "stupid." Rumours about me spread like wildfire around the school. I noticed that no one else I knew at school was scorned as much as I was. So I decided there must be something wrong with me.

I desperately searched for ways I could earn respect from everyone. I behaved well in class and worked hard, which made me the teacher's pet most of my school years. I thought that if I couldn't get respect from my peers I could at least earn the teacher's favour, which would hopefully get me some protection from my enemies. I tried displaying my talents to give everyone a reason to like me. I sang in all the school talent shows, had my drama plays shown in assembly, and tried getting the best marks in class. With some people it worked. One guy even fell in love with my voice. But for most of my peers it made no difference. I still had to face the same public humiliation day after day.

I tried my best to make friends. I would put all my time and effort into a friendship, only to watch it go to waste. I tried to please everyone with the hope that someone would take a liking to me. Once or twice I even resorted to buying people things or giving them homemade snacks.

There were two popular girls whose personalities I liked, and for a brief period of time we seemed to get along. One day, they agreed to let me hang with them at break. The trouble was that I had no clue how to socialise or what to talk about. I tagged along as they walked over to a big group of guys sitting on the grass. As soon as the guys saw me coming, they got up and left. I felt what was left of my confidence slip away.

After eleventh grade, I found the answer to a lot of my questions. My psychologist and a psychiatrist diagnosed me with Asperger's syndrome. Asperger's is a mild form of autism. It's a neurological, developmental disorder in the brain that changes a person's whole perception of life. The main symptom is difficulty in socialising and understanding what behaviour is appropriate for different situations. Usually people with the syndrome are intellectually superior to people their age, but they lag behind emotionally and physically. I felt shocked, like I had been hit by a bus. But it was a defining moment for me — I was relieved. I finally knew why I had been a social outcast all my life, and why I struggled more than others to make friends.

My newfound knowledge made it easier for me to endure the

humiliation I experienced at school. I now understood that my problems in society were not caused by a lack of character, and I stopped judging myself all the time. I stopped my endless efforts to please people. Instead of living my life in fear with my head hung low, I began to hold my head high and make myself heard.

I plucked up the courage to confront my bully. I made up my mind that I would show him I wasn't going to accept his abuse. So when the usual "retard!" came my way the next day, I rebuked him with, "Take a hike!"

I decided to tell him about the syndrome, in the hope that he would leave me alone. One day I saw him in the library alone and I took the chance.

"Listen," I began. "I've been diagnosed with Asperger's syndrome. So if you think I'm weird, that's the reason. Please just leave me alone." He was amazed. He didn't only leave me alone, but he actually defended me after that. He told me later that he felt privileged that I had trusted him with confidential information. I was shocked at how he had a total change of heart.

After I left school I realised that I was better off not being one of the popular ones at school. Most of them gave in to peer pressure to please the crowd, and did things that weren't very smart, while I made a few good friends who accepted me for who I was. I was more concerned about my future success than pleasing everyone.

I've learned to embrace the things that make me different, instead of obsessing over them. Even if everyone else sees me as strange, that's okay, because if I try to be who I am not, I will stumble for the rest of my life. I am no longer afraid to express my individuality, no matter what anyone says. If you always follow the crowd, you end up hiding who you really are inside.

~Shellique Carby

# Gotta Be This or That

*Knowing yourself is the beginning of all wisdom.*
~*Aristotle*

I was sixteen when I snagged my first job as a cashier at a discount department store. Most places I applied weren't interested in an applicant with no experience. At least, that's what they told me to my face. Realistically, I don't think they liked my look—thick black eyeliner and shadow, black nail polish, even black lipstick some days.

The other girls at Faceless-Corporation-Mart dressed and talked just like the ones at my school. They were all about the designer jeans and the tops so low-cut you could see their bras. I tried to stay out of their way, but couldn't always manage.

One day I walked into the break room and the Girl Brigade was hunched over a bridal magazine. I tried to be nice, to "make conversation" as my mother puts it. I asked, "Who's getting married?"

They looked at me like I had three heads, and one girl said, "Nobody." Everyone else laughed, but I didn't get the joke.

"Don't you read bride magazines?" a university student, Samira, asked. "I've had my wedding planned since I was, like, five!"

"I'm don't want to get married," I admitted.

Mistake.

Samira fake-coughed the word, "Lesbian!"

The other girls joined in: Cough. "Queer!" Cough, cough.

I didn't react, except to open the bathroom door and camp out in the end stall until break was over. Wouldn't life be peachy if they were right? Being a lesbian would have been easier than being whatever I was. Bisexual? I never liked that word, because it implied there were only two genders. I believed in gender fluidity. Male and female were only extremes. There was so much in the middle.

After break, I went back to my register, still trying not to cry. I wouldn't give those girls the satisfaction. That afternoon, I was scheduled alone at the mall entrance, which was never very busy. That's where I met the customer who changed my life.

In my mind, I call this person "Sheila." I never found out her real name, or even if she thought of herself as male, female or somewhere in between. Sheila was thin, hunched over a bit, grey hair thinning on top, wearing a typical old lady skirt and blouse. What set her apart from other women was her thick white stubble, hairy arms and legs (and ears and nose!), men's glasses and orthopaedic shoes. Sheila obviously had a male body, but seemed to want the world to acknowledge her as female. I was happy to oblige.

I knew what the magazine girls would have thought, and honestly, some of those judgments entered my mind, too: lazy crossdresser, senile man wearing his dead wife's clothes, queer. That's what everybody called me — queer.

There was a sparkle in Sheila's eyes, a proud and knowing glimmer. I envied that. Nobody was at my register, so Sheila set tubes of lipstick on the black conveyor belt. "Can I ask your opinion, dear? Which of these shades would suit my complexion?"

I laughed, and right away worried she'd think I was laughing at her. "Sorry, just... nobody's ever asked my opinion about make-up. Most old people are scared of me." That came out way ruder than I'd intended. "Not that you're old..."

"Of course I'm old," she teased, flicking her wrist as if to brush off my anxiety. "I'm ninety-three."

Her cheerfulness put me at ease, and I joked back, "You don't look a day over ninety."

She chuckled and drew my attention back to the make-up. "Which do you think?"

I read the names of all the shades and let her chat about this and that. The more we spoke, the more I admired her. When I asked why she hadn't talked to Tracy in the cosmetics department, who knew more about make-up than I ever would, she said, "Oh, I didn't want to waste the girl's time."

I knew what that meant—Tracy wouldn't give Sheila the time of day.

Even after she'd left the store, I kept thinking how brave Sheila was. I wondered if she was oblivious to the dangers of going out in public looking not perfectly prim-and-proper feminine or burly-butch masculine. It was a dangerous world out there. Was she just too old to care?

Sheila came into the store again about a month later, and ambled straight to my cash. I was busy, so I couldn't chat. I was glad to see her happy and healthy, but irritated by the snickering whispers from others in line. After Sheila had left, the woman behind her said, "What a freak."

I tried not to respond.

But I couldn't help it. I said, "Maybe you're the freak," and she left in a huff. I was lucky she didn't ask for a manager.

For months I didn't see my ninety-three-year-old idol. I wondered if she was okay. Then one day I had to go to the Science Centre to work on an independent study project. When I hopped on the bus, who did I spot? Sheila!

I was so happy to see her. She had on a long skirt and polo shirt, those same orthopaedic shoes and thick-rimmed glasses. Her face was shaven and her make-up was as neat as any ninety-three-year-old could manage, but that still couldn't compensate for the bald patch on her head. There were a lot of people on the bus, but everyone was standing away like Sheila had some kind of disease.

So I sat beside her, and to my surprise, she remembered me. She told me she lived with her son and his family. Today she'd been visiting her niece. There weren't many people in the family who would put up with her "quirks," but her son and daughter-in-law were tolerant enough. "I can't shave myself anymore because of the palsy," she told me, "but Danny helps when he's got time, and Nancy helps with my cosmetics."

It struck me, in that moment, how lucky we both were. My family was pretty nonchalant about me being bisexual. Sheila's daughter-in-law helped her with make-up. Not everybody who seeks acceptance finds it, but we two had.

I asked if Sheila had ever considered wearing a wig, or stockings, or women's shoes? She'd pass better for a female if she did. Nobody would stare and snicker. She told me she'd tried all that when she was younger—in her sixties—but she was too old for confining wigs or pinching shoes.

"I'm ninety-three," she told me again. "Sticks and stones may break my bones—and if they do, I've lived a good life anyhow." Sheila clutched her purse, her hands shaking slightly. "Besides, the old song was wrong—'Gotta be this or that.'" She sang a bar in a wavering voice. "You know the tune?"

I nodded.

"After ninety-three years, I should know you don't gotta be what you aren't. Does you no good. You must always be true to yourself."

Though she hardly knew me, Sheila seemed to see where my pain was. She gave me words to live by. And that "insult" the other cashiers hurled at me—queer? That's how I identify now, out loud and proud.

~Giselle Renarde

# Every Single Flaw

*Labels are for cans, not people.*
*~Anthony Rapp*

I used to be unsure
Of who I really was.
I never really thought
That I was good enough.

I never talked to people.
I feared what they would think
If what I said was wrong
Or I made a huge mistake.

It made life kind of lonely
Having no real friends.
No one to be there for me
Until the very end.

I'd be walking down the halls
And smile at someone from class
But they'd never see me.
They'd always walk on past.

I never knew where I fit in
Or who I'd want to be.

Everything I tried
Was never really me.

When I heard metal music
I liked it from the start.
I also have discovered
My love of making art.

I'm fine not being popular.
I'm not obsessed with fashion.
Now I've figured out
Art and music are my passion.

I listen to my iPod
Or write songs of my own.
It fits me so much better
Than dressing like a clone.

I've really changed a lot
From who I used to be.
Not only how I dress
But I ignore when I get teased.

I don't care about designer clothes.
I wear skinny jeans and band shirts.
People may not like that
But I don't let their teasing hurt.

People call me goth or emo
But that doesn't hurt at all.
I'm proud of who I am.
Every single flaw.

~Carissa Smith

# Tough Times for Teens

**Chapter 6**

## Grieving

# Ripples

*It is from numberless diverse acts of courage and belief that
human history is shaped. Each time a man stands up for others,
or strikes out against injustice, he sends forth a tiny ripple of hope.*
~Robert F. Kennedy

Hundreds of people stared at me, waiting for me to speak. My family sat in the front row, followed by a few rows of close friends and neighbors. The rest of the audience was made up of distant acquaintances and complete strangers, and as I looked out at them, I felt my words freeze in my mouth. They wanted me to say that everything would be okay, but how could I comfort a room full of strangers?

"I'm not a very good musician," I began. "When I learned the trumpet, my brother found a pair of my dad's noise-canceling headphones. I thought he went a bit overboard. I mean, those babies were meant to drown out the sound of a table saw."

There was nervous laughter in the front rows, but most of the audience looked uncomfortable. Was I making jokes at a funeral?

"I had an overweight teddy bear when I was young," I said. "I called him Fatso Bear. Clive soon got the same bear, and he gave his the clever name of Fatty Bear."

More laughter. My audience was warming up, and I felt the lump in my throat begin to dissolve.

"We played a game when we were kids," I went on. "It involved cars and rotten eggs. Clive would hide in the bushes, and when I gave the word, he would throw eggs at the cars that drove past. The game ended when our neighbor drove by in his vintage Jaguar Roadster."

This time laughter washed over the entire room, and I had to wait for it to die down before I could continue. Most people might not understand why I was making them laugh, but why should they? Some people hid behind silence, or harsh words, but my defense mechanism was comedy. If I made them laugh, perhaps we could forget why we were there. If I made them laugh, perhaps they wouldn't see that behind my smile, I was dying of a broken heart.

It had been a week since my younger brother killed himself, and I still hadn't cried. I didn't cry when sad women flocked to my house like doves, or when I caught my mother crying in his bedroom. I didn't shed a tear when my father's friends came over to rip up the living room carpet in great sobbing howls, or when they nailed down a shiny hardwood floor. People mourn in different ways.

Now, standing before a room full of strangers, I felt tears prick my eyes. It was the first time since my brother's death that I had felt anything at all—how strange that jubilation and calming support from hundreds of strangers would summon my tears. I felt elation rise and die in my chest, and for the first time in a week, I realized that my heart was still beating.

Still, it wasn't easy to tell five hundred guests things they already knew. Clive was unhappy. Clive was a weird little kid with an imagination, and there weren't enough other weird little kids in our town. Clive didn't fit in, and he thought that nobody wanted him. Didn't he know that every strange beauty finds a calling and a kindred heart?

I looked out at my audience and began again. I told them stories of Clive's adventures and fearless ambition, about how he could muster the courage to do a back flip on solid ground or just stick up for himself. I gave them a Clive they had never known, because I didn't want Clive to end inside that room. I wanted everyone to leave with things they had never known about him, so that he would live on inside their hearts. Funerals are too often reductions of untold personalities, and I wasn't going to let that happen.

Tears welled up in my eyes, and this time I didn't stop them. I stood in front of a room full of friends and strangers, crying without shame.

"He's here," I managed, after a long moment of silence. "He's here right now. Let me explain what I mean."

I glanced at the friends from Clive's elementary school, his old best friends from whom he had drifted, the friends he only saw once a year.

"If he ever told you something he didn't share with anyone else," I said. "If you know something about him that nobody else in the entire world knows, then there are pieces of him left to discover. There are hundreds of untold secrets in this room, safe within your hearts and minds."

A woman I didn't know covered her face and shook with quiet sobs.

"There are a hundred things I want to ask him," I said. "I want to ask him if he read *Franny and Zooey*, and if he liked it. I want to ask him if he ever fell in love, because I don't know. I read his journal once when I was mad at him... it was full of poems about gerbils and stuff, but it didn't mention love."

Sad laughter.

"So you have to help me," I said. "Tell me about him. I thought it was too late, but standing here, I remember that it's not. I want to know my brother, and every one of you knows something about him that I don't know."

As distant acquaintances and new friends stepped up to embrace me and offer their words of sorrow, I discovered a community I had never known. It was a community of hundreds, woven together by the invisible threads of my younger brother's life. How absurd to think that he never felt he belonged, when hundreds of strangers found each other through being his friend. If he had opened his eyes and seen the ripples he created in hundreds of lives, he would have weathered the storm and landed safely on the other side.

Four years have passed since my brother's death. I no longer mourn only the spirited sixteen-year-old boy I lost, but the twenty-year-old young man he would have become. The once fragile ties binding me to his friends have grown stronger over the years, and we have created friendships of our own. A month ago, an out-of-state friend I had never met flew to California to spend the week with my parents and me. We spoke of Clive, but we also spent the week laughing and discussing our daily lives.

I wish I could have told Clive what I know now. You are not yet yourself. You are only the boy you have known for two years, when the sadness began. That version of you will die on his own, if you let him. He will fold and take a bow, then retreat into the darkness. It will be a hard act to follow, but in the years to come, you will know that it is worth it.

~Jill Barry

# A Knock on the Door

*Dad, your guiding hand on my shoulder will remain with me forever.*
*~Author Unknown*

I went to sleep the night before
With no worries or concerns.
That morning there came a knock at the door.
I looked through the glass and my worries soared.
We answered the door and the news came fast.
It was like an atomic blast.

"Your husband was killed in a car accident this morning."
I looked at my mom, who started crying.
I stood there in so much shock and all I could think
Was, "This can't be happening."
In an instant our lives changed forever.
No more father daughter dances or hanging out.
No more family dinners or trips.
Our lives were turned upside down.

I do not remember much from that day,
So many people who didn't know what to say.
That day changed me forever.

Never did my dad see me start high school.
Never did he see me graduate.
Never will he walk me down the aisle,
Or see his grandchildren run and play.

My life will never be the same.
I miss him more and more each day.
Somehow I am dealing with the pain
Of living without my father.
The one who I looked up to and love,
The one I call my hero.
Never take for granted one single day,
Because you never know when it might all go away.

~Meaghan D. Scott

# The Summer

*If I had a single flower for every time I think about you,*
*I could walk forever in my garden.*
*~Claudia Ghandi*

It was one of the hottest summers our province had ever seen, and instead of hiding inside an air conditioned building like most sane people, we were unprotected in the blistering heat working ourselves, and our horses, into a sweat.

At seventeen I'd already been riding and competing since I was seven. I met Chris when I was eight, through a mutual friend and trainer. We trained at the same barn for a number of years, but since he was the only boy in the barn and three years older than most of us, all the young girls silently fought over him. We had our share of laughs; at ten, during one of his signature water fights, I attempted to jump over a trailer hitch. And bailed. Badly. I completely ripped up one of my knees on the gravel, and like an embarrassed little girl, hid in my parents' car. On the ferry ride home, we pulled out a game of checkers. And, in his typical "no mercy fashion," he beat me. In the nicest way possible, of course.

After a couple of years, he and his parents moved on and purchased their own farm, where Chris became his own trainer, and took on horses as clientele. I continued to train with the trainer where we had met.

As fate would have it, several years later, I was invited to help out at his farm's open house. I had recently purchased a young horse and hadn't been doing much in the horse world, so to say I was ecstatic to spend a few full days on a farm was a bit of an understatement. It was an amazing few days for me. I got to spend time with some of the most amazing people and horses. It was so great, in fact, that we arranged for me to bring my horse to him.

Over those few days, Chris and I had spent a lot of time working as a team—exercising horses, clipping them, sanding feet, bathing, getting them ready. And we made a great team. Ultimately, we decided in exchange for helping him at the farm, he'd help me with my young horse. It was a perfect arrangement.

But we made such a great team because we went beyond professionalism and genuinely got along. There were days when I just needed to get away, so he would come pick me up at seven in the morning and we'd spend the day working horses and just talking. He was probably one of the best people I could ever have gone to for advice; he never turned me away or rejected me when I needed help or someone to listen.

We spent more hours preparing for the horse show that summer than anything else, and we learned a lot about each other. The horse show, of course, was amazing. It was a week spent camping out on the show grounds, going to bed at 1 a.m. and waking up at 5 a.m.

I remember days sitting in the arena at the farm, where Chris would make me laugh so hard that I would be in tears. That's something everyone loved about him—his humor and his laugh. Of the dozens of memories I carry with me every day, his laugh is one that will forever be the strongest.

Unfortunately, as that summer came to an end, my young horse injured her leg. Chris was there every step of the way, for the vet visits, the ultrasounds, everything. He repeatedly helped me do things with her, because it was too hard for me to handle what my horse was going through. Due to the severity of the injury, it was best for us to remove her from the training facility, and take her to a farm where her injury could be rehabbed. So with that, we moved on. We kept in touch for a while, but as the horse world goes, we both got busy and lost touch. We would see each other at horse shows and talk, and I intended to bring my horse back to him when she was better.

Then one Sunday, I was taking my lunch break at work. My phone started ringing, and it was my best friend Conley who was in Saskatchewan at a National Horse Show. I don't usually answer my cell phone, but she usually doesn't call me, so I picked up, assuming she must have won her class.

All I remember from that phone call is one sentence: "I'm not sure if you've heard, but it was just confirmed that Chris Peeler was killed in an ATV accident." I thanked her for the call, hung up, and ran outside, unable to control the tears and the heaving.

Just days before, I had been thinking that I should call him. But I didn't. I assumed that I would get another chance. In life, you just never know when it will be the last time. All I have now are memories. Days spent on the farm just lounging around watching movies because we were snowed in, or the way he managed to make my veggie hot dogs so they actually tasted good.

I always think of this quote by Flavia Weedn when I think of Chris: "Some people come into our lives and quickly go. Some stay for a while, leave footprints on our hearts, and we are never, ever the same." Ten years with him is what I got... and I will never, ever be the same.

~Gabrielle Miller

# Life Stolen from Him

*If we can put a man on the moon, we can end drunk driving. But it starts with one person at a time.*
~William Elliott

The halls had never looked so dead and sad as they did that day at Centralia Washington High. The students were quiet. The teachers were murmuring. Everyone had heard the morning news through the loudspeakers: "Students and teachers. We are sorry to inform you that we lost a member of our tiger family. Michael Conine was killed in a car accident yesterday morning."

After those words, conversations died out. Everyone started crying, people departed for their homes in tears, teachers comforted each other, and it felt like someone had pushed pause on the school remote. Never had a school day felt so slow, so empty, so... dark.

I had not known Michael Conine, age seventeen, junior, nicknamed "Bucka." I'd seen him occasionally in the hallways, always with his friends and smiling. But I had never talked to him. Why would I? Aside from the fact that I was a timid girl, I was also a sophomore. I didn't usually try to make friends with people older than me, mainly because of my shyness and low self-esteem.

For some odd reason, his death pained me in ways I could not explain. It was as if I had lost a good friend. I had a heavy, aching feeling in my chest.

Some people would later say, "There were no words to express how I felt." Yet for me, there were and still are many words to express how I felt and still feel. The word that stands out from all the rest is pity.

I felt sorry that he had gone with his friends on Saturday night to a party. Sorry that they had gotten drunk and the driver wasn't thinking as he started his Bronco. Sorry that the driver lost control and swerved off the road. Sorry that they had all survived miraculously except the one in the passenger seat, Michael.

My sympathy for the parents remains fresh in my heart. I pray that they can overcome this tragic event in their lives. I hope others will learn from this accident and think before they drive intoxicated. Not just for them but for their passengers who are the victims. Michael will no longer be able to attend the school Pep assemblies on the last day of every month. He won't laugh with his friends. He won't say, "I love you" to his girlfriend, who still mourns for him. No, life was yanked from him at the age of seventeen.

If your friends or people you know are having problems with drinking, talk to them. Don't let your school go through an accident like my school did. The next Michael could be your closest friend.

~Diana Torres

# Hang in There

*We acquire the strength we have overcome.*
*~Ralph Waldo Emerson*

t was a warm sunny day in July. My family and I were up north in Bellaire, Michigan, along with my brother's girlfriend, Nicki. As we were swimming and playing in Lake Bellaire, we decided to pull out the jet skis. We only had two, so while Nicki and I doubled up on one, my brother Chris jumped aboard the other. We took off to the middle of the lake, laughing and having the time of our lives, going close to eighty miles per hour. Chris began to fishtail us, moving his jet ski in a way that would splash loads of water to the side, until suddenly he lost control and spun around, doing a complete three-sixty. We then hit him head on.

I woke up to Nicki screaming my name in the water. I had no idea how long I was out, or what exactly had happened. I looked behind me and saw my jet ski had been demolished into a million pieces. To the left, I saw my brother, floating. Nicki and I swam to him as fast as we could, hoping he was only playing a joke on us. It was far from that. As we lifted his head from the water, his feet were dangling, his eyes were rolled back, and he was turning purple and blue. Nicki held him, and I swam to his jet ski, which was also wrecked, in an attempt to find help. I stood on it, waving my bright red lifejacket, and a boat came our way.

The family on the boat grabbed Chris from our arms and pulled him aboard while Nicki and I jumped on behind him. After laying him down, they began CPR. In the meantime a lady was trying to distract me, but there was no way I was about to take my eyes off my brother. I held his hand, crying in shock and whispering in his ear. I told him he was going to be okay, and I prayed and prayed for God's strength. Suddenly, I heard him cough, and I thought the nightmare was over, but it had only just begun. Blood was coming out of his ears and his mouth. Before I knew it, we were at the dockside with ambulances and my parents waiting.

The paramedics quickly rushed Nicki, my mom, and me into the beach house to assess our injuries, and told my dad to wait outside with them while they worked on Chris. I couldn't see much from inside, but I could feel the fear shivering through my body and down my spine. When I asked my mom if Chris was going to be okay, she shook her head, bawling her eyes out, and told me, "I don't think so." After hearing that, I couldn't breathe. I was in shock and couldn't control my body. I was put onto a stretcher and rushed to the hospital, where my brother's ambulance quickly followed behind mine.

I awoke in the hospital to the doctors putting needles and IV's into my arms. I heard a boy scream, and I yelled, "What are they doing to my brother?" The doctor told me everything was fine, and to sit back. But I knew he wasn't telling me the truth. Then a grief counselor came in with tears in her eyes, looked at me, and talked with the doctor. She walked out of my room, looking back with every step she took. Something wasn't right. I knew it.

Finally my dad walked into my room. He sat down and said, "I can't lie to you Becky. Chris is dead." I looked my dad in the eye, tears streaming down my cheeks, and screamed. I screamed and screamed until there was nothing left in me. My dad held me, and my mom rushed into my room to hold me as well. But I didn't feel their warmth. I didn't feel anything. Only disbelief.

My brother was only seventeen years old, about to be a senior in the fall. How could this happen to such an outgoing, all around awesome kid? He was my hero and my best friend. He always understood the real me, and accepted me for who I was. I didn't think God would ever do such a thing.

The next few days, our family received more support than we ever imagined, and we were beyond thankful for it. We had people by our sides constantly, crying and grieving with us. The funeral was hard, but I was still in disbelief and shock. It was like a constant nightmare.

Over the next year, I felt so guilty for what happened. So many different thoughts ran through my head. I shouldn't have been going that fast, I should have turned the jet ski one quick move, I shouldn't have gone out that day. Even though people constantly told me it wasn't my fault, it didn't matter. I still felt responsible for my brother's death.

I became suicidal, wanting to end my life too. I began by cutting my arms, because the pain made me feel alive. The fact that I could still hurt made me feel good. But it got worse, much worse. I began to cut my wrists to the point where they wouldn't stop bleeding and they got more and more infected every day as I continued to cut. I abused all types of medicine and pills, hoping my life would end soon. My parents realized what I was doing to myself and sent me to a psychiatric hospital.

I hated it there. I felt out of place and I didn't think anyone could help me. After many days and nights, I was finally released and able to go home. Seeing my parents made everything better. Although I wasn't completely cured, I realized what I was putting them through in addition to my brother's death, and that was enough to break my heart.

After sending our story to *The Montel Williams Show*, Nicki and I were invited on TV to talk with Sylvia Brown, a famous psychic. I was so anxious and thrilled to hear this, I didn't know what to do with myself. We had the experience of being on national television and talking to a lady who spoke directly with my brother. She said, "He doesn't blame you for his death. In fact, he knew he wasn't going to live long. He lived his life to the fullest." After, I felt like a whole new person.

It has been eight years since my brother died, and I'm okay now, something I never thought possible. I never thought I would smile again or even be happy. No one could ever replace Chris, but I have had moral support from everyone I know. I haven't forgotten about my brother, and I thank him for the person he has made me. I look at life in a new way, and approach every situation with a different perspective.

I am not writing this just to get my name in a book. I am writing this for anyone and everyone who has ever lost someone special in their life. I want them to know that as hard as it is to believe right now, soon enough, things will work themselves out and you will be okay. It gets easier, and after everything I have personally been through, I am promising you that. Hang in there.

~Rebecca Cattaneo-Harris

# 58

# Chicken Soup for the Soul

# This Too Shall Pass

*I have sometimes been wildly, despairingly, acutely miserable, but through it all I still know quite certainly that just to be alive is a grand thing.*
~Agatha Christie

If you're waiting for the end of the day
Walking around with your smile stretched thin
If you're building those walls around yourself
Fearing that sooner or later they'll close in

If there's always something missing
And nothing ever seems right
If the weight of the world is on your shoulders
And you can't quite seem to find the light

If your good intentions come to no good
And you let the best things slip away
If you don't know who to trust anymore
And you're hoping to make it through to a better day

If you're feeling alone
And if ends never seem to meet

If you're finding it hard
To wake up to reality

If you're trapped inside
Wondering how long it will last
Just breathe, don't worry
For this too shall pass

~Nayantara Dutta

# 59

# Saying Goodbye

*To live in hearts we leave behind*
*Is not to die.*
*~Thomas Campbell, "Hallowed Ground"*

I walked passed my classmate a little confused. She was leaning against the wall with another girl and she was crying hysterically. She must have broken up with her boyfriend, I thought.

I reached my first period class early. As a high school senior I drove myself to school and always arrived earlier than the school buses so I could get a good parking spot. No one was in the classroom yet. I dropped my backpack on my desk and returned to the hallway. I decided to go to the computer lab and check my e-mail before school started. One of my friends had graduated the year before and went into the military. E-mail was still fairly new and we found it easier to use to communicate than writing letters.

I passed several more students who were younger and they were also sobbing. What in the world was going on? I decided someone in their grade must have been in an accident.

I signed on to the computer and it wasn't long before another of my classmates joined me.

"Did you hear the news?" he asked as he approached the computer next to mine.

I shook my head no.

"Keith drowned last night at the river."

My world froze as I tried to make sense of his words. Although

I wouldn't say we were great friends, Keith and I had some classes together and talked often.

How could this happen? We were two weeks away from graduating. Some of us were going to college. Keith was joining the military. We were all too young. Kids don't die!

I walked back to my first-period class feeling numb. The hallways were now filled with people talking and crying. I sat at my desk and stared off into space as my mind tried to digest the information I was hearing.

Railroad trestle jumping was popular among the teens in my community. There was a train bridge thirty-five feet high that they would jump off into the Shenango River. It was dangerous, of course, but it was rare that anyone ever got hurt. On Memorial Day, some of my classmates went. Keith had a successful jump. He was swimming to shore when he was suddenly pulled under the water. He called for help once, then disappeared. The group searched for him to no avail. Another classmate, who was a volunteer fire fighter, helped pull Keith's body from the river ninety minutes later.

I don't know what happened in my first period geometry class that day. All I remember is the bell ringing and hauling my backpack to the locker room. I changed into my gym clothes, went into the gym, and sat up against the wall, staring at the shiny yellow floor. I couldn't think of anything other than Keith and, finally, I cried. I retreated to the locker room to be alone.

By the time the bell rang dismissing class, I couldn't even think. I stood in the hallway lost. I couldn't remember what my next class was or where it was located. I started to panic and then I saw a group of my classmates head outside to the courtyard. Not knowing what else to do, I followed.

We sat there in the warm May sunshine in silence. Someone started the Lord's Prayer and we all fell into sync reciting the words, our voices echoing around the small space we were in.

The principal or someone must have seen us because our entire senior class was called to the auditorium. I think this was a way to contain us so we weren't all wandering around the building hopeless and lost.

Classes resumed the next day as normal. Another student took up a collection to help offset Keith's funeral expenses.

The viewing was held a few days later. The line extended away from the building, a great length down the sidewalk. Keith was clearly loved and would be missed by many. I stood in line watching the people around me. A lot of classmates were hugging and crying. People found themselves in the arms of people they didn't normally talk to at school. The cliques were gone. We were all hurting and we all needed each other.

The only viewings I had been to before were for older relatives who had passed away. I was never sad at these. I barely knew them, and common knowledge was that old people were supposed to die. Seeing a seventeen-year-old lying in a casket was one of the hardest things I ever had to go through.

At our graduation ceremony they announced Keith's name. We gave a standing ovation as his younger sister walked the stage to collect his diploma. Even with him gone, life went on.

I had a recurring nightmare for close to a year after Keith's death. In it, I was standing by the river and he was walking towards the water. I kept yelling for him to stop, to not enter the water, but he always did. One night the dream was different. After I yelled for him to stop, he turned to me and smiled saying, "It's okay. I'm alright." Then he disappeared into the dark water.

After that, the nightmares were gone and I was finally able to let him go and start healing. Oddly, I found out that another classmate had a similar dream. I think Keith knew that we missed him and he needed to come to us and tell us it was okay to move on.

~Valerie D. Benko

# Gone

*Although it's difficult today to see beyond the sorrow,*
*May looking back in memory help comfort you tomorrow.*
*~Author Unknown*

If you were going to leave,
I wish you'd gone in the autumn,
When everything is dying anyway.

Or in the winter,
When cold and bitterness seep deep into the skin,
Leaving an icy chill
That countless mugs of hot cocoa could never melt.

I wish you'd folded the shirts in the basket,
Putting the creases in all the spots
I'd always failed to find.

I wish you'd kissed the children
Sleeping peacefully in their beds,
When the late spring breeze
Drifted through their open windows,
Offering a hint of lilacs
And the promise of freedom.

I wish you'd fed the dog,
Or at least scratched behind his ears
When he followed you to the door.

If you were going to leave,
I wish you'd told me,
So that I might have said goodbye
Before you couldn't hear me
When I did.

~Jennifer Lynn Clay

# Learning Regret

*If tears could build a stairway,*
*And memories a lane,*
*I'd walk right up to Heaven*
*And bring you home again.*
*~Author Unknown*

As a teenager, I thought regrets were for old people. People who had lived long enough to make huge mistakes and live with the consequences. In fact, regret was the furthest thing from my mind at seventeen, when I met Roman.

I was a first year university student in a male-dominated program, and I was looking for a place to fit in. I joined the campus Solar Team and put my name down for their mechanical team, specifically the aerodynamics subdivision. I was one of three girls in the large, multidisciplinary group. It was easy to feel intimidated by the older students, especially when my knowledge of tools barely extended past a nail file. When the engineering team manager led me over to the head of the aerodynamics group, I was desperate to please. I worried that my new leader would take one look at my pink sweater and my high-heeled boots, choke back a laugh and send me out to buy the snacks. Instead, I was introduced to Roman.

A couple of years older than me, Roman was a tall guy with curly hair, glasses, and a sardonic sense of humour. Instead of scoffing at his new recruit, Roman patiently tried to explain what he was working on. He could probably tell I understood less than ten percent of what he was saying, but he assigned me a task nonetheless: to work on the fairing design. I was ecstatic, and a little bit nervous. I wasn't doomed to be snack girl—I was a designer! I scribbled his suggestions in my logbook frantically, all the time thinking, just what is a fairing?

I needn't have worried. For the next eleven months, Roman shared all of his aerodynamic knowledge and experience with me. He taught me how to use modelling software, how to use the shop tools, and even how to play poker. I spent the summer covered in dust and foam, learning how to create a body lay-up right in our own shop. Along with two of our friends, we were the Brotherhood, responsible for manufacturing the car in four months. We wrote nicknames on the back of our coveralls and argued over whose music to play while working. I was the only girl in the Brotherhood, and I was proud to be a part of it. One of my favourite ways to take a break was to sit on a stool at Roman's side and watch him work. Wearing his signature navy coveralls over his equally signature flannel shirts, he was always ready to chat and joke—and he always smelled good. He became the older brother I never had, and I wouldn't have minded more from him.

I went away for vacation at the end of the summer. When I came back, I discovered that things in the Brotherhood had changed. A recent graduate, Roman had landed his dream job in another country. I didn't see him in person again, and he left before I got to say goodbye. We e-mailed each other often at first, and then only occasionally, and then rarely. By the time Roman had been gone for over a year, our contact usually consisted of a Facebook "poke." We were both caught up in our regular lives; him with working as a mechanical engineer, me with getting through school and finally becoming mechanical manager for the Solar Team. When we did e-mail, we had lots to share, but I always figured we'd have time to catch up later on. The last time I heard from him, he was going to live in Wales for six months for work.

Two and a half years after I met Roman, I received a devastating message from one of the Brotherhood. A longtime lover of hiking and spelunking, Roman had disappeared while hiking alone on a mountain in Wales. The search and rescue team later found him dead at the bottom of a 200-foot drop. I was the one to break the news to Roman's friends and colleagues still in university. I broke down within seconds of choking out the story. The weeks that followed were tough. Sympathy messages and hugs flew back and forth between new and old team members. The Solar Team held a beautiful memorial in Roman's memory, right in the workshop and garage. His parents hosted a memorial service for friends and family, encouraging us to celebrate Roman's life, not mourn his death. Getting to know Roman's parents helped heal the pain I was feeling, but throughout everything, I kept thinking that I never got to say goodbye.

Why couldn't I have taken ten minutes out of every day to e-mail him? Why didn't I stay in touch? Why didn't I see him during his last visit home? Regret infected my mourning. Even months later, I had to leave the fabric section of a store after touching a bolt of flannel and tearing up. His last Facebook poke is still sitting on my homepage, waiting for a response. I leave it there as a reminder of Roman, and as a reminder to keep in touch with those I care about. I hope wherever he is, he knows how much his mentorship and friendship meant to me. Even in death, he taught me a valuable lesson about regret, and to treasure each moment I'm given with the people close to me.

~Emily Ann Marasco

# The Grieving Time of Grass

*While grief is fresh, every attempt to divert only irritates. You must wait till it be digested, and then amusement will dissipate the remains of it.*

*~Samuel Johnson*

It had been nearly two years. It wasn't supposed to hurt anymore. Everyone else seemed to be coping and getting over it better and faster than me. I felt alone... so terribly alone.

None of my friends from college knew Rachel; she didn't live that long. The cancer claimed her life a few months before she would have graduated from high school. She was two months away from celebrating her eighteenth birthday.

Each time I went home, I visited her grave. I thought seeing her name on the cold marble would help me heal, but it didn't work. I thought after the one-year mark it would get easier, but it only got worse. I felt guilty because I was still mourning. I was supposed to be strong. Rachel wouldn't want me to be so sad; she would want me to go on with my life the way she wasn't allowed to and remember that each day is a blessing. But I just couldn't do it.

Everything reminded me of Rachel. I'd hear her favorite song and instantly burst into tears. All of my friends suddenly seemed to want to go to the restaurant where Rachel had worked. I even caught glimpses of her in crowds only to be disappointed by someone of similar appearance.

Things that were supposed to be fun and exciting for me only made me hurt because I knew Rachel never got to experience them. While registering for my second semester of college classes, I couldn't help but break down and cry, thinking how she never got to have even her first day of college. I didn't want to go on with life without Rachel, but everyone was expecting things of me. I couldn't handle the pressure; I just wanted to stay in my bed all day, and for a while, that's exactly what I did. I had friends who would literally have to pull me out of bed and convince me to go to my classes or even eat. I started seeing a counselor, but the pain just wouldn't go away.

Once, while visiting Rachel's grave, as I stood shivering in the cold October wind, I noticed something totally new. I found beauty in the graveyard. As I surveyed the vast expanse of graves surrounding Rachel's, I discovered a difference. Rachel's grave was still not covered in grass. The grass was scarce and it was more dirt than anything else. Other graves had lush green grass on top of them, but not Rachel's.

I started to cry, but this time not out of desperation or misery. It was hope and joy that made the tears fall. The earth itself had not yet completely healed from Rachel's death — what made me think that I should? Since her death, there have been times when the grass grew fast and thick, but then something would happen, like a storm would come and destroy some of the progress. The earth was forced to start over again. How much grass there was growing on her grave varied by the day.

I almost couldn't handle how perfect the metaphor was. For the first time in two years, I suddenly felt at peace with my grief. I knew that since even the ground hadn't healed yet, there was no need to rush my mourning process. It was okay to take a few steps back just when I thought I was getting over it. I used to think this meant that I was a failure, but I was wrong. No one could feel my pain but me. I couldn't rush through my grief. I had to take every day as it came and move forward as I could.

Though I still miss Rachel dearly, I have been able to heal at my own pace without worrying about what I was supposed to be doing or feeling. I know it will always hurt a little bit, but I also know there is hope for the future. Things will get in the way and sometimes there will be more dirt than grass, but I am the only one who can work through my grief, and in time I will do just that.

~Sarah Sawicki

# Tough Times for Teens

## Silver Linings

# Lovesick

*Love is a symbol of eternity. It wipes out all sense of time,*
*destroying all memory of a beginning and all fear of an end.*
*~Author Unknown*

In the past six years of my life I have spent countless hours in
a hospital. Going to appointments, having tests run, getting
surgery, and now that I know how it feels to be there, spending my time visiting other patients and volunteering my time with
the ASYMCA and at the kids' holiday parties. When you've spent so
much time around the staff, they, like other patients, become your
family. Out of all these people who have touched my life in some way,
there is one who touched my heart and who I will never forget.

It was a year and a half after I was diagnosed with superior mes-
enteric artery syndrome when I met Kevin. It was springtime and we
were both in the hospital for treatment. Kevin was larger than life,
always joking and playing pranks on the hospital staff. By the way he
acted you'd never think that he had leukemia. He did though, and
as our friendship grew stronger, so did his disease. He was so much
fun to be around, and neither of us had to hide our sickness from
each other. We'd gone through some of the same tests, some of the
same nurses had cared for us, and we knew all the ins and outs of
the hospital.

Some time passed, and Kevin went to a hospital in Seattle, where
they were hoping to perform a partial bone marrow transplant. All
of us who knew Kevin hoped and prayed that they'd be successful.

Kevin and I sent messages back and forth while he was away, but one day I received a message from Kevin's father. He told me, "Kevin and I have lots of time to talk up here, and you're all he can talk about. Whatever you talk about in your messages is making him very happy, and I thank you for that." Unknown to me, Kevin had been hiding his true feelings. Although I had a boyfriend, the stress and anxiety over Kevin put a strain on our relationship and we soon broke up, leaving me available for Kevin.

Halloween came and I was at the hospital helping with their party, when my mother pulled me aside and told me Kevin was coming home. He was too sick and there was nothing that the doctors could do. I remember a few minutes later, crying on the phone as Kevin told me himself when he'd be home. When tears kept Kevin from being able to speak, I continued the conversation with his dad. As we rolled into November Kevin finally asked me to be his girlfriend and I promised to be there until the end.

I spent the next weeks by Kevin's side at the hospital, and at his house. Holding his hand every step of the way as I slowly watched him fade. He was no longer able to walk or lift his arms and eventually lost the use of his hands too. When Kevin's anxiety attacks hit I was sometimes the only one who could get him calm enough to sleep.

Kevin was still the same person—cracking jokes, making others laugh. He still had a happy outlook. Thanksgiving rolled around and I spent the Friday after at Kevin's house. He was drifting in and out of sleep, so I sat by him holding his hand, singing or talking to him whether he heard me or not. That night when I left after he fell asleep, I kissed him on the cheek, told him I loved him and that I'd be back tomorrow. Little did I know that was the last time I'd see him.

I was at the mall with my mom and older sister hitting the after Thanksgiving sales. We were finishing up when Kevin's dad called. I knew then that something was wrong. Kevin had gone to the hospital that morning to get another round of platelets; it was then that the cancer took over. I don't know if he ever asked for me—I was too scared to know the answer. I had almost been with him that morning.

I was planning on going with him to the hospital, but my sister's desire to start shopping early postponed my plans. I think God knew I wouldn't have been able to handle it. All the tears I'd been holding in the past few weeks would have spilled out. I needed to be strong for Kevin and, in not being there when he passed away, he never had to see me afraid and crying. For that I'm very thankful.

At Kevin's memorial service I remember playing the harp but having to have my younger sister take over as my fingers were trembling too much. I remember Kevin's mother coming to hug me and trying to comfort her as we cried. I remember Kevin's sister going from person to person, giving out hugs. She reminds me so much of him, especially now that her hair too is gone due to chemotherapy. She's going to make it though, and I know if Kevin were here he'd have given his life to save her.

Some times are harder than others, and life doesn't always seem fair. I don't know why hardships seem to enter the lives of those who least deserve them. But through Kevin I have become a better person. I've learned to look at the good even when faced with illness, love wherever I go, and laugh as much as I can. I thank God every day for Kevin's influence in my life. I was able to give Kevin the one thing he wanted before he died—a girlfriend. I feel honored that God chose me to play that role. It's been four years since Kevin was called home, and there's not a day that goes by that I don't think of the kid in glasses who made me laugh. I still cry sometimes, but I know Kevin's watching over those he loved. His memory reminds us to never lose faith, laugh often and love whomever we meet, for you never know what battle they're facing.

~Latira Anderson

# Revelations

*The willingness to accept responsibility for one's own life*
*is the source from which self-respect springs.*
*~Joan Didion*

The wind was swirling the leaves on the ground when I entered the hospital doors. I was ushered into a tiny room where a blond, pale nurse arrived shortly to ask about my health history and to run a few minor tests. She left and came back after a brief absence.

"Everything looks normal. However, your urine test reveals that you're expecting. Did you know you're pregnant?" she asked. She held a pen poised over her clipboard.

I nodded assent.

"You didn't tell me that before."

"Sorry," I said. "I didn't think it'd matter that much."

The nurse frowned at my answer. "Do you know how far along you are?"

I shrugged. "Maybe like two months? I don't know."

"Okay. We'll figure that out more closely based on your last period. How do you feel about being pregnant?"

I glanced at the wall and lied. "Fine."

"Can you remember what you've had to eat today?"

I thought back to the day's events. I had gotten up at six in the morning and eaten a chocolate long john donut. For lunch at school, I'd eaten a few slices of turkey from a sub sandwich—I'd thrown the bread, lettuce, and tomato slices away—and I'd drunk a Coke. That was all I could remember.

"The fainting spells are not going to go away," the nurse said. "You probably fainted today because you didn't drink enough fluids. And healthy foods are especially important for you at this time."

She looked up from her clipboard and observed the dull expression on my face. "You know all this already, don't you?"

"Uh huh." My reply was monotonous and half-hearted.

She stared at me, her forehead creased with subtle lines. For a long time, there was nothing but silence between us. She said nothing at all, only stared at me with hard, blue eyes. Then, very bluntly, she began.

"Hellooo! You're not just getting up and going about your daily activities anymore. A tiny baby is forming inside of you! Do you realize that? Every day for the next seven months, there's something new developing."

She paused, and for a moment, I thought she was going to cease her loud lecturing. I stole a quick glance at her face. She glared at me and then started up again.

"Think about it. A heart to pump blood, eyes and ears for your baby to see and hear with, a brain to learn with. Think about what's really important. There's a baby growing inside you. I don't care if you like it or not. It's happening, and you'd better realize that you're not just living for yourself anymore."

She had worked herself up to the point where her face was a red, flustered glow. I gawked at her, dumbfounded and not sure what to make of it. Then anger began to well up inside me.

I left the hospital in a horrible mood, brooding over the nurse's rudeness. How could she behave that way towards me? How could she judge me like that? She didn't have the right. First of all, she wasn't my mother, and secondly, I was pretty sure it wasn't a part of her job description to scold patients.

I went home and rested in bed for the night, unable to fall asleep. Although my anger had subsided a little, it was still there simmering in the background. The nurse's words continued to replay in my mind. The creation of a tiny human being was going on inside me. It was really happening. The thought struck me as oddly surprising, and I pondered that for a long time. It must have been around two in the morning when another realization popped into my head.

This was real.

It was more real than I had ever imagined anything to be real in the seventeen years of my life. This little fetus inside was dependent on me for its growth and health. Its survival depended on me. It was a daunting idea and the responsibility a bit overwhelming. More than anything, though, I was awed. How had I failed to see this pregnancy that clearly before?

I suddenly felt guilty for not knowing the extent of the responsibility that this baby's conception brought upon me. This child's life was now to become my life. Its happiness would be my happiness, its sadness my sadness. We would share a life together; we already were. This should have all been so obvious, yet it had been so mysteriously hidden in the crevices of my seventeen-year-old mind.

A few months later, I saw the image of my baby through an ultrasound machine.

"Does everything look okay?" I asked with hesitation.

I could feel the cold gel spread around my belly as the technician moved the wand around.

"Yes. Everything looks perfect from head to toe. Do you want to know the sex of the baby?"

I nodded.

"It's a girl."

I couldn't help but smile as I watched her turn over on her side and kick.

~May Nou Chang

# Learning How to Love

*Let no one who loves be unhappy... even love unreturned has its rainbow.*
~James Matthew Barrie

At age sixteen it is hard to see past your first love. It can be all consuming, it can be great, and it can also turn out to be the worst heartbreak you have ever experienced.

His name was Evan, and he was a friend first. His sister was my best friend all through elementary school, and I always thought that her brother was the coolest guy. They lived just down the hill from me. Sure, Evan would tease us, but when he invited us to hang out with him and his friends we really felt like we were part of the cool kids. His basement, where we would all hang out, had dirty carpet and posters of rock and reggae musicians. Everyone wanted to be around him—he just had this personality that drew people to him. Everyone wanted to be his friend because he was so smart and always had something interesting or funny to say. He knew everything from dumb movie quotes to philosophy.

He told me that he had never had a girlfriend before, although he was very popular. He just didn't think that girls liked him. But he was so wrong. He was the most attractive person in the world to me. I felt like his personality and mine went so well together. I knew already that I was in love.

We were all hanging out in his basement one night when he took me aside and told me that he had feelings for me. I was ecstatic, and after that we were inseparable. Since it was summer, we spent every moment together for three months. We had so much fun, having sleepover parties with his sister, watching The History Channel, and just talking and laughing all night. Whenever I looked at him I would get this feeling... I knew this wasn't just puppy love. It was real love, and he was my first.

When we finally said that we loved each other, I took it to heart. Then school started back up and our relationship changed. We didn't get to see each other as much, and it killed me. For him, seeing all his friends made him want to spend more time with them and less time with me. I knew I was being too clingy but I couldn't help it. I was still so in love with him and I didn't know how to handle my feelings.

Everything seemed to be spiraling out of control. All I could do was cry. I hated fighting with him and I could not see the light at the end of the tunnel. I couldn't eat or sleep. My parents were so worried about my depression that they checked me into the hospital. They put me in a smock that was pretty much like a burlap sack, gave me a book and a bed, and locked the door. I couldn't use the phone. I wanted to know if Evan and I were breaking up or not. We had fought but there was no resolution.

When I got back, my mom told me that he had been trying to call. She said that he had asked me to come over, and it gave me some hope. I was there in a heartbeat. When I got to his house, he told me he had feelings for another girl. He broke it to me so coldly. I was so angry with him for having feelings for this new girl. How could he leave me for someone else? I felt totally betrayed.

Two weeks after our break-up, I was finally starting to heal when my whole life was flipped upside down. I was watching TV in my living room when I heard the wail of sirens. I saw a parade of police cars going down the hill. I didn't think much about it at first, but when ambulances started coming I really took notice and I retreated to my room to avoid the noise.

A few minutes later my mother came and knocked on my door. She had a very solemn look on her face. "It's about Evan," she told me in a quiet voice.

"I don't want to talk about him, Mom!" I hollered back. I was still so hurt about our break-up. I knew if she brought him up I would start to cry. I had no idea how right I was.

She wouldn't take no for an answer. Then she broke it to me as gently as possible. "He passed away. He passed in his sleep. They think it might have been a brain aneurism."

I was so confused... I didn't know what to think. I was still mad at him for breaking up with me, but the process of forgiveness started right there. How could I be mad when the person I loved had just passed away? I was heartbroken all over again but I began to appreciate all of the things he had done for me. He taught me how to love, and he gave me love in return. A first love is such a huge milestone in someone's life and to have shared that with such an amazing person was a blessing.

~Julia Valentine

# Change in Plans

*We are made wise not by the recollection of our past,*
*but by the responsibility for our future.*
~George Bernard Shaw

As a small girl, my mom always told me, "You will never know how much I love you, until you have a child of your own." I never understood those words, because I didn't think I could love anyone as much as I loved my mom. But then I gave birth to a blue-eyed, curly-headed baby boy. When they laid this little, perfect person on me, I felt the warmest, most loving feeling anyone could ever imagine. And right away, I knew my mom was right.

The journey began nine months before. I was a senior in high school and I had been dating the same guy for about two years. We had just ended the semester for Christmas break when I found out I was pregnant. A wave of emotions flooded me and I felt overwhelmed. I was excited, of course, but I was also scared. To be seventeen and having a kid while you are still being a kid can be a very scary thing. As much as it hurts to say this, I felt like there was so much I wouldn't be able to do. My plans were to be a dancer in college, and to go to nursing school. My plans did not include being a teenage mother.

Some people looked down on me and treated me as though I was wearing a scarlet letter, which, I guess, is a burden all teenage mothers must face. But my family, including my Church family, was so supportive and good to me. They understood that everyone makes mistakes and that no one is perfect. My friends were great as well. They stood beside me the whole time. I was so thankful.

Now, as for the father of my child, the first four months were close to perfect. He was supportive and promised that he would stand by me the whole time. But as winter passed and the flowers started showing, so did I. And as I started showing, the pregnancy became more real to all of us. The whole thing became all too real to him, and it was too much for him to bear. He decided to inform me he wasn't going to be a part of my life, or my child's, in the McDonald's parking lot. Which, by the way, is where we first met.

The rest of my pregnancy was interesting. I finished my senior year and graduated six months pregnant with my head held high. In June, I had my shower and received more presents than anyone could ever imagine. Then, the day before the Fourth of July, I found myself in early labor. I was excited that my precious boy was about to arrive. Sadly, they stopped the labor and sent me home. But I knew only a few more weeks and the day would arrive.

On Sunday, August 1st, I went into labor again and there was no stopping me this time! Luckily, my doctor's plane from his vacation in China landed just a few hours before I went into labor. My whole family and all my friends came to be with me through the entire event. The end of my journey had finally come and I was so grateful! My labor and delivery went smoothly and, finally, I gave birth to Tavin Bentlie. He had my nose and my mother's eyes. He was my brand new baby boy, and he was such a miracle.

Unfortunately, after he was born, the doctors informed me that he had jaundice. At first, we tried a biliblanket to help his condition, but it only got worse. He had to stay in the hospital. While he was there, his dad came to see him. After talking it over, I decided he could come back.

Eventually, Tavin's dad and I got back together. Now it feels like we are a happy family. We are definitely not your average family, but a special one in our own way. Hopefully, one day after college we will get married and be on our own. But for now, we are taking things slowly and, together, raising our precious little blessing. I didn't have the typical senior year I thought I would have, but I wouldn't have had it any other way.

~Kirstin Paige Fitzgerald

# An Awesome Gift

*When someone you love becomes a memory, the memory becomes a treasure.*
*~Author Unknown*

"She was only sixteen years old!" I cried. "Why does someone so young have to die?" It was one of those questions that no one can answer. Well, no one but God. Sometimes though, if you really listen carefully... He'll give you the answers.

Her name was Laura Melany Valentine, and I'd known her since she was fourteen years old. That's how long she was in ChemoAngels. ChemoAngels is an organization that brings support to people with cancer. Each patient in the program is required to check in every month with the monitor they are assigned. I was Laura's monitor. Every month she would let me know how she was doing. So, for two years, I rode that roller coaster with her. The ups, the downs, the celebrations and the tears, as she went from treatment to treatment desperately trying to fight the cancer beast.

In between all the tests and the treatments, Laura just wanted to be a normal teenager. She attended school whenever she was able and she had a lot of friends. She loved hockey and became a well-known fan of the Peoria Rivermen. Everyone who knew Laura loved her. Despite her illness, Laura still seemed to find the energy to volunteer, to reach out to anyone who needed her. She was the youth chairman for Relay for Life, a personal attendant for children with disabilities, she volunteered for St. Jude's and Children's Miracle Network, she was active in her church, and she even received the Young Hero Award from the Illinois National Guard. She loved life and wanted so desperately to stay.

I guess God had other plans for her. After four reoccurrences of cancer, Laura completed her final journey here on Earth and finally went "home." She fought so hard. I was so sad to hear that she passed away. It was really important to me to go to her funeral visitation. I wanted to pay my respects to Laura's family and I wanted to say good-bye to my friend. Her visitation was from five to eight in the evening. I arrived there shortly after five. The line at that time extended all the way outside the funeral home. I stood in line for almost two hours, that's how many people were there. Friends, classmates, hospital staff, and fellow patients—it was endless. The line moved at a slow but steady pace, but there were just so many people. It was clear how many lives she touched after going to her visitation that night.

All week after I heard about her death, I had been struggling with feelings of anger and wavering faith. Wondering why someone so young, who fought so hard, had to die. Someone who should have had so many more years of life left. Who accomplished so much and touched so many people. It just didn't make sense to me. I was angry at how cold and callous cancer is. I was angry with God because I didn't understand why so many wonderful people are taken from us too soon.

I walked into that funeral home with all these feelings. But you know what I walked out with? I walked out with awe. Awe at the simple fact that each and every person in there was truly blessed to have known Laura. What an awesome gift from God! He placed Laura in each of their lives. And even though her time here was short, the gift of Laura's presence in their lives will stay with them forever. I looked around that room and each one had a story to tell of how Laura touched them. It was amazing to me that someone who was only here for sixteen years could do so much. I can only hope that when my time is finished here I touch at least half the number of people Laura touched.

I walked into the funeral home that evening wondering why Laura had to die. But I didn't walk out asking that same question. Instead, I walked out knowing in the deepest part of my soul... why she lived.

~Amy S. Rolfs

# Seeing Through the Haze

*Sometimes in tragedy we find our life's purpose —
the eye sheds a tear to find its focus.*
~Robert Brault, www.robertbrault.com

Through the haze of anesthesia, I could see my mother and father sitting by my hospital bed, eyes red and swollen from crying. Just as panic came creeping in, my mother said the two most life-changing words I would ever hear: "It's cancer." My head was instantly swimming with fears and questions, though all I could stammer was "Will I lose my hair?" and the answer, of course, was "Yes."

No more than a week prior to this, I had been a happy, lively sixteen-year-old, gliding through life without a care, yet here I sat surrounded by talk of chemotherapy, procedures, and tests. I had already gone through countless scans, MRIs, blood work, ultrasounds, and even a double oophrectomy, the surgery to remove the ten-pound tumors that had consumed my ovaries. At that moment, as I sat there barely conscious of the world around me, I realized that my journey was far from over and I broke down in tears.

"Dysgerminoma," the doctor called it — a very rare form of

ovarian cancer found in young girls. She also told me that I was lucky. When I first began noticing changes to my body, I kept it to myself for fear of embarrassment. Months went by before I confided in my mother about the things I noticed. I had been losing weight, yet my stomach was growing larger every day. I experienced back and abdominal pain and it burned when I used the restroom. After I told my mom what was happening, she brought me to a doctor who rushed me into surgery. She told me that, had I come in for surgery days or even hours later, my tumors would most likely have ruptured and spread the cancer throughout my body. What she considered luck, I considered a miracle.

It took three weeks for me to heal from the surgery that permanently scarred my stomach from top to bottom, and then the hard part started. I took the most aggressive chemotherapy they could offer—seven days a week, five hours a day, for three months. My hair was gone a week into my treatment. I remember looking in the mirror at the wig shop and what I saw terrified me. It looked like one of the kids from a hospital commercial, pale and thin with hideously dark circles under my eyes, looking as if death was mere seconds away. It couldn't be me in the mirror. Tears soaked my shirt as my mother tried to comfort me. It was then that I knew I had to make a decision. I could continue wallowing in self-pity, or I could stand up and confront my future with strength. I left that wig shop without a purchase, and without fear of what was to come.

The months ahead would not be easy. I couldn't eat; I couldn't sleep; I couldn't leave my home or have visitors. Despite the constant nausea, aches, pains, and crippling fatigue, I managed to maintain a positive attitude and a smile. I laughed with the other patients at the office and reminded them often of God's plans for us. I didn't cry or question the Lord about why this was happening to me or why I had to go through this. My trust was placed in Him and I surrendered to His plans for me.

Somewhere along the way, I came across this verse from the Bible and it became my mantra: "We rejoice in our sufferings, because we know that suffering produces perseverance; perseverance, character;

and character, hope" (Romans 5:3). I firmly believe that I experienced all of this for a reason, that my suffering had a purpose. Not only did it give me the strength and hope that characterizes who I am today, but it also gave me the opportunity to touch the lives of others. And because of that, all that I went though, every single day was worth it. I am a survivor. I am truly blessed.

~Alyssa Guthrie

# Birth of a New Me

*When you are a mother, you are never really alone in your thoughts. A mother always has to think twice, once for herself and once for her child.*

*~Sophia Loren*

I opened my eyes, and a rush of pain shot through my body. I'd finally awoken to this bittersweet moment in my life, and although my body ached with inexplicable pain, I couldn't help but feel happy and joyful. The night before had been frightening, but with the future approaching, it was well worth it. My bad decision was about to be the best thing my young life had ever given me. I peered over at my precious new life. Everything was about to change.

Brandon's first two days were spent in a nursery while his young new mommy had time to recuperate. The time we spent in the hospital was great, and I didn't know what to expect for the days ahead.

A high-pitched cry screeched out of the dark. I turned to look at the clock: 3:17 a.m. I wasn't expecting to wake up this early, but what other choice did I have? I stretched over to grab the seven-pound, five-ounce infant. It was time for another feeding, and I was fuming. Who said I had to wake up so early to feed him? Nobody told me to, but I had to do it because no one else would.

A couple of weeks later, it was around 12:30 a.m. and Brandon hadn't fallen asleep yet. He cried and cried at the top of his lungs. His painful cry didn't cease until around 5 a.m. I began getting frustrated and at that very moment I realized how selfish I was. I didn't want to take care of my responsibility — my own child. So many women would do anything to give birth to a child, but I had been given that opportunity. Taking on this full-time responsibility was my choice, and I had no other options.

Waking up every three to four hours to feed a newborn, missing out on the biggest parties, and losing my teenage years may have been frustrating, but as a parent it was my duty. As Brandon's mother, I had to make sacrifices because my child had become everything in the world to me. My child needs me, and I had to learn to be there for him.

Since those early days, I have realized that my life isn't just my life anymore. I belong to someone else. I have to sacrifice for Brandon to be sure that he has everything he needs. With the birth of my son, I also began a new way of life. Rough times will come, but my love for my son will always remain.

~Kharmisha Cummings

# Weathering the Storm

*When written in Chinese the word "crisis" is composed of two*
*characters—one represents danger and the other represents opportunity.*
*~John F. Kennedy*

In April, a deadly tornado hit our small town in North Alabama, destroying everything from houses and other buildings to the lives of the people inside. On that day my family and friends had no idea just how much we would go through in the following months. Sorrow and heartache have been plentiful. But we were not left hopeless. In fact it's times like these when we realize just how much hope we have. It's times like these that teach us how to be strong in our faith and in our love for one another.

Although the house we sought shelter in was destroyed, my family and most of my friends' lives were spared. But we weren't spared from the aftershock that comes with a catastrophe of this size.

When the storm was on its way, my family and I were blessed enough to have some friends not too far down the road with a basement. They called and said we were welcome to come down and stay there while the storm passed. My mom, who never really wanted to leave during a storm because she didn't think it would get that bad, was conflicted. I believe her gut feeling was telling her to go, but past experiences were telling her not to worry. I remember looking at her while she was trying to decide and saying, "If we don't go, we might regret it." I had no idea just how right I was at the time. Finally, we decided to go.

At our friend's house, we made our way into the rooms that had been designated the safest. Not thirty seconds later, the angry storm started moving slowly over the house. At first all we heard were thuds and bangs here and there. I was in a closet under the staircase with most of the little ones, who were terrified. Audible prayers went up as we all clung to each other. I don't remember hearing wind or the house above us being destroyed. I don't remember a sound like a freight train like so many people say they hear. But what I do remember is being flooded with adrenalin, being so alert and terrified and confused that no thoughts could form in my mind. There were only feelings, which quickly went from, "This won't be that bad," to, "Will we live through this?"

But we did, thank God, and when we came out of the closet we had been hiding in, we saw that the room we had been in not two minutes earlier was covered in insulation, boards, leaves and branches. Then we looked up the stairway and saw nothing but sky—something I'll never forget.

In the aftermath of the storm, we have learned many lessons. Lessons that, without going through something like this, we would never have learned.

The little community I live in is, for me, a little piece of heaven on earth, with beautiful scenery, smiling faces and loving people. So it's hard now to go out every day and see the destruction that is still everywhere, and the heartache on the faces of everyone. But, if I could go back and change anything about that day, the only thing would be the lives lost. Because our town has learned some hard lessons, but they've made us stronger. And we're better for it.

We've learned that, in order to realize how much we need each other, we have to get rid of everything that keeps us from each other. Sometimes to see how truly blessed we are, we have to have everything ripped from our hands. Because when that happens we learn to cling to all we have left. Material things are just that—material things. And they mean nothing in the grand scheme of life.

We've learned that a strong will and positive outlook are very important qualities to have.

We've learned to find joy in simple things: a sweet smile, a hug from a friend, a listening ear or just watching our little ones play and be completely blissful in the innocence of their youth.

We've learned that life would be dull without hardships, and to be thankful for them. After all, where would we be without trials and difficulties? Would everyone be blissful all the time? Probably not. But that's why we go through trials and difficulties, to build our character and make us stronger.

We learned what it was like to be the ones who, instead of lending a helping hand to those in need, were the ones searching for a helping hand to pull us up out of this devastation and help us get back on our feet.

I've always had a strong need to relate to, and help, people as they recovered from natural disasters. But until now I never knew what it was like to be on the inside looking out. I didn't know how it felt to look around and see so much heartache, or a pile of rubble where your home used to be. Sometimes—many times, in fact—it got to the point where I just wanted to sit down and weep. But always, when the weeping was over and I was ready to look up again, there was a kind, smiling face waiting to help and encourage me in any way they could.

This storm has restored my faith in humanity. It has made me realize that not everyone is always good, but everyone has good in them.

We all have storms in our lives, whether they are big or small. Mine just happened to be in the form of an actual storm. But we can't let them beat us. I have learned that you always need to get back up and take another step, because the more steps you take, the easier it gets. Soon, you'll learn how to walk again.

~Chelsey Wright

# Tough Times for Teens

## Chapter 8

## Family

# Finding My Happy Place

*If I had to sum up Friendship in one word, it would be Comfort.*
*~Terri Guillemets*

I can hear the door slamming and curse words being yelled. I feel alone in my room with my pillow over my head. With tears running down my face, I swallow my sadness and try to find my happy place. But where is my happy place? It is hard being a teenager, but it is even more difficult being a teenager with a father who's an alcoholic.

Being in a position like mine, you have to find ways to cope with situations like this. I sometimes try talking to people who care. Andria has been my best friend since I was four. Now I'm fifteen, and I can't believe we've been friends for eleven years. There is one downside to talking to Andria. She lives 216 miles away. Somehow we manage to stay close. In fact, her move brought us closer than ever. When I talk to her about my dad, I just want to cry because I wish she could be there sitting next to me while I hide in the room from everything... my dad, the alcohol, my life.

The recent years have been especially rough. My dad is always drunk, arguing with everyone, blaming everyone else for his problems. Someone who was close to me passed away recently, and, of course, Andria moved away, making everything harder. Some days

I wake up crying. I had to be taken out of class one day because I was crying too hard. None of my friends have an alcoholic parent, so when I attempt to vent, they don't respond as I wish they would. They don't understand; they don't know what I'm feeling.

I began to see a counselor. It helped me feel better and more confident for a while but then I began to feel like I didn't need that anymore, I needed something different. I needed to talk to someone who understood me, someone else just like me—someone who also has an alcoholic parent. So my mom showed me something called Alateen. Alateen is for teenagers whose lives have been affected by someone else's drinking. When I go to Alateen meetings I don't feel lonely anymore. When I sit in that room with all those other kids, I know that I can be open with my feelings and I feel safe because I can trust them all. It is easier to talk to someone when they have been in your position at some point and time in their life. Alateen may be my happy place.

Sometimes I cope with my anger, frustration, and loneliness by writing. I like to write songs—not too many people know that about me. I didn't even tell Andria. I also like to listen to music. It distracts me, just lets me listen to the beat and stop focusing on all my stress.

If you have an alcoholic parent, I'm sure you would sympathize with a lot of my experiences and feelings. It's really frustrating. I know that I cannot do anything about it. It is my dad's choice and he is the only one who can change it. All I can do is pray that my dad gets help, because if he doesn't he will lose his family. He will lose us. Family comes first... not alcohol.

I have realized that my happy place can be anywhere I want it to be. All I need is to be confident and positive. I will stand up for myself and my family, and I will learn from my dad's mistakes. I will not let alcohol take over my life and I will live life to the fullest. I know that there will be rough days, but all I can do is remind myself to take one day at a time.

~Ava Hope

# For Good

*We must embrace pain and burn it as fuel for our journey.*
*~Kenji Miyazawa*

I stood, waiting off stage. My head was spinning, and I could feel my palms getting sweatier by the second. I prayed things would go more smoothly than the night before, when I broke into sobs midway through my song. Taking a deep breath, I started stroking the silver bracelet with a heart-shaped clasp that I wore continuously.

My heart was pounding as the emcee announced my act.

"Next up, Lisa M. singing 'For Good' from the musical *Wicked*!"

I thanked myself again for asking to save the second part of the announcement for after I performed. It took almost all of the courage I had to stand up on that stage in my school's gymnasium.

I heard the first chords being played from the piano track and took a deep breath. As I started to sing the lyrics, I found my mind straying to the past weeks and everything I had been through.

It had started as a normal day in March—nothing out of the ordinary, except that I had forgotten my lunch. I ended up borrowing money from a friend. But when my gym teacher, whom I had known since kindergarten, asked me to come to the school office, I was scared, as any fourteen-year-old would be.

"Am I in trouble?" I kept asking.

She just kept assuring me I wasn't in trouble. Then a horrible thought came to my head. Was it my grandfather who had been in the hospital for cancer a month earlier?

Seeing my mom, my brother and sister, and our close family friend crying in the principal's office wasn't too reassuring.

"Dad was cleaning his gun," my mother said, tears welling up in her eyes, "and he accidentally shot himself."

What happened next was strange. People tend to say that they have out of body experiences in circumstances like these. I always thought they meant above themselves, looking onto the situation, but I felt like I was pushed to the back of my head. I remember sitting down and my leg involuntarily shaking. The rest is a little foggy.

I remember being confused as to whether my mother meant my dad or her dad. I didn't know my father or my grandfather owned a gun. However, when I got home, my grandpa was waiting for me. It felt like a nightmare.

After I ate a little food to make my mom feel better, I went to my bed to sleep. As I was lying in my bed waiting for sleep to come, one thing kept coming to my mind.

Dad never talked about his shotgun.

I tried to talk myself around the unthinkable.

There were directions to a shooting range printed out, I reminded myself.

My mind was stuck in this back and forth conversation about two horrendous possibilities.

I felt so alone. It was as if all of the happiness in the world had gone wherever my dad was. What if the shooting wasn't an accident? What if you weren't good enough?

As I fell asleep, I prayed and prayed that I would wake up and it'd all be a dream.

When I woke up about an hour later, I noticed my phone lighting up. I checked my messages and found a surge of texts and calls from my friends from school. I thanked my lucky stars that I didn't have to tell anyone from my close-knit private school. The only people I had to tell were my friends from my choir. Both my school and my choir had been reaching out to me with so much love, it brought tears to my eyes.

Despite the support, sometimes I still felt extremely alone.

Many people had sent cards, and as I was arranging them on my desk, I saw a blue card with butterflies on it that had "Love you, Daughter" on the front. The inside said:

Lisa,

*Have a great birthday.*

*I Love You,*

*Dad*

I broke down in tears as I read the familiar chicken scratch handwriting. It had been the birthday card my dad had gotten me a month earlier. Immediately, I felt comfort and warmth in my heart. I knew that no matter what had happened, my daddy loved me, and that was all that mattered.

Onstage and in the present, I prepared for my big note. I felt strength from the bracelet he had given me as I sang. Tears were welling up in my eyes, but I held them back. Tears would not ruin this song.

As I sang the last line about how knowing that I had been changed by his presence in my life, I let go of the last note and let the piano chords ring out. The crowd burst into wild applause, and once again I felt the radiance of love coming from the audience for my father and for me. I gave the audience a quick smile before walking off stage as the emcee announced:

"Lisa has dedicated this song to her father."

~Lisa Millar

# This Time

*As you grow older, you'll find the only things you regret
are the things you didn't do.*
*~Zachary Scott*

My footsteps echo as I walk down a cold, dimly lit corridor. The fluorescent lights cast deep shadows in the forgotten corners of this place. I glance at my dad walking beside me, and see the deep, grim set of his jaw, his face taut with stress, his eyes bloodshot from lack of sleep. The rest of my family follows us. No one utters a word.

I slow as we reach our destination and turn to face the doorway I have come to know so well, familiar as the face of a good friend. Or a dreaded enemy. I am on the fourth floor of the hospital. The oncology ward. Hospital halls aren't foreign to me; that's not the source of my trepidation. My dad works here after all. I've visited countless times before, but it's never been like this.

Cold fear creeps into my stomach as I wonder how different she'll look this time. Will she recognize my face? Will I cringe at her labored breathing, acutely aware of her suffering? Will I understand her slurred speech as she imparts the last words I may ever hear her say?

We linger at the threshold for a long moment before my dad reaches up and turns the handle. As the door swings inward, we crane our necks around the corner, mixed emotions of dread and hope mounting in our hearts. Dread that she may look worse, be worse, than yesterday. Hope that she can communicate clearly, comprehend our words, remember our names.

My grandpa glances up as we file into the cramped hospital room. "Hi." His tracheotomy wheezes and sputters as he struggles to speak. He has attended her patiently almost every day since she moved to her new room. Standing up slowly, he greets and hugs each of us, tears glazing his eyes. He turns away quickly so no one will see.

I turn to survey the new room. Despite the cold hospital feel, it is nicely decorated: a small blue-green couch under the window, a rolling office chair at the desk in the corner, a high-backed armchair situated next to the bed. Notes and cards from grandchildren adorn the surrounding walls and get-well-soon roses fill a table opposite the door. To my relief, the sterile smell of a recently remodeled room permeates the air, not the rank hospital stench I had expected. The muted tones of The History Channel, her favorite, emanate from a TV near the ceiling, punctuated by the artificial breathing of the oxygen tank next to the bed.

Finally, we all turn our eyes upon Grandma, asleep as usual. She looks so petite and feeble in that big hospital bed. Sunken eyes and temples have forever altered the face that was once so familiar. Her typical boisterous manner has been replaced by an abiding silence from which she emerges only occasionally. Her hair is thinner and whiter. A sallow hue has colored her skin, now hanging loosely off her frail bones.

"I love you, Grandma." Sarah, my little sister, gives her a gentle peck on the cheek, to which my grandma utters an unintelligible reply.

"What?" Compassion filling her voice, Sarah bends down, her ear closer to Grandma's mouth, and lifts up her oxygen mask.

"I love you, too," she whispers faintly. She reaches up to push the mask back onto her nose but can't, so my dad reaches over to help. I wait patiently as each of my siblings takes a turn by the bedside, until finally it is my turn.

I approach her tentatively, unsure what to say. Finally I whisper,

"Hi, Grandma." She tries to answer and I imagine her response is the usual "Hi, kid." Her gray-blue eyes search my face for some sign that I comprehend what she's attempting to communicate. A sad smile turns up my lips and an irrepressible film of tears coats my eyes. I would say "I love you," but I can't for fear that any speech may cause an outpouring too private for the surrounding witnesses. So instead, I simply lean down and plant a kiss upon her down-turned mouth. She takes my hand, her grip surprisingly powerful for one so sickly. Her skin gives easily in response to my gentle squeeze. She loosens her grip and I turn away, making room for the next person.

I make my way to the couch and settle down, trying to get comfortable on the slightly-too-firm cushions. Outside the window, the patterned red brick of the adjacent wall catches my eye. As I study the rough, rectangular patchwork of blocks, my mind wanders to a painful place. Why didn't I spend more time with her when she wasn't ill? Why didn't I take advantage of her closeness to our house? She only lives twenty minutes away. Why was I always so selfish? Not wanting to visit because of the thick, stifling cigarette smoke saturating the air. "No, I'm about to go to youth group. I can't show up smelling like that...." "I just took a shower; I can't go in their house and get dirty again." It wouldn't have been so bad if she had been able to come outside. But she couldn't. She's been in a wheelchair for as long as I can remember.

"Rachel, it's time to go."

My dad's voice pulls me from my reverie as if from underwater. I glance around the darkened room and realize everyone has left except me.

"Grandma's sleeping; we should let her rest."

I heave myself off the couch and silently draw near the side of the bed. I slide my hands along the waist-high bedrail, the smooth, tan metal cool under my palms. Bowing low over the coverlet, I softly press a kiss to her forehead. Before I turn to leave, I close my eyes and envision her as she used to be, not necessarily healthy, but better than now. That is how I want to remember her. "I love you, Grandma." My voice seeps out as little more than a breath, hardly even audible.

After giving my grandpa a hug, I turn to leave. The door inches slowly shut, but before it closes I steal one last glance at my grandma, sleeping so peacefully. I hope I get to see her again.

But it is not to be. My grandma dies later that week. I will never forget her, and I will always regret making so little effort to spend time with her before she was sick. The next time I walk down a cold, dimly lit hospital corridor, visiting another grandparent, I hope to do so without such regrets.

~Rachel Nolan

# Despite Her Problems

*The first thing in the human personality that dissolves in alcohol is dignity.*
*~Author Unknown*

I've come to terms with my mother's relationship with my stepfather. Their marriage has been doomed from the beginning, but they go through periods where they can speak to each other without fighting.

Part of the problem is that my stepdad, Tom, is an alcoholic. He and my mom like to go out and drink. One night, they went to a bar or something with some of their friends. Actually, I'm only assuming that's what they did because there was so much going on at home that I didn't even know what they were up to. All I know is that they came back drunk.

At about six or seven in the evening, my mom left my baby half-brother, Thomas, with me and my sisters, Lindsey and Logan. By eight o'clock, a storm had blown in and the electricity was out. I remember calling her to let her know what was going on, but it was so loud wherever she was that we couldn't hear what she was saying, so we hung up. We had nothing better to do so we all went to bed.

Mom came home at around two in the morning. I didn't hear her come in, but I was awakened anyway by the sound of the house alarm. The storm had set it off and my mom was on the phone with the company trying to get it turned off. The only problem was that she was so drunk she could hardly speak, much less read the buttons the poor man was trying to get her to push.

Finally, with help from my sisters and me, my mom was able to shut the alarm off. We all gathered in the kitchen to say good night. My mom, who was swaying back and forth, managed to break a glass before she staggered off to bed.

Even though I was bone tired, I still wasn't able to sleep. Texas is just too hot without air conditioning and a fan going, so I alternately stared at the ceiling and the backs of my eyelids.

It must have been about an hour later when I began hearing the knocking on the door, but I wasn't about to get up and answer it. Mom and Tom's room was closer and they would be better able to deal with it. It went on for a while and I was just getting up the resolve to go and answer it when it stopped.

Not five minutes later I heard shouting from the living room.

My legs were shaking and I felt like throwing up as I opened my door. I stood in the hallway for a moment as two of Grand Prairie's finest blinded me with flashlights. They explained that they had come to check out the house after the alarm went off, and they got worried when no one answered the door. I imagine they were even more worried when they found the back door unlocked and glass scattered all over the kitchen.

I was extremely embarrassed standing there in my pajamas explaining to them that we were all there and that my mom had broken the glass and been too tired to clean it up. I was worried about why my mom hadn't answered the door. I walked the officers to her bedroom door and went in to wake her. She was even drunker than I had first realized because her initial response was, "Turn off that alarm." Then when I told her again that there were police here, she tried to wake Tom up to tell him to turn the alarm off.

I left the room with tears running down my face. I'd never felt so let down. Not to mention embarrassed that the police officers had picked tonight of all nights to come over. They asked me what was wrong and I told them I was just tired and I couldn't wake her up, which was at least partially the truth.

They went in with their flashlights and woke her and Tom up. My mom had forgotten about the glass on the floor and thought one of the windows was broken. The police officers watched as they examined the kitchen window and tried to determine whether it was broken or not. One of the officers turned to me and asked if they'd been drinking and I told them they had.

The next morning my mom was up bright and early. I found her in the usual spot, just outside the back door, smoking. She tried to laugh off what happened with the police. She was complaining about how they'd tracked mud in all over the carpet. I told her she'd embarrassed me and that I hoped she was happy because she made herself look like a fool.

She apologized and though I can't say that she hasn't gone and gotten drunk again since then, I can say that my mom really meant that she was sorry. I can also say that I forgive her. My mom loves me and supports me in every way she can. I can't change who my mom is, but I can learn from her mistakes and love her despite her problems.

~Emma Copeland

# Missing Thomas

*Earth has no sorrow that Heaven cannot heal.*
*~Author Unknown*

It was August when everything started. I was in Arkansas with my dad at the time of the accident, attending my great-aunt's funeral. My dad and I got a very unexpected call at about six in the morning. I could tell by the strain in my dad's voice that what I was going to hear would not be something I wanted to hear.

I heard my dad ask, "Should we come home now?" and I became very worried. My dad was supposed to be a pallbearer at the funeral, so for him to suggest that we leave had to mean something horrible had happened.

He hung up the phone, took in a deep breath, and sat down on the bed in the motel room. I wasn't prepared for the next words that came out of my dad's mouth.

"Thomas is in the hospital," he said, looking back and forth between my eyes and the ground. Thomas was my cousin.

"Wha—what happened? Is he going to be okay?" I asked, holding back tears.

"He has third degree burns on over seventy percent of his body." He paused. "He and a few of his friends snuck out and were playing with fire. The next thing they knew, Thomas was on fire. They took him to the hospital and then he was airlifted to a special burn unit hospital, which is where he is now." His eyes were very solemn.

The whole ride home was completely silent. I didn't know what else to do so I looked out the window and cried. All that was running through my head were memories of Thomas. I tried to remember the last time I'd seen him, but I couldn't. I didn't get to see Thomas a lot, but we were still close.

It took us two hours to get to the house, and from there my grandpa picked me up and drove me to the hospital so I could see Thomas.

"Are you sure you want to do this? He doesn't look at all like himself," my grandpa said while he drove.

"I know, but, well... he's my cousin and I want to see him in case..." I didn't dare finish the sentence. I couldn't look at my grandpa.

Walking inside felt almost impossible, but somehow I made it to the fourth floor and into the waiting room. The hospital had a sterilized medical scent that sent chills down my spine. Seeing all the familiar faces in the waiting room just put more sadness in my heart.

I took a seat next to my aunt and my cousin Krissy.

"Do you want to go to his room to say some words to him?" my aunt asked me as we sat there. "He is unconscious, but the doctors say he might still hear what you're saying." She was nervously fiddling with her thumbs. I nodded and obediently followed her into the hallway.

Due to the risk of infection, we had to put on blue plastic gowns and gloves before visiting Thomas. My aunt helped me put mine on, and we headed inside.

I was shocked when I saw Thomas. He no longer looked like himself. He had tubes in him, helping him breathe and eat. His whole body was swollen from the fire and he was completely wrapped in blankets except for his face, the only real part of him I could see. His lips were swollen and a dark purple color. He looked nothing like the cousin I used to see riding his bike down the street with a mischievous grin and dimples showing. The one thing that made him look a little like himself were his freckles. You had to look really close to notice them, but they were there. My aunt and grandma began to say a prayer for him to let him know they were with him.

When it came my time to talk, all I could say was, "Umm, hey Thomas. It's me... Anna." That was all I was able to say without breaking down. My grandma put her hand on my shoulder and we walked out of the room.

Two weeks later, we were given amazing news. Thomas had been moved to Cincinnati, Ohio, where he was able to get skin grafts done on his hands. They also discovered that he had been sixty percent burned by the fire instead of seventy. The back of his head, a small patch on his back, and his feet had been spared. Within a week they had woken him up from his medically induced coma, and a few days later he was talking and opening his eyes.

Everything was definitely looking up. All the prayers and turning to God helped more then anyone could have ever imagined. Thomas shouldn't have been alive, according to the doctors. It was a miracle he had pulled through this far.

Now, I wish I could say that Thomas made a full recovery, but he didn't. I wish I could say he was still here with me today, back to his old kind but stubborn self. But the truth is, he isn't.

Late one night my mom came running down the stairs with tears in her eyes. She held me tightly in a hug for a long time and told me the words that would haunt me for the rest of my life.

"Thomas passed away," she said. I couldn't do anything, I couldn't even move. I was in shock. My cousin, who was supposed to make it through this, was gone, and he was never coming back.

I learned an important lesson that night. I may have learned it the hardest way possible, but I learned it. We should always tell everyone we love that we love them, because you never know when it's going to be too late. My family believes that God took my cousin from us because of all the pain he was going through, both mentally and physically. Skin grafts and recovering from burns are incredibly painful. On top of that, Thomas remembered everything that had happened to him, every part of it. He was a strong kid, but even he couldn't — shouldn't — have had to live with all of that pain.

I miss and love my cousin and he will never be forgotten. There will always be a piece of him in the hearts of many — including mine.

~Anna Martin

# 76

# Through the Valley

*Grieving is a necessary passage and a difficult transition
to finally letting go of sorrow — it is not a permanent rest stop.*
~Dodinsky

Tears stung my eyes and cheeks as they flowed down my face. I could feel them burning the back of my throat in a hot, salty lump. Despite the number of times I wiped my eyes, the deluge refused to stop. My brain tried to comprehend all that had happened, but could barely keep up. It had only been one week since Victoria drowned. Now here I was, standing in the first pew singing worship songs at my sister's funeral.

After being found facedown in the middle of the pool six days earlier, Victoria was rushed to the emergency room. From that moment everything went by in a blur. The doctors tried everything they could to revive her, but nothing seemed to work. They stepped back from the table when her heart would not start, apologizing for not being able to do anything else. I felt like I had been slapped and had the wind knocked out of me at the same time. This couldn't be possible.

My parents and I walked toward Victoria's still form on the gleaming table. Haunting purple-pink eyelids stood out on her pale face. The grim set of her mouth and expressionless features looked out of place on her usually radiant, smiling face. I looked up to catch sight of Dad stretching his hand out over her and closing his eyes. I followed suit as he started praying, echoing those desperate words in my mind. All of a sudden, a beep sounded from the monitor, and jagged lines formed on the screen. Was it possible? Evidently the doctors thought so, because they were quickly stabilizing her, saying she was going to be moved to a room in the Pediatric Intensive Care Unit soon. I prayed hard while the doctors worked. I prayed harder than I ever had before.

And I prayed all through the next four days in the PICU. Prayer was my constant companion then and in the days, weeks, and months following the announcement of her death. Without a doubt, I know this is what got my family and me through. It was also those who were standing in faith with us, and for us, when ours failed. Their support meant more than words could say.

Looking back, I remember a thick, disorienting fog descending on me, making it difficult to think or act. Tears came fast and easy then, with no warning whatsoever. I wondered how I was going to get through this, because everything looked bleak and hopeless. At the young age of thirteen, the future, which had seemed so bright and promising, was momentarily obliterated, and forever altered. By learning firsthand about pain and death, I grew up overnight, losing a piece of my childhood. I had to deal with issues, and make decisions that required maturity, many of which I should not have even had to think about at that age. I felt lost as I wondered around aimlessly, looking for the light at the end of the tunnel.

It was during this time I realized just how important prayer and outside support were. Having people to talk, cry, and share with kept me afloat. These people the Lord brought into my life were a lifeline, an invaluable source of support. Few things are more important in the midst of a tragedy than having a strong person to hold onto while walking through the valley. Their presence and words of comfort were priceless.

Despite what anyone might say, healing does come through mourning and sharing with others. It helped bring me closure, a sense of peace, and a way to adjust to my altered life. It is also true that time mends painful wounds. While I will never forget the beautiful and bubbly girl who was my sister, time has served to ease some of the intense pain. It is still sensitive, but it does not hurt to the same extent.

There is no doubt that I learned about the fragility of life the day Victoria drowned. I also learned that despite my lack of understanding as to why, I had a choice. I could either be angry, turning away from God, or I could trust him with whatever plan he had. It was not an easy decision, nor was praising him in my pain, but it was worth it. While not always easy to see, I realized he always has a plan. It has been a long journey since that sunny day in June, and I have learned more than I ever imagined. Now, I can say I have been through the valley, with its shadows, hopelessness, and darkness, but on the other side there is light; there is hope.

~Rachel Vachon

# 77

# The Year Without My Brother

*Siblings are the people we practice on, the people who teach us about fairness
and cooperation and kindness and caring—quite often the hard way.*
~Pamela Dugdale

"I f you leave, don't you... don't you ever come back!" I
screamed at my seventeen-year-old brother. "If you leave, I
will never forgive you!"

My brother Damon just looked at me, his eyes sad and angry.

"Goodbye, Brianna," he said, his voice hard. Then he was gone.

I cursed as loud as I could, not caring that my mother was asleep.
How could my brother do this to me? How could he just leave us like
this? He knew I was too young to take care of our mother, who was
sick. He knew I needed help getting off to school in the morning and
cooking dinner and all of that. I was only thirteen at the time. I was
just a kid. How could I take care of my deathly sick mother when I
could barely manage to take care of myself?

I felt tears spring into my eyes but I didn't let them spill over. I
had to be strong for my mother. I had to.

"Brianna? What's the matter?"

I spun around and saw my pale-faced mother looking at me, her eyes big.

"Damon is gone, Mom. He..." I couldn't finish.

My mother gasped softly, then she nodded. "I knew it was bound to happen some time."

"That's all you have to say?" I snapped.

"He's seventeen, sweetie. He shouldn't have to take care of his old mother and little sister. He has his whole life ahead of him."

"So you're saying that it's okay if he doesn't want to take care of you — us — but I have to?"

I was so angry with my mother. How was it fair that I was now responsible for her and me? How was that fair?

My mom nodded at the door. "If you want to leave, leave."

I scowled at her. "You know what, Mom? Goodnight!" I stomped over to the couch and sat down, clutching a green pillow to my chest.

I heard my mother murmur something before retreating to her bedroom. When I heard the door close softly, I began to cry.

It was only a year after that horrible night that my mom was diagnosed with cancer. Not even a month later, she was gone from this world.

It was really hard for me. I didn't have anyone. My friends just didn't know what to say to me, and my other family members... well, I love them dearly, but I didn't want to live with them. The only person I wanted to live with was my brother, but he wasn't around. He hadn't even shown up for the funeral.

I was forced to live with my great-aunt Laura, who was like a second mother to me, but was really strict.

After two months at Laura's, things got better. I was doing well in school, had made new friends, and even had a boyfriend. But I still missed my brother, my best friend. Did he even know our mom was dead? Did he care? No, I thought. If he cared, he would have stayed. Or at least called to make sure we were both okay.

Then I remembered it.

"If you leave, don't you ever come back!" I had yelled at him. "If you leave, I'll never forgive you."

I felt horrible. My brother had stayed away because of me. If I had just let him go without a word, he probably would have come back.

I was about to start crying when I heard a knock at the door. I wiped my eyes and ran to open the door.

"Yes?" I asked as I flung the door open.

"Brianna?"

"Damon?"

I stood there for a moment in shock. Was my brother really here?

He gave me a small smile and his eyes were filled with tears. "Hey, kid."

Then we were both crying and hugging each other and murmuring apologies. I had never felt so happy in my life. My brother was back. Maybe for good.

After a few minutes we pulled back and I took a good look at him. He had grown an inch taller and his hair was shorter. My brother had always been very handsome. All the girls at school adored him.

"Don't leave again," I whispered. "Please"

"I wont, I promise."

He kept that promise to me. He bought an apartment up the street from our aunt's house and walked me to school every day. When my aunt died six months later, the court said I would be allowed to live with my brother.

To this day, two years later, my brother and I get along great. He's really more like the father I never really had. And his soon-to-be wife is like my big sister. I never thought I would see my brother again, and at first, I didn't even want to, not after what he did. But now that he's back, I'm happier than I've ever been.

~Brianna J.

78

# True to Myself

*How many cares one loses*
*when one decides not to be something but to be someone.*
~Gabrielle "Coco" Chanel

was really good at lying back then. Of course, I have to lie a lot less now, but I learned very early on to keep secrets because I could not trust my parents.

I went to primary school in Australia. And the thing about Australia is that you can take Christian Indoctrination religious education classes as part of primary school, unless your parents choose to opt out of them.

My mother did.

Not, I hasten to say, because she didn't believe in Christian education—she just didn't agree with mainstream Christian education—it wasn't zealous enough for her. That might explain what I was growing up with in the house. My mother's church was an Old Testament church, capitals intended. Our food was nearly kosher, we went to church on Saturday (the "real" Sabbath), we fasted often, and we spent a weeklong "Feast of Tabernacles" away from home every year, being sermonised to.

I find that one of the questions people always ask is, "When did you know you were gay?" and I can never give a succinct answer to that question. I don't think I ever had a single light bulb moment where I knew. It was more a smaller series of moments coupled with a final moment of acceptance.

Followed by a life of secret-keeping and, eventually, coming out.

For most of my high school years, my school functioned on a house system; you went into one of four houses at the start of your seventh year and you stayed in that house for your entire high school career. There was one guy in my house—let's call him Samesh—who was always doing just a little better than me academically. I think he was probably one of the smartest guys I've ever known. For some time, we were friends and rivals. Mostly rivals actually. But before the last two years of school, they began grouping students by year instead of house. Suddenly, we were mixed up in different home-room groups, and the change spurred a new group of friends, pulling together myself, Samesh, and about four others.

Of all of us, Samesh was still the smartest, and another friend, Ashley, and I generally traded off for the next spot. Samesh would try to pit Ashley and me against each other, while pretending not to care about his schoolwork. If you tried too hard, you weren't cool. If you made an effort, you weren't cool. Soon, everyone around Samesh began to slip academically. I don't know if it was deliberate or if Samesh was just naturally sneaky, but he had gathered his closest rivals and taken them down by convincing us it wasn't cool to be good at academics.

I remember one ordinary Tuesday, sitting in my usual seat at what had become our table, when I realized what was happening. We were in cheap plastic seats by the door, bags and cricket bats thrown up on the ledge at the top of the corridor wall. I remember watching Samesh and everyone else laughing about something. Then I looked at all of us and thought, "Why am I doing this?" Why was I so needy for affirmation from a guy I didn't even respect or like very much, to the point that I was willing to play his game and sacrifice my own happiness and academic achievement?

So I stopped playing.

First, I went back to trying my best, and my grades improved immediately. Then I stopped mouthing along to his lines and jokes. I changed the playing field and started excelling at things I cared about:

theatre and debating—the latter of which I stole top honors from his trophy shelf. The funny thing was, when I broke away, Ashley joined me. It seemed like I wasn't the only one noticing how stuffed up the situation was.

I guess the point is that things got better. I made a decision to be true to myself, and things got better.

There were other ways, however, that I was not being true to myself. I had made leaps and bounds standing up to Samesh, but there were still some hurdles to conquer. My family was in Singapore for some religious holiday and we—along with a few of Mum's Christian friends—were lunching at a brightly lit café in one of the city's homogenous shopping malls. They were talking about a spot somewhere in town where "they" went to do the "immoral" things that "they do." The implication, of course, was that these were gay men going somewhere to do terrible things. The judgement being passed was that gay people were bad people, and they were inferior to my mother and her friends.

My sister lost it.

She was amazing. She first blasted them for being judgemental, and then challenged them on how they could possibly know what gay men actually did. Did they have any gay friends? No, of course they didn't. Did they personally know any gay people? Well... not that they knew of. How, then, did they have any possible way of being reliably informed as to what gay men did or did not do? She had gay friends, and from where she sat, Mum and her friends were being ignorant bigots. What on earth—she asked—what on earth would Mum say if my sister turned out to be gay? Or me? What would they say to that? How would they deal? Gay people were just like anyone else.

She was one of the first people I came out to. Close friends first, and Internet friends before those I knew in person, and then her. I don't remember what we were talking about—I almost chickened out—but then I just came right out and said it.

The first thing she said was "Are you sure?" The next thing she said was "So, does this mean that I get all the jewelry you would have given to your wife?"

I thought that was pretty cool.

Things aren't perfect now, but they're better. I came out to my parents, but my mother's still a highly religious individual, and my dad has yet to meet my partner properly after over a year of living only five minutes away. But that's okay. I may want their love and approval, but I don't need it. I just need to remind myself to be me.

And strangely enough, I'm happy. So I know I must be doing something right.

~Matthew Lang

# My Sister Sarah

*Making the decision to have a child is momentous. It is to decide forever to
have your heart go walking around outside your body.*
~Elizabeth Stone

Three years ago, my sister Sarah got pregnant. She was only
seventeen and a senior in high school. Being her younger
sister, I kept the secret from everyone as long as I could. I
even got angry when people would ask me about her. I didn't want to
blow the top off the lie; I wanted Sarah to tell everyone. After school
one day, my sister went to my grandma's house and my grandma
scared her into telling the truth. My grandma then told my dad and
my dad flipped out! I remember him being so angry at Sarah, but I
knew that he must have already known. She was six months pregnant at that point. I'm almost certain that I'm not the only one who
saw that belly growing underneath her shirt.

I didn't go with Sarah to her first doctor's appointments but I did
go to the third or fourth. The first time I heard the baby's heartbeat,
I was so happy I almost cried. I also remember Sarah coming home
with her sonogram pictures. She was so happy to be telling everyone
that she was having a little girl. When I heard this, I went right to
work on helping her find a name. I printed out three and a half pages
of baby girl names that I liked. We read them over with my mom and
one really stuck out: Chantelle.

In October, my sister was taking a hot shower. After her shower,
she came into our bedroom and kept making noise, so I asked her

if she was okay. She looked at me with a worried face and said no. I followed her into the living room and she knelt down in front of the couch with her hand over her back. I started rubbing her back and asking her what was wrong. Her hair was falling over her face so I pulled it back. Then I called my grandma and told her that something was wrong with Sarah's back and that she needed to hurry over. I went into my dad's bedroom to wake him up. When we got back to the living room, my grandma had helped Sarah onto the couch, but Sarah was still bent over. My grandma looked up at my dad and said, "We might be having a baby today."

My dad then rushed to the bathroom and put on some sweats but my grandma told him to just stay home with my little brother because Sarah might be having false labor contractions. Then Grandma turned to me and said, "Want to come just in case?" And of course, I said yes! So my dad helped Sarah into my grandma's car, buckled her in the front seat and kissed her head. "Call me when you get to the hospital," he said to my grandma. She nodded her head and we were off.

The hospital was about fifty-five minutes away. When we were in the town, but not yet close to the hospital, my sister started crying. I didn't want to scare my sister so I kept quiet and kept rubbing her back like she told me too. We got to the hospital emergency parking lot and my grandma went in while I helped Sarah get out of the car. The security guard helped me get her up the walk and into a wheelchair. Then everything happened so fast.

By the time we got into a room, Sarah was already dilated to six centimeters, and she was bleeding. She was crying and I felt so bad for her. Soon enough, the doctor came in and checked Sarah and Chantelle's heartbeat, telling us it was almost time to meet Chantelle. He left, but maybe ten minutes later my sister told my grandma that she felt like she needed to push. I rushed into the hallway and called the nurse to get the doctor. Not long after that, Chantelle was lying on my sister's chest.

My dad made it to the hospital and I went to get him in the waiting room. My grandma said the first time he saw Chantelle, his eyes lit up and the anger towards Sarah disappeared.

Babies are a wonderful thing, but since I am a senior in high school now, I can only imagine how stressful it was for my sister before and after Chantelle arrived. She didn't do it alone—we always helped her with Chantelle and my aunt Breanna even babysat her for free until Sarah got home from school at noon. Still, I'm very proud of my sister for being a great mom, for finishing high school on time... and for giving me my niece, Chantelle.

~Jordan Mata

# Never Gone

*In the night of death, hope sees a star, and listening love can hear
the rustle of a wing.*
~Robert Ingersoll

T his is a poem I wrote a week after my grandma passed away. I read it to my family at her wake, and although extremely difficult, I got through it.

Today I prayed to God,
As I began to cry,
I asked him once, then twice,
If things would be all right.

I stared out of the window,
Sniffed and blew my nose,
Hot tears stung my face,
And I knew that we were close.

We showed up at the entrance,
I already felt so weak,
And then I saw her there,
Lying still, unable to speak.

I had never seen my grandma,
So broken or so strange,

Unrecognizable to me,
Hooked up to everything.

There were monitors and tubes,
She was speechless, lying still.
I just stood in silence,
A silence that could kill.

My mother said, "Hi Mom,
Don't worry, we're all here."
She then told me to speak,
To say hello, that I was near.

I said hello to Grandma,
And waited to hear her voice,
But I knew that in her condition,
She would make no noise.

I choked on my hello,
Listened to my mother talk,
Didn't know quite what to do,
So I paced back and forth.

The day progressively grew worse,
My family members came,
We cried on each other's shoulders,
With not one person to blame.

My grandma remained quiet,
Eyes fluttering now and then,
And when discussions ceased,
The crying would start up again.

I've never felt so helpless,
As I watched my grandma die,

Nurses took turns coming in,
The time inched slowly by.

Every second was so precious,
We knew this was goodbye,
And as they wheeled her into surgery,
We all began to cry.

They asked us if we wanted,
To say farewell one final time,
And as my mother stroked her hair,
My grandma opened her eyes.

They seemed so very pleading,
So alert and so aware.
For a second I wondered if,
She saw Grandpa standing there.

My mother told her thank you,
For everything she's done,
We gathered all around her,
A family that was one.

Her eyes began to water,
As if she already knew,
That this would be the end,
That her life would be through.

We watched them wheel her away,
Tears streaming down our cheeks,
And walked into the waiting room;
Things began to look so bleak.

The TV was turned on,
We sat nervously in our chairs,

And after half an hour,
We heard our worst nightmare.

The doctor walked on in,
And said her colon and intestines rotted,
That there was nothing they could do,
Once the problem had been spotted.

So they closed her right back up,
And sent her back to her room,
He said she had a few hours left,
And that she would be gone soon.

My aunt fell to the floor,
As she yelled "Oh my God!"
It was at that very moment,
That we all began to sob.

I've never felt so broken,
Or lost inside my heart,
As I imagined my grandma gone,
So weak and falling apart.

We mourned for quite some time,
Lending a shoulder to those near.
Out of every word in existence,
Those were the ones we feared.

We walked back up to her room,
And gathered around her bed,
Bible verses were being recited,
So that to Heaven, she would be led.

We watched the monitor screen,
As the readings began to lower,

And then her lungs gave out,
And God's will took over.

Severe weather hit us,
And we had to leave her there,
Crying with each other,
Leaving her to God's care.

I will always love her,
My grandma was one of a kind,
But now she's in a better place,
With my grandpa in eternal life.

I know that God will love her,
And take care of her while we're here,
For He has a brand new angel,
That will always be so near.

My grandma is in our hearts,
Her memory will carry on,
For when you arrive home,
You are never really gone.

~Stephanie Michelle Pabst

# Living, Losing, and Loving

*Adversity is like a strong wind. It tears away from us all but the things that cannot be torn, so that we see ourselves as we really are.*

~Arthur Golden, Memoirs of a Geisha

When I was in eighth grade my mom was hospitalized. It wasn't for more than a week or so, but to me it felt like months. She had an irregular heartbeat and required surgery. Every day after school my dad would drive my brother and I to the hospital to visit her.

It's absolutely horrifying to see someone you love lying pale on a hospital bed with a brave, false smile plastered across her face. It's a scene I would wish upon nobody, and a sight I will never forget.

My aunt Kim and my grandmother came and lived in our house to help us manage while my mom was absent. We hadn't noticed it, but in our busy concern for my mother we had neglected simple yet important tasks like laundry and washing dishes, both of which were piled high.

Auntie Kim did all that she could to ease our load, generously taking on any task that she saw, no matter the size or difficulty.

I started having nightmares and I feared that this arrangement would become permanent. I foolishly wished my relatives would leave so that my mother would come home. I didn't appreciate the time and effort they devoted to my family, and I took for granted their unconditional love. I only wanted my life to go back to normal, and I wanted it desperately.

It's sad that it's only when we're faced with tragedy that we realize what's really important in our lives, and only the threat of losing something can make us truly appreciate it. I never appreciated my mom more than when I thought I might lose her.

I was lucky. My mom recovered and my life resumed over time. Years went by, and I graduated high school an optimistic, energetic girl, ready to begin the rest of her life.

But my family received news that shook us deeply. My Auntie Kim, my father's only sister, who had so carefully and devotedly helped us in our time of need, had been diagnosed with stage four lung cancer.

Hearing this news did not strike me with fear, as some would expect. Rather, I was hit by waves of regret and helplessness. I flashed back to those nights when she had swept the floors and washed the windows in my own house, helping my family in any way she could. I regretted never thanking her, and I regretted never fully appreciating her sacrifices or her love for my family. And I felt helpless because no matter what I could do for her or her family, no matter how many loads of laundry or swept floors, I could never heal her. I could never give her back her old life. And I know no matter how many meals I cook or how many dishes I wash, I can never give her children — my cousins — their mother back. There's only so much that chores can fix.

I know how it feels to fear for your mother. And I know how it feels to want her — or any loved one — back at home. I know how it feels to crave your normal life with every fiber of your being. And I know how much it hurts when there's nothing you can do but clean, and pray.

Just as it took hospitalization for me to appreciate my mother, it took tragedy for me to fully realize my appreciation for my aunt. It's wrong, and it's sad, but it's the truth for far too many people — just like me. I realize now that I have been incredibly, unbelievably blessed. I was blessed to have Auntie Kim back in eighth grade, when she cleaned and cooked tirelessly to help my family cope. And I am blessed to have known her throughout the years in her health. I am blessed to have known her love.

Even now, as Kim faces incredible struggles and embarks on a difficult and painful journey, she faces each new obstacle with grace, dignity, and — incredibly — optimism. I can't even begin to imagine the unbelievable strength that she possesses and demonstrates every day, just as I was unable to understand the depth of her love for me, my brother, and my parents all those years ago. I have been truly blessed to witness the heroism of this woman, and I am honored to have her as a role model in my life. I only wish that I had been able to fully appreciate her sooner, before I was faced with the threat of losing her forever.

~Brianna Abbott

# Forgiveness

*Forgiving is rediscovering the shining path of peace that at first you thought others took away when they betrayed you.*

*~Dodinsky*

large bush all but covers the small stone engraved with Dad's name. I have to duck down to enter the little opening. Once inside, I sit next to the stone.

Someone has placed a fresh, new American flag at the head of it. Brushing the debris from the gravestone, I trace the letters of my father's name with my fingers.

Tears fill my eyes as I'm suddenly struck with an intense longing. There's so much I'll never know about him. He took his own life when I was twelve. He sexually abused me for years.

I heard somewhere that one of the greatest gifts children can give to their parents is forgiveness. It was something I needed to do. Tears choked my voice as I spoke to the father I lost years ago.

"Dad, I do love you," I told him, my hand on the cool stone that bore his name. "I forgive you for what you did to me. I wish things could have turned out differently. I'm sorry we never had the father-daughter relationship we should have. I'm sorry, Dad, for what never was. But I will never forget you."

Embraced within the arms of the overgrown bush, feelings and emotions long forgotten begin to surface. Good memories overshadowed by painful ones. Going fishing as a family. Dad teaching me how to drive the tractor. Dad coming home with small toys for my sister and me. I smile and allow myself to enjoy these memories for a while.

Then I rise from my position by the grave and notice a bird's nest on the ground nearby. I realize that birds must have nested in the towering, neglected bush that shelters Dad's grave. There is life here, in a place known for having none.

Brushing twigs and leaves from my clothes, I turn and begin walking back the way I came. I feel more closure now than ever before. The birds in the trees overhead seem as though they are singing just for me, and their beautiful melody comforts me. There's a new freshness in the air as the breeze picks up. I breathe deeply of the sweet summer air.

As I approach the cemetery gate, it occurs to me that I never had the opportunity to say goodbye to Dad before he died. Glancing back at his grave, I stand silently for a moment.

All is silent except for the birds and the light breeze whispering through the trees. A tear slides down my cheek.

"Goodbye, Dad."

I am free.

~Denise A. Dewald

# Tough Times for Teens

## Chapter 9

## Love Gone Wrong

# Ow

*If you really put a small value upon yourself, rest assured that the world will not raise your price.*
~Author Unknown

Ouch. Why? This hurts. But he loves me. Doesn't he? Am I bleeding? Is it going to bruise? Will people notice?

"I'm sorry."

He's sorry. He didn't mean it. He loves me. He's doing it because he cares.

"But you just can't act like that."

He's right. I can't act like that. It's my fault. Why I am so stupid?

This was my life for over a year.

I was always strong, always okay, always the caretaker, not the "caretakee."

So when my all star cross-country, A-student, nice guy boyfriend hit me, I refused to believe it was real.

I thought I was being strong, getting through it. I thought giving up on us because of a few slaps and shoves would make me the human exemplification of weakness. Meanwhile, I was dating it.

Over the fifteen months we dated, I got to know a darker side of him. He was easily infuriated, didn't like any of his friends, and was terribly insecure.

I thought about breaking up with him hundreds of times. Every time he laid a hand on me, I thought about it. But I was always faced with a waterfall of questions that lead to doubts.

Who'd believe me? He took all AP classes, ran track and cross-country, and volunteered at Give Kids the World. The teachers thought he was bright and clever. And, well, he was. My friends thought he was sweet and caring. And sometimes he was.

I couldn't step back and realize the problem with this: they didn't know what I knew.

What kept me with him more than anything else, though, was the fact that despite this, he loved me. That was how I justified it for myself. He made himself my life, slowly. By telling me how much he detested all of my friends and asking me kindly not to pursue theatre anymore. But, I insisted to myself, that this was only because he loved me.

So, when he broke up with me out of the blue in a forty-second phone call, my heart broke. There was no one to go to. He was it for me; my world had crashed.

I called him for the next few weeks. He didn't answer. I tried to talk to him in the hallways; he ignored me.

Finally, I went to a friend. I told him everything. I spilled my heart to him. He believed me and he confirmed what I secretly knew all along: it was not okay.

Weeks after, he came to my house with roses and apologies and tears. And I looked into his sad, blue eyes, and I remembered all the joy he brought to my life. And then the pain. And I walked away.

I am so proud of that moment. My school's motto — Vires, Artes, Mores — means Strength, Skill, and Character. That day, I embodied Vires in a way that always fills me with pride. I had the strength to walk away.

~Alessandra Shurina

# Giving Up the Past

*It took me a long time not to judge myself through someone else's eyes.*
*~Sally Field*

On the wall outside my health class is a poster. It asks, "Is your relationship based on control? Or love?" I was fourteen the day I saw that sign. I wish I had read it.

When I met Mark, he was sweet. A senior to my freshman, we dated for almost seven months before he changed his mind. Though Mark was sweet about the break-up, I hated him for it. I wanted to be angry and so I was. I spent nights out partying with my two new best friends, Christa and Vanessa, the old ones long gone. They showed me how to do a shot properly, how to keep my dress from riding up, and many other useless skills that only mattered when I was sneaking out at midnight to go to another party. I thought I was free—free from my parents and my sister, free from all of the people who held me captive in this cage of who I was supposed to be.

Vanessa and Christa were constantly in trouble. They took me with them, and before long I was the epitome of the fallen girl. Teachers gave up on me, old friends walked away, and still my family noticed no difference.

Declan was just a friend, or at least he was supposed to be. For a few months after my break-up with Mark I had a best friend who asked nothing of me. Then one night, while hanging at his house, I kissed him. I, a fourteen-year-old high school freshman, kissed a twenty-one-year-old college student.

My life became a high-speed chase in which I was sitting shotgun. The love between Declan and me felt real. My falling grades improved and I aced Spanish, a class I hated... but Declan loved.

If only it had really been that sweet. Sometimes Declan scared me. He pinned me to walls and on the bed, daring me to fight back. The look in his eyes was dangerous, as if he would love to put me in my place if I tried to move. He controlled me, made me bring my cell phone everywhere I went so he could contact me. I couldn't talk to other boys, and eventually my new friends too. I skipped class to go to his house, and pretty soon the entire relationship was an ever-expanding secret we kept from everyone.

Declan insisted I never cut my hair and never dye it from it's natural red. He hacked my Facebook and e-mail to check up on me. It all seemed normal to me. This was what normal relationships felt like, wasn't it? Yet I also felt ill, useless, stupid. I thought I was in love.

Then one day my parents found out. They moved, quickly isolating me from Declan and everything connected to him. All I had were two songs we loved and a few journal entries about him. My father was furious, my mother cried, and I screamed. I told them how unfair it was, how I hated them. I lied to protect the man I loved.

Weeks later, after having no contact with Declan, the ties broke. The vice grip he'd kept on my life loosened and fell away. I realized who I could be, and I knew I was going to be someone who had nothing to do with Declan. Slowly, I regained my life. I watched old shows he didn't like and called up friends he didn't approve of.

The last step came a few weeks before school. My hairdresser stood behind me as I deleted two songs on my iPod, cutting away the long locks that once upon a time were red but now were dyed brown. In that moment, I shed Declan and the control he held over me. I escaped that world, but Vanessa and Christa did not. Vanessa is nineteen and still lives with her parents, has no job, and uses drugs.

Christa is facing jail time for stealing a credit card and charging it to the limit. Declan, last I heard, was arrested for statutory rape.

I have no desire to get even with any of them for how they dragged me down. The past belongs to them—they can keep it. But the future? The future is mine.

~Bailey Baer

# Green Eyes

*Damaged people are dangerous. They know they can survive.*
*~Josephine Hart*

My freshman year of high school started with "I love you" and ended with "I hate you." Stretched between the two was an abusive relationship that I survived.

I moved to Indiana the winter of my eighth grade year and hid in the shadows of my new school until summer, leaving for high school without a friend by my side. The summer before high school I joined marching band in an attempt to find my niche for the next four years of my life. It was there that I met Mike.

Our relationship was, in every way, a normal teenage relationship: we went to the movies, held hands at the football games, danced at homecoming. I spent the first few months of our relationship happy. I was so in love with him; I did not think things would ever change between us.

Around Christmastime, though, they did.

On Christmas Eve, Mike invited me to church with his family. I wore a light pink sweater. I sat in the pews while he played with the worship band. When service was over, Mike's family drove me home and Mike walked me to the door. He had a frown on his face.

I asked him what was wrong. "Nothing," he said, "I'm just dating a whore is all."

I looked at him, hurt and confused, and asked what he meant.

"That sweater! You just had to wear something to get all the attention, didn't you?"

I just stared blankly at him.

"I read somewhere that girls with green eyes are always looking to hook up," he said.

I looked away from him. Suddenly I was so ashamed of my bright, green eyes. I asked him what exactly he wanted.

"I wish you would just blend in. No one notices girls with dark eyes or clothing. Why can't you be like that?"

From that day on, I only wore black clothing. And I decided my eyes were brown.

I usually spent all my time without Mike at home alone, so that he wouldn't accuse me of cheating on him. But in January, I agreed to usher at a music festival at school just to get out of my house, even though I knew I would miss Mike's call. I had returned from showing some friends their seats in the balcony and was walking back to the doorway to pick up more programs. As I turned the corner, I was pushed hard against the wall. I looked up and I saw his face. He looked like he was about to hit me. I watched his arm tighten, his left hand coiling into a fist. I searched for something to say, but he opened his mouth first.

"Why didn't you call me?"

I frantically looked to my side, hoping someone would come down the hallway.

I lied and said I forgot. I was afraid to look him in the eye. He had me pressed to the wall with his hands on my shoulders. He was hurting me. He didn't hear a word I said.

"I called you at 5:30 and your sister told me you were here." I checked my watch as he faced the stage; it was 5:45. "And I started freaking out because I knew you'd be here with another guy." I was staring at him, at a complete loss for words.

I opened my mouth to give some sort of excuse, but I never got a word out. His hand hit my face. My skin started to burn, my eyes watered. The lights in the theatre dimmed and I started walking away from him. He yanked me to him by the waist. I started struggling against him and his grip tightened. I sat down in my seat as a bruise on my side formed underneath his hand.

Over the next few months, he kept abusing me until I didn't even know who I was anymore. After he saw how my face swelled when he hit me the first time, he learned to hit me where it would be hidden. I walked around with a bruised pelvis for two weeks after spending the night at a girlfriend's house and not telling him. I had knuckle-shaped bruises on my ribs for not texting him back right away. After every hit, I hated myself. It would take weeks for me to gain the courage to dump him, to finally be rid of him, but then he would apologize, kiss my battle scars, and tell me he loved me, that he'd never do it again.

And I always believed him.

It wasn't even spring when he first brought up sex, but I always put my foot down. The Friday before the Super Bowl, Mike presented me with a silver ring on a silver chain. The silver band was inscribed with "True Love Waits"—a sign, I thought, that Mike was getting my message. He asked me to marry him, something I said yes to out of both fear and longing. It was a sick attempt to get what he wanted, and it wasn't long before "True Love Waits" turned into a million reasons why we shouldn't.

That Sunday, Mike and I went to a Super Bowl party at a friend's house. On the ride over, two days after our engagement, Mike had beaten me in the back for not "putting out" for the man I was going to marry. When I got down to my friend's basement, I stretched out on a couch because I was in so much pain.

The couch was towards the back of the basement, far from the TV and the other party guests. During the second quarter, Mike came over and lay on top of me, pinning me to the couch.

I tried to stop him but he grabbed my hair and pulled my face closer to his, whispering, "You're going to like it." I was so afraid and humiliated. I looked at the backs of all of my friends' heads, their eyes glued on the football game, and I did not cry out. When he was finished, he held my face in his hand, wiped my tears and told me I had the most beautiful brown eyes he'd ever seen.

That was the way my life was for eight months: beatings, sexual assaults, verbal abuse. I figured Mike was so busy with me, it never occurred to me to wonder what he was doing while I waited at home for his calls.

I got a call one evening in the summer from a concerned mother, warning me she was pressing charges against Mike for raping her daughter. More calls came after that; formal charges followed. He was taken out of school and placed under house arrest.

It was then that I finally took a look at myself. Really saw myself. I stared at my face in the mirror and saw my eyes: green, bright and hopeful. They were the only things he couldn't change, no matter how hard he tried.

My green eyes gave me the courage I needed to go to my parents. They were my reminder that I was not who he made me—who I let myself become. My parents helped me. There were court hearings, orders of protection, police cars parked in front of my house, and, finally, restraining orders. I haven't had to be around Mike for a long time now.

It was not easy, and it still isn't, getting over what happened. I talked with counselors. I learned to accept that things would not always go according to plan. Mike never saw a day in prison; he went to college, just like me, and is living his life elsewhere.

When I was with Mike, I forgot how much I love who I am. I forgot that it's my imperfections that make me who I love. If I ever forget how to love myself again, I'll end up in that grave he made for me. And I'll never go back there again. I am Ally, a writer, a musician, and a survivor of abuse; my eyes are green, they are beautiful, and they will never change.

~Allyson O'Donnell

# Homecoming Queen

*Let your tears flow and where they go, let your sorrows follow.*
*~Dodinsky*

As she stares at the pavement
And the people pass by,
She envisions a life
That doesn't come with goodbyes.

So she sits in her bedroom
And starts sobbing in vain.
The man of her dreams
Has forgotten her name.

While everyone's dancing,
She climbs into bed,
Trying to get the thoughts of him,
Out of her head.

Her tears hit the pillow,
So she flips it again
And curls up with her favorite
Stuffed animal friend.

Soon the crying exhausts her,
She drifts to a dream,
Of a place where she is,
Her own homecoming queen.

~Laura Campbell

# i'll Be Ready

*To conquer fear is the beginning of wisdom.*
*~Bertrand Russell*

Thump-thump. Thump-thump. Thump-thump. I wake up to the sound of my heart racing and sweat running down my neck. When would he stop haunting my dreams? In my dream, his brown eyes were full of anger. He was coming after me, to hurt me. But every time I tried to get away, he always got to me. That's when my eyes flew open and I sat up in bed. These nightmares came monthly.

He didn't start haunting my dreams until a little over a year ago. Our friendship began the summer I was going into seventh grade. I helped his mom at a summer camp in June. We had a lot of fun together. We soaked each other with water balloons and got in trouble for talking too much, even though it got a little awkward at times. Our friendship grew when school started. I saw him almost every day after school. He was a year older, and I knew he'd never like me. I had feelings for him anyway.

We had so many inside jokes and we were constantly laughing. There wasn't a day when I went home without a smile on my face. We were always making fun of each other. He started to open up to me, but that didn't last long. In late March, things began to turn. He was always angry about something and took out all his anger on me. The playful hits turned into hard smacks on the shoulder. He threw anything at me that he could get his hands on, yet I still stayed around. I thought that maybe, just maybe, he'd calm down and open up.

Things just got worse. The teasing got more hurtful every week. He started calling me names, and meant it. I stood there and let him talk, but he'd turn around and snap at me. It hurt to know I couldn't help. I felt like a punching bag. I came home with bruises at least every other week.

That summer I helped out at another camp for his mom. He continued to throw everything at me, but he seemed to loosen up a little. We had our laughs. It started out like the last camp session, but then things turned bad again. He came after me on more than one occasion. He attacked me in the girls' bathroom. When I got free, I slipped and ran into the wall. That was one of the few moments I wished I wasn't clumsy. He came after me again. His eyes were full of anger. I couldn't understand what I had done wrong.

It was weird to think that, just an hour before, he had been very open with me. "When I learn to drive I'm out of here," he had said before. I shook my head as if I understood. He was serious. There was more going on in his life than I knew.

After the bathroom incident everything seemed to go back to normal. The rest of camp flew by. When all the kids left I helped put things back in his mom's car.

He came after me again as I was walking back into the building. I found myself up against a cold white wall, his knee slammed into my butt, his hands grabbing me, my heart racing. I couldn't figure out how to get free. Everything happened so fast. I was suddenly off the wall, and stepping into my mom's car. She didn't see a thing.

I sat there shaking. What just happened? Later that night I found bruises on my body. That was the start of the nightmares. I was scared of other guys. They could hurt me too. Every time I saw him, I ran the other way. I didn't want to talk to him. I told a friend everything that happened. Her older sister told the school counselor, who called me in to talk.

"Sarah, it's not your fault he hurt you. He shouldn't have sexually harassed you. You need to tell your mom so we can all sit in here and chat," she said to me.

Somehow, I found the guts to tell my mom. I ended up leaving school because of all the rumors running around. I met with a therapist, who eventually helped me overcome my issues.

I still struggle every once in a while. I still have nightmares, but they have changed. Instead of him coming after me, I'm asking him why he hurt me. I'm more confident and not afraid of guys anymore, but I still wonder what would happen if we ever meet again. If we do, I'll be ready. He made me into a stronger person, and he helped me set my boundaries. I will never let a guy hurt me like that again.

He made me realize what I want to do after college. I want to help people who went through what I did. I know what they've been through. I know I can make a difference. If someone ever harasses you, or touches you inappropriately, tell your parents. You can't live your life without telling them. You'll just live in fear. I'm starting high school tomorrow, and I'm ready to begin a new chapter. There's no more fear of him left in me—just the hope that someone will help him get better.

~Sarah Catherine

# 88

# A Wolf in Sheep's Clothing

*Everything will be okay in the end. If it's not okay, it's not the end.*
*~Author Unknown*

wo weeks into freshman year we had a student transfer into our biology class. The teacher had us make nametags for our desks to help everyone learn our names. That was how I learned Kyle's.

As the week continued, I would see him glance my way and smile. I always smiled back just to be friendly.

After a couple of weeks of hanging out between classes, he asked me to be his girlfriend. With complete joy, I said yes. A couple of months went by and we became inseparable. I learned a lot about him and who he was as a person... or at least, who I thought he was.

I eventually learned that he came from a violent and abusive background. His father drank a lot and would beat up his mother. He had been watching this since he was a child. Once his parents divorced and his father moved out, his siblings became violent towards him. He constantly had to defend himself. At the time, I thought nothing of it. I felt sorry for him.

After about six months, our relationship began to change. We started to argue a lot over minor things and he became very jealous.

At school, he tried to control who I talked to and hung around with. Sometimes he would ask me to meet him in the hallways and if he was talking to one of his friends he would introduce us. Then, when his friends saw me in the hallways, they would stop me to say hello, but once Kyle started seeing this, he got mad and accused me of trying to "steal" his friends. He would always say in a stern voice, "Those are my friends, not yours."

He insisted on walking me to class every day to ensure that I didn't speak to anyone he didn't like or anyone I wasn't supposed to.

During lunch he would watch me like a hawk just to see which guys I would talk to. If I disobeyed him, he would yell at me and make me promise that it would never happen again.

On some of the days we spent lunchtime alone together, we would laugh and joke around. But on other days, he turned into a controlling, jealous monster. He would grab my phone and go through my text messages and phone calls. If he saw any male's name, he would either throw my books on the ground or tear apart my binder and folders as if he were a five-year-old throwing a temper tantrum. He became so furious one day that he punched a brick wall and broke his knuckles. He blamed me for his injury because he said if I hadn't done anything wrong, then he wouldn't have hurt himself.

One day, outside my English class, a school counselor saw Kyle raise his voice and put his hands on me. The counselor saw me struggling to get out of his tight hold, so he called Kyle over and I hurried into the classroom. I later found out that the counselor talked to him about inappropriate behavior. Kyle blamed me for getting him into trouble.

This went on for months. The arguments became more serious and more physical. He would grab my arm and raise his voice, but not loud enough to cause a scene. The more I tried to resist, the tighter his hold on me became. He would leave bruises I tried to cover up and make excuses for. But sophomore year was when things really took a turn for the worse.

On a Friday the thirteenth, Kyle told me before school started that his dad was going to pick him up early in the day, but he would be back in time to spend lunch with me. When lunch started, I met up with him. I could tell that something had upset him. He told me that he and his dad had got into an argument so he was in a bad mood. He accused me of ignoring him and began to yell at me. Since he was sitting down next to me, I turned the other way. I wasn't in the mood to argue with him. This made him extremely angry so he grabbed me by the face and bit me right on the cheekbone with all his might. I started crying from all the pain and told him to stop, over and over again. When he didn't, I started hitting him. After a good minute, he finally let go. Some of my friends saw me bawling but thought it was because of an argument. I went three periods without anyone seeing me cry and without noticing the giant welt that was beginning to form on the side of my face.

I had to stay late that day to get a project done, so when my parents came to pick me up from school, it was dark. I didn't mention what happened earlier that day because I didn't want Kyle to get into trouble; I was protecting him. My family and I were headed out to eat and I knew once they saw the bruise on my face, they were going to question it. Before they had the chance to notice it, I came up with an excuse to make it seem like a freak accident. My parents knew better than that. I confessed to the terrible fight that had occurred between Kyle and me.

My parents called the police and they soon arrived. They took pictures of the black and purple welt. The policemen told us they were going to visit Kyle's house and question him about the situation. We were going to pursue charges.

Three months after the incident, Kyle and I went to court. The judge gave him a slap on the wrist. I didn't feel like justice had been served but there was nothing I could do about it.

After everything that I endured, I had to go to counseling to help cope with the situation and move on from what had happened.

My grades had dropped tremendously after the incident, so to help with that, I switched schools. I needed a fresh start where no one would know my past.

I never once realized that I was a victim of dating violence. It took a really traumatic fight to see it, but after all this time, I've finally been able to find the good that came out of the situation. Because of him, I am now a stronger, wiser person.

~Kristen Lianne Elias

# She Told Me So

*The best conversations with mothers always take place in silence,
when only the heart speaks.*
~Carrie Latet

I was eighteen, standing in a Holiday Inn parking lot in Murfreesboro, Tennessee. My mom was in a moving van filled with the remains of my failed marriage. The driver's side door was open so I could give directions. The goal was to line the van up horizontally in the truck parking area. I'd say, "Back up a little," not really confident that's what needed to happen, and my mom would back the van up an inch. I would survey the situation again and say something like, "Forward a little." She'd slide her green eyes sideways at me. We'd both dissolve in hysterical laughter. After twenty or so tries, the frustration caught up with us, and the laughter turned to tears.

There we were, mother and daughter, forty-two and eighteen, both attempting the kind of job that the men in our lives had always done for us. Both left alone by the men in our lives.

The year before, two weeks after high school graduation, I had shocked everyone who knew me and married the boy my mother hated, perhaps just because she hated him. Days before my one year anniversary, I sat on the floor of a one bedroom apartment, sobbing, the phone cradled between my ear and shoulder. I listened to my mother's comforting voice in one ear while his fury raged in the other.

"You stupid bitch! Get out of my house!" My well-worn copy of Chaim Potok's *The Chosen* whizzed past my head and hit the wall with a thud.

"Amy, are you okay?" My mother's voice was a mix of anger and concern and sadness. A stifled sob was the only response I could manage. I could not believe my mother was hearing him speak to me this way. I was mortified. I hung up the phone and then picked up the receiver again, confirmed there was a dial tone, and left it lying on its side on the battered second-hand coffee table.

The rest of that night is an empty spot in my memory, as though someone pushed the delete button and erased the entire file. All I know is that I somehow made it to the next day, when I broke down in tears, bent over the back sink at Hardee's, my tears falling on greasy dishes. Ruth, the sixty-year-old woman who was breading chicken behind me, pulled her hands out of the sticky mess and wrapped me in her arms.

Before long, I was blubbering to everyone who'd gathered around about how my husband didn't want me anymore. I kept the parts about the bruises and late-night hospital visits and police knocking on the door to myself. He may not have wanted me, but somehow this group of men and women, most of them teenagers as well, whom I'd known for just a few months, came to my rescue. All the hugs and smiles and offers to take me in fixed me up enough to finish the shift.

At 11 p.m., my heart was pounding as I drove home, thumping in time with Mindy McCready's "Ten Thousand Angels" on the radio, bolstering my confidence. I had exactly fifteen minutes to pack what I could and go. Hair dryer, curling iron, clothes, shoes, and books spilled out of the pink and green striped canvas bag my mom had bought for me a couple of years earlier. As I turned the corner into the bank parking lot, I couldn't believe I was really leaving. Shaky fingers, surely not my own, inserted a credit card into the flashing ATM slot and retrieved the last hundred dollars from the joint checking account.

By 11:07, I heard the operator ask if my mother would accept a collect call from me. For some reason, I told her where I was—on the side of a busy street in the worst part of town—and where I was headed—a stranger's house. "I'll get a flight and be there in the morning. Get in the car and lock the doors now. I love you."

Somehow I made it to Tanya's house, sat awake and alone in her and her husband's tiny, cozy living room. I managed to call work and quit over the phone, fighting back tears. I'd just received an award for employee of the month. I gathered the strength to return to the tiny apartment, to sort and pack our things. I watched as we dismantled our budding life together, turning it into a series of "Your family gave us that," or "That came from your mom."

By evening, everything was tucked into boxes, our names written neatly on the side in big black letters. I drove to the airport, blinded by tears, sobbing the entire way. When her plane landed, though, I was dry-eyed and had reassembled the walls around my heart. I thought I'd hear "I told you so." I didn't. Her arms reached out as she came near, but I bristled and pulled away. I did not want to fall apart in front of her. She looked hurt. She said nothing. We gathered her bags, and I drove us to the hotel room I'd spent the last of the money on. I fell into bed, and for the first time in days, I fell asleep, my mother's soft breathing the most reassurance I'd felt in a very long time.

The real journey began the next morning when we loaded the van and left my now ex-husband standing alone in the apartment complex parking lot. The tall, deep green trees that lined the highway filed past the windows, bidding us a solemn farewell.

When the rolling hills gave way to steep grades, my mom's knuckles strained against the steering wheel, as white as her face. "Shut the radio off," she ordered through clenched teeth. I watched the familiar set of her jaw as I twisted the radio knob, silencing Garth Brooks. I knew a meltdown was about to happen.

"Come on, John! You should be here right now! Why'd you leave me to deal with all this?" My mother's shrieking prayer to my dead father sent chills up my spine. Her face, white earlier, was now flame-red and streaked with tears.

"It's okay, Mom," I whispered.

In a gas station in Asheville, I slipped away to a pay phone and made the call. I'm not sure why, but I had to hear his voice one more time.

"Hello."

"Hey." My voice was too soft; I regretted it the instant that one word rolled off my tongue.

"What do you want?" His voice was steel.

"I... um... I was just going to let you know where we are." My fingers traced the grimy grout between the truck station's chipped tile walls.

"Why?"

"I don't know." I could feel the tears beginning to burn my eyes. "I have to go."

"I need you to sign over the title on the Toyota."

I set the receiver back on the hook.

"Who was that?" my mom asked. Her eyes met mine, and I knew we both knew.

"No one," I said, and we climbed back into the truck.

That night, laughing and crying in that Murfreesboro parking lot, we were two women who needed each other equally. It took two hours, but that moving van was in the truck parking area. It may have been crooked, but we were proud of our hard-earned accomplishment all the same.

Now, when I look back, I just have to smile. My mother never said, "I told you so." In all the years that have passed, she's never once uttered those words. Maybe because she didn't have to. Maybe because she took one look at me in the airport that night and knew that my hurt was her own. Whatever the reason, we were no longer simply mother and child. We were both women on the journey toward friendship.

~Amy F. Miller

# Tough Times for Teens

## Second Chances

# 90

# Best Days of Your Life

*Good judgment comes from experience,*
*and often experience comes from bad judgment.*
*~Rita Mae Brown*

**W**hen I roamed the halls of Triton High School, back when I'd hastily scribble out homework assignments during homeroom and sleep until noon on Saturdays, there was a single phrase that always made me cringe: "These are the best days of your life."

As a teenager, I imagined adults never left the house unless armed with this nugget of wisdom. It came from all directions. My mother, father, grandparents, aunts and uncles—even the deli guy down at Pathmark felt the need to play the sage one day as he sliced my provolone.

They could have delivered the message in Pig Latin for all I cared.

Did they really expect to convince me of this? I mean, I spent most mornings in geometry class, locked in an epic battle between gravity and my eyelids. I'd sweat through three shirts every afternoon running sprints on Coach Reilly's baseball field. I stocked away most of my evenings on the shelves at Drug Emporium, right beside neatly lined rows of mouthwash and deodorant. Life didn't seem like much of a paradise.

Furthermore, adults couldn't know how it felt to have college essays and applications pile into a mountain of guilty procrastination. They couldn't know the emptiness the first time you realized that someone who interested you greatly didn't have the same interest in you. They couldn't know the fear of being invisible — to be a nothing in an environment where status meant everything.

They could never know. Or, at the very least, they could never remember. Could they?

Something happened at the tail end of my junior year that changed my outlook on life forever. There was a baseball game. I stood at my usual post at second base, watching a base runner dangle dangerously off first. There was a bunt — a bad one — that took one hop before the pitcher scooped it up.

"Two! Two!" I called as I covered the bag. The pitcher, a bit surprised by my risky strategy, spun around haphazardly and fired a bullet that was destined for the outfield. I dove to my left and felt the ball cradle for an instant in the webbing, and then BOOM!

My bones chattered all at once as they struggled to absorb the blow, and my insides lurched violently against my spine.

"That's it," I thought as I tried to focus on the blurry images of my teammates circled above me. "My ribs are shattered."

In the waiting room, after a bumpy ride to the hospital in my dad's car, my parents filled out paperwork while I grew weaker and weaker. I had apparently timed my injury to coincide with the busiest day in medical history. One hour turned to two. Two to three — until the throbbing pain in my gut took a sinister form. I struggled to convince myself that a six-headed alien was not about to burst through my abdominal wall.

"Mr. Morelli, we can take you now," called a weary nurse. My parents wheeled me to an examining room where two more nurses took turns poking and prodding my ribs with their index fingers.

"Does this hurt?"

"No."

"This?"

"Nope."

"Well, Mr. Morelli," one of the nurses said, "it looks like your ribs are tip-top. You're free to go."

Free to go? Did she really just say that? Don't get me wrong, it's always good news to find you're in perfect health—but the pain? It didn't lie. However, the most extensive medical training I'd received up to that point involved Neosporin and a Band-Aid, so I followed doctor's orders. I struggled out of the hospital bed on wobbly feet and began the painstaking process of pulling up my pants.

That's when fate intervened. A resident, who was passing through my examining room on his way to a cup of coffee, happened to glance in my direction. Then, with eyes wide and brow wrinkled, he did a double take

"Son, get back in bed immediately," he said sternly. "Nurse! Let's get an MRI on him this instant." They wheeled me down a hallway at breakneck speed and stuffed me inside a weird, tube-like contraption, all in one motion.

When the doctor returned with the findings he said, "Mr. Morelli, you're suffering from internal bleeding due to the fact that your spleen has been severely ruptured."

"What the heck is a spleen?" I asked.

"Well," he said, "It's an organ that provides support to your circulatory system. You can live without it, much like the appendix. But we need to act fast if we want to avoid a transfusion. You've already lost a significant amount of blood. We don't have the facilities to perform a splenectomy here at the hospital. We'll have to fly you to Cooper. It's a trauma center."

As if on cue, the rapid chop-chop of a helicopter punctured the air as it descended onto the hospital roof. The nurses wheeled me outside and two paramedics quickly folded up the legs of the bed, shoved it inside the transport, and strapped me down. The ride to Cooper was a blur of sweat and clenched teeth.

Long tubes of fluorescent lighting whipped past me like the dotted lines on a highway as the paramedics wheeled me through another bustling waiting room and into the prep station for surgery. The room was lined with hospital beds, maybe six or seven wide, all occupied by patients with injuries ranging from heart attacks to gunshot wounds. For a tense moment, the heart monitor attached to the gentleman beside me bottomed-out and a medical assistant rushed over to erase the flat line.

"I'm going to die," I whispered to myself for the very first time.

And then I was briskly wheeled out of the prep room—ahead of all the others—and down a long corridor to the operating room. The surgeon lowered a bright light from the ceiling, injected something into my IV, and told me to count down from ten.

"Ten, nine, eight..."

I woke up the next morning with twenty-six staples and a jagged incision blazing a trail from my sternum to my waist. It was at that moment, with my family huddled around me and the rush of panic long removed from my body, that I had a most peculiar thought: Maybe, in their own way, the adults had been right all along. Maybe these were the best days of my life. Maybe it even went beyond that. Maybe the single best day of your life is the one you're currently living.

My road to recovery was a long and winding one indeed, but the experience itself remains indispensable. Since then, not a single day has passed that I haven't enjoyed, respected, and cherished. I'm now certain that each day we're living is a priceless collection of moments to be treasured.

~C.G. Morelli

# 91

# Angel in Disguise

*Angels can fly directly into the heart of the matter.*
*~Author Unknown*

All the details of my plan were finally ironed out. The appointment for the abortion was scheduled and keeping the entire situation a secret from my family seemed to be the less painful choice for everyone. At nineteen years old, raised with very conservative Catholic ideals, being an unwed mother meant only one thing—shame. I would be ruining my parents' lives. I'd be an embarrassment to my brothers. Everyone would know that I had had premarital sex—something I was not emotionally mature enough to share with the world.

So, the plans were set. The only glitch was that I'd have to take time off from my new job for the appointment. My mom often called me at work just to say hello. What would the office staff tell her? If they told my mom that I was at a doctor's appointment, Mom would question me, as I was still on my parents' medical insurance plan. This would only force me to add more lies to the heaping pile I had already started creating.

Laurie, the office manager at the dental office where I worked, was also the wife of the dentist. We weren't exactly close and more often than not, there was tension between us. But, Laurie was going to play a part in my plan—although it was not the role that I was expecting her to play.

My plan was to take her to lunch, confide in her, and ask her to please "cover for me." If my mom were to call the day of the appointment, Laurie could just say I stepped out for an errand. Easy as pie.

The day I took her to lunch, we took my car. As I drove I began to explain the situation to her. While my emotions were at the surface, I tried to keep things as matter-of-fact as possible. "I found out that I'm pregnant. My family would never understand the situation. I don't want to be a mother at nineteen. I made an appointment to terminate the pregnancy."

I was expecting things to go smoothly, for her to understand her role in my plan, and to simply nod and say, "Okay." That didn't happen.

Instead she asked me to pull over. After my car was stopped on the side of the road she began to tell me a story. When she was fifteen, she found out she was pregnant. She too was raised in a very conservative Catholic home, only twenty years earlier. Her parents quickly had her whisked away to another state to live in a home for unwed pregnant teenagers. It was in this place were she endured alone the stages of her pregnancy and the difficult labor, only to have the baby taken away from her and given up for adoption. Laurie was sent home to live out the rest of her high school years pretending to be a normal teenage girl. She had never forgotten that baby or the fact that she was a mother or the fact that her parents gave her no choice in her situation.

The last thing she said to me was this: "Kristin, I know your parents. I've met them. They are good people and they love you. Your parents are not my parents. They will love you unconditionally no matter what. I want you to do one thing for me—I want you to tell your parents. No matter how they react, the decision to have the abortion is still yours, but I want you to trust me and talk to them. I won't agree to your plan unless you agree to mine."

I was shocked and in tears. Tell my parents? That was my worst nightmare. I couldn't bear to see the pain in my mother's eyes or the shame on my father's face in learning their only daughter was unwed and pregnant at nineteen.

The next few days were an emotional blur as I wrestled with

the situation and tried variations on the "announcement." I prayed continuously, it seems, for the fear and shame and guilt that flooded my body to go away. I imagined this unborn child and debated the impact that either choice would have on this little being.

The day came. I remember being at my parents' house and telling Mom that I needed to talk to her. We went into her bedroom and sat on her bed. I began crying and told her that I was pregnant and about the appointment for an abortion. I don't remember exactly what I said, but I do very vividly remember the look in my mother's eyes and the first words she spoke. There was nothing but love from my mother. She hugged me and whispered in my ear, "Well, the first thing we need to do is cancel that appointment. I'm going to be a grandma!"

It took us a while to gather our emotions and then gently she said, "You need to go talk to Dad." He was in the living room watching TV in his favorite chair. I sat on the couch across from him and struggled to say, "Dad, I need to tell you something important. I found out that I'm pregnant," as tears rolled down my face. And, as I expected, I will never forget his face or the words that he said, but not for the reason I thought. He smiled with only love and said, "Do you have any idea what this is going to cost me?" He stood up, walked to the couch and just hugged me and loved me.

And with that, I was going to be a mother. I wasn't going to be another girl who had an abortion. Instead I was going to be a young mother who had the unconditional love and support of my own parents. It was going to be hard—I would have to keep working and finish college and raise a child. And it was hard. But motherhood, as all mothers know, has been full of joy, happiness, love, lessons and surprises.

My daughter, born when I was twenty years old, recently graduated from our hometown high school where even my own father graduated. I've never seen my parents more proud! She has headed off to college out of state, ready to tackle the world. We have the best relationship I could ever have asked for—we are best friends.

I have tried and tried over the years to track down Laurie but every attempt has failed. I wanted to thank her and tell her about the beautiful life that she helped bring into this world—the strong, beautiful, ambitious young woman who has filled so many lives with love and joy. She was an angel sent into my life to help steer me onto a better path.

~Kristin Goffman

# The Life Not Taken

*Here is the world.*
*Beautiful and terrible things will happen.*
*Don't be afraid.*
*~Frederick Buechner*

I stumbled over my feet as I halted in the middle of the gravel parking lot under the warm light of the moon. I had one thing on my mind: Am I far enough away? People swarmed out of the double glass doors of the gym, running, like me, in a sea of panic. My feet moved and my brain followed, across the gravel, up the stairs, and into the restaurant. Was he still back there?

They say things happen for a reason, and before that night I thought it was true. Now I'm trying to figure out, decipher in my mind, why my life was spared.

•••

I examined my Facebook chat list, hoping for a single person to be home. No luck. Mom was out of town, and there was something about sitting at home with Dad in the middle of the summer watching reruns of the Stanley Cup Playoffs that didn't sound exciting to me, so I resorted to the gym. I recalled that new class that my mom and I had tried once before, Latin Impact. I looked at my thighs and forced myself to go.

I swung open the glass doors of the gym. "Two-seven-eight-two-seven-two-two," I confirmed my number harshly as I dug through my oversized periwinkle purse for my membership tag. The gym was packed, as usual. I pulled out my *Anthem* book and read a few pages before I noticed people gathering around the door to the aerobics room. I better get over there. I took my place in the very back, perfectly angled so that I could see the instructor but wouldn't call attention to my lack of rhythm. I hugged the wall. I was clearly the youngest one in there.

A woman leaned over her "are-you-fat-or-are-you-pregnant?" belly, fiddled with the speakers and secured her microphone headset.

"Hey everyone! I didn't just go and get fat. I'm going to have a baby! This is my last class," she said with a giant smile on her face. Never mind. The air was sticky and hot and I couldn't wait for the class to begin so it could be over. Finally, we began. "Head down... touch your toes... roll your shoulders..." We snapped and popped our butts to an upbeat Spanish song as we turned in circles. I laughed at myself and shimmied off the embarrassment.

In the mirror I saw him walk in. Tall and thin, freshly shaved. His black sweatband matched the huge duffle bag that hung over his shoulder. What the hell was this guy doing here? I disregarded the creep and kept dancing; maybe he would be my glimmer of hope that I wasn't the worst one in there. My glimmer of hope didn't last long.

"Shimmy, shimmy, cha-cha-cha!" I followed Mary, the instructor's voice and footsteps when I was cut off by sudden darkness. Cool! I thought. This is a good idea for the routine! Dancing in the dark! My thoughts were naïve. Warm-ups were coming to an end when my stomach dropped to my feet and I jumped. What was that? Did the speakers blow?

POP! POP! POP! The ringing in my ears drowned out Shakira's voice. I could feel a gust of wind blow across my left shoulder and push some hair into my face. All I could hear was my heartbeat and the glass shattering. I snapped my neck to see where the commotion was coming from. The fiery sparks caught my eye first. And then there he was. Only six feet from me, he held his arms extended, weapons in hand. More pops, more fiery flashes, more broken mirrors.

When your life flashes before your eyes, do you really see your life from birth to that moment, or do you see your inner strength and your ability to persevere? Fight, flight or freeze, is there really a choice? My brain went on autopilot as I flew to the double doors, paying no attention to the man who was trying to shoot me. To some, turning your back to danger is more dangerous. For me, it was my only option and potentially saved my life.

I snuck out the back doors, trying not to catch the eye of the shooter while he single handedly wounded and killed my classmates. There was no time for emotion; I couldn't go back. My lungs had an unlimited supply of air as I sped through the main lobby. Gym-goers and fit employees stared me down as if I was losing my mind. I swung open the double glass doors for a second time that night, only with a different motive than the first. The gravel crunched under my Adidas sneakers as my legs took over and pushed me forward. I stopped. When I turned around a flock of people rushed out of the building. I'm not far enough away, I thought. I have to keep going.

Through the parking lot, weaving in and out of cars, and up the stairs, I finally came to a stop again. A younger woman who worked at the gym linked arms with me and pulled me into a full sprint. When something terrible is happening, it is amazing how people stick together, even complete strangers. Together, we busted through the doors of Peter's Place, a nearby restaurant.

"SHOOTING SHOOTING! CALL 911! LOCK THE DOORS!" I screamed. The customers were gathered around in the lobby. Why are they not freaking out? I wondered. I broke down. "I need a phone! I need to call my dad!" I said. An older waitress kindly took me by the hand to a back room, and we locked ourselves inside. I dialed my dad's number. Please answer please answer please answer.

"Daddy! There's a man! He's shooting people!" I could tell Trey, my brother, was scared when I heard him scream, "I'M PUTTING ON MY SEATBELT!" in the background. The usual ten-minute drive from my house to LA Fitness turned into a two-minute drive. Those were the longest two minutes of my life.

What if he goes through my purse and finds out where I live? What if he is in this restaurant, coming back for me? What if I don't make it out of here? I contemplated at least fifty possibilities. After what seemed like a lifetime, but was really only twelve minutes from the first shot, my dad pulled into the parking lot. I heard the sirens of ambulances arriving in the parking lot. The windows in the car were fogged with humidity, but I refused to unlock the doors or open the windows. We finally left.

We passed my driveway and continued to grandma's house. Dad called 911 in her driveway, hoping that I could get my purse back from the crime scene. Bad move. The police ordered me to go back to the building. I was horrified to find out I was one of the few women unharmed in that class.

The drive back was almost as nerve-wracking as the drive home. I focused on the sound of the radio and the sound of my heavy breathing rather than the sound of passing ambulances and additional police cruisers. News vans, cops, ambulances, and crowds of curious people blocked off the entrance to the gym. I was escorted by an officer into the building. I felt important. I'd never seen the gym so empty. I imagined it would look like a crime scene equipped with heavy layers of caution tape. I was wrong. I had to step over puddles and trails of blood that led to the aerobics room. Had I known the dead bodies—which included the shooter himself—remained there in that room, I would have never gone back.

They asked me everything about the night. Pointless questions like, "What were you wearing?" I was asked to recall everything about that night. I wasn't so thrilled to have to try and relive it. After standing there in that cemetery of a building for almost an hour waiting for everyone to be interviewed, the detectives finally released me. Once we were back at my grandma's, I waited for my mother to come home from Titusville. She was doing much worse than I. I'm glad she wasn't there with me though; things could have turned out differently. We sat there for a while in front of the television and watched the same thing over and over again—but it never got old.

A week prior, I could watch the news and hear of a mass shooting, and think, "Wow, that sucks." I never thought I would be the news. That night, and for many nights to come, I slept with my mom. Somehow, being near Mom when night falls gives me a sense of security, knowing she can protect me from the unknown dangers of the world. But, deep down, I know I can protect myself. Something bad happened to me. Someone tried to kill me. I've witnessed death. And I'm alive.

~Jordan Elizabeth Solomon

# Living and Learning

*Just because you make mistakes doesn't mean you are one.*
*~Author Unknown*

Since I was a little girl, people always told me to learn from my mistakes — my parents, my teachers, everyone who was older and wiser. Only now do I feel like I am starting to understand the concept, but it took a string of events to bring me to this point, the first of which happened when I was fourteen.

My parents got divorced. It wasn't a surprise — I felt as if we had all been waiting years for it to happen. At first I didn't feel that sad, mostly just relieved they weren't going to be married anymore. They had fallen in love young, gotten married fast and never stopped to think that maybe they were two completely different people. After they divorced, my dad disappeared, and in a way, so did my mom. She had to work all the time to take care of her five children. That was when I got sad. I felt really alone.

When I was sixteen I started dating a boy. Being with him was better than being at school, better than being at home — better than being anywhere, really. We used to stay up all night and sit in his car and listen to music and smoke cigarettes and he would tell me I was the most amazing girl he'd ever met. We would stay up till we saw the sun and I would miss school in the morning and I didn't care. Nothing mattered anymore.

I dropped out of school when I was sixteen. I didn't get to graduate with any of my friends, but at the time it didn't bother me because I felt as though they were looking down on me for my choices anyway. I ignored everyone who was concerned about me, but mostly my mom. I thought I knew everything and felt like she was trying to tell me how to live my life, so I pushed her away. I spent less and less time at home; sometimes I would be gone for days or even weeks at a time.

I left home when I was seventeen. My mom had had enough at that point and she gave me the choice to get my act together, stop disappearing and go back to school, or leave her house. I was feeling like I didn't "need" her for anything at that point. So I left.

The next two years were the toughest. I never saw my mother, and I saw my younger brothers and sisters only once every few months. Every time I saw them they looked more grown up. My brother would be taller and his voice a little deeper, and my sisters would be more mature and beautiful than I remembered. A tension began to form between my boyfriend and me. He wasn't the same person that I met and fell in love with while blowing smoke rings and watching the sunrise. But I guess I felt like I could save him, and we could do all the things we had planned and dreamed. We fought a lot and I hated the person I became when we did so.

We broke up when I was nineteen and I didn't even know him, let alone love him, anymore. I didn't know or love myself either. We had changed so much since the days of being sixteen and starry-eyed; I felt like I had changed for the worse.

I packed my life into a few duffel bags and cardboard boxes and slept on couches till I could get my own place. I spent most of my money on bills and partying. There were many times I couldn't remember coming home; it felt nice to be numb to my own feelings. Sometimes I couldn't afford food so I would buy cereal and milk with my last five dollars because I knew it would fill me up. Other times

I couldn't afford toilet paper so I would go to the convenience store down the street and hoard a huge wad of napkins.

On the odd night that I didn't go out drinking, I would stay home and cry, looking back at the years since I was fourteen. I cried for my parents, for my mom, and for leaving her when she needed me. I cried because my siblings barely knew me, but I felt like such a horrible person I wasn't sure I wanted them to know me at all. I cried that my boyfriend and I hadn't loved each other better, and for the awful things we had said to each other. I realized I had forgotten what it felt like to smile a real smile. I was empty.

It was close to my twentieth birthday when I got fed up with crying. Maybe it's because I was getting older and more mature, or maybe it's because I had literally expelled every tear of sadness and self-pity from myself. I woke up one morning and knew that I had to start putting together the pieces of my jigsaw life. I kept a journal and every day I would write down things I was grateful for and things that made me a good person. I also wrote down my biggest regrets, and all the mistakes I wanted to undo. I felt more alive than I ever had, as if the sad weight I had been carrying around since I was fourteen had been lifted.

Over the next few years I tried to right all my wrongs. For the very first time my life seemed colourful and full of promise. My mom and I rebuilt our relationship from the ground up and we are best friends again. I spent a lot of time getting to know my siblings and gaining their trust, and now I see them every week. I called my ex-boyfriend to apologize for the way things turned out and to let him know that I was happy we had that time together. I sincerely wanted to thank him for everything he taught me, because what I went through with him allowed me to better appreciate my new boyfriend, who I eventually married. I finished high school and went on to university.

By no means do I have it all figured out; I don't claim to be an expert on how to live your best life. But I am starting to know that there is nothing I can do to control what happens to me, and which of my choices turn out to be good or bad ones. This acceptance has given me peace and purpose that I never knew existed. And now I really believe that nothing is a mistake as long as you learn from it; that every tear you shed, every test you fail, every love you lose or regain—it all makes you a better and stronger person in the end.

~Josephine Cruz

# Hitting Rock Bottom

*Happiness is a form of courage.*
*~Holbrook Jackson*

"Were you trying to hurt yourself, Tracy?" My lungs constricted, my face grew hot, and I couldn't catch my breath. What had I gotten myself into? The social worker's face loomed above me, repeating her question over and over again. Her accusing eyes looked deep into my soul and it seemed as if she could read my thoughts. YES. Yes, I was trying to. Happy now?

It was six o'clock in the morning on what should have been a fun-filled half-day of school, but the reality of what I'd done to my own body the previous night was coming back to haunt me. The hospital room's walls were closing in around me as my parents exited through the curtained doors. Don't leave me with her. Bring me home. Please... it'll never happen again. I'm so sorry. I wanted to scream for them to stay, but the tears glistening in the corners of my dad's eyes silenced me.

"Hello Tracy! I'm Dr. Johnson, and I'm going to ask you a few questions," the petite, tanned women hovered over me, eyeing the scars on my wrists and the IV in my arm. I simply nodded, fearful that if I opened my mouth, I would spill all my secrets and troubles to this strange woman, who would just write them all down on that little notebook in her hand, and report that I was "crazy" to some superior officer. "Your doctor tells me that you've admitted to taking over forty Tylenols last night, and stealing some antidepressants. Is this true?" I picked a spot on the wall and focused hard, nodding my head up and down one single time. I couldn't open my mouth, I wouldn't. I refused to admit my weakness to this woman I had just met, a woman whose only goal was to gather incriminating evidence against me, so she could lock me up in the "freak ward."

"Tracy, you don't have to answer any questions you don't feel comfortable answering, but I do need you to talk to me. You almost died, sweetie. We need to figure out what happened." A small smile played at the corner of her lips, giving me the impression that she was a person I could trust. For the first time, I looked her straight in the eyes, and tears slowly began to flow from mine.

"I think... I don't really remember... I don't know." My voice was shaking and no matter how hard I tried, I couldn't find the right words to describe my innermost feelings and fears. Dr. Johnson smiled encouragingly and sat back in her chair, as if settling in for a long road trip. I took a single, steady, deep breath, searching for the words to explain myself.

"I wanted to die. I know I was trying to kill myself last night, I just... don't... remember." My throat closed around the words that had just flowed from my mouth, trying to choke them back in. "Everyone keeps asking, 'Why?' Why would I do something so drastic? And I can't answer. I don't know why I did it, I just... don't know. I'm sorry."

I saw Dr. Johnson writing ferociously on her pad of paper, a tiny hint of a smile on her face, and it was then that I knew. She wasn't there for me; she wasn't even asking these questions to help me. She was just doing her job, and by getting me to confess, she could now complete her task. "Please, don't send me to Linden Oaks. I swear... I'll never do this again. I'll be better. I promise. I'll be happy. I just want to go home. Please, don't send me there." Though I would have sworn it impossible, the tears came even faster, my whole body shaking with sobs until my eyes ran dry. "Please, please, please. Don't do this. Please. I'm sorry. I'm so sorry," I screamed at first, my voice screeching and cracking until the sound was just a whisper. I fell asleep with tears dried in lines down my face, whispering silently how very sorry I was.

The white walls of the room blinded me when my eyes fluttered open again. The sunlight was still streaming brightly through the windows, telling me I had only been asleep for a few hours. As my eyes readjusted to the daylight, I saw my parents sitting lightly on the edge of my bed, holding hands. My mother's head was buried in my dad's chest, as if she was trying to hide her tears. No matter how hard they tried to conceal their pain, it was plain to see they'd both been crying. Oh God. What had I done?

Before this point, I'd only seen my dad cry once, so I had always viewed him as the strongest man in my life, and here he was, crying over the mistakes of a little girl. Though both adults had tears in their eyes, my parents looked so peaceful in that moment that I wished I could just freeze time. Hands intertwined, comforting each other, I had never seen them look so in love. But the joy I felt in that moment was shattered the second my leg twitched and my dad glanced over, his eyes widening with surprise when he saw I was awake.

"Hi pumpkin. Feeling better?" he asked, attempting to smile. My mom straightened her back, plastering on her "happy face," though I could clearly see the pain in her eyes.

"I feel fine. Can I go home now?" I knew I sounded like a whiny five-year-old, but I couldn't help it. I missed my normal life. My parents exchanged a look, one that I knew well. It was that glance where in a split second, your parents telepathically communicate, arguing whether or not to tell you the truth, and then deciding who has to be the bearer of bad news.

"Sweetie, you're not going to be going home for a while," my mom spoke softly, refusing to make eye contact. "The doctors have decided that it's in your best interest to spend a few days at Linden Oaks. You haven't been medically cleared yet, but once that happens, you'll be transferred over there. I promise Dad and I are doing everything we can to make your stay as short as possible. I'm sorry Trace, but you have to do this." The room was silent as the reality of my situation set in.

"NO! I can't go there!" I nearly screamed, attracting the attention of every nurse on the floor. This couldn't be happening. What if my friends found out? They'd think I was some suicidal freak. Once again, tears poured out of my eyes. I pulled my knees to my chest and rocked back and forth, trying to shake the truth from my brain. I am a suicidal freak. I belong in Linden Oaks.

My mom stood up and rushed to the head of the bed, wrapping her arms around me and holding me close. We stayed like that for a while, just hugging each other, and doing our best to hold one another together.

When I finally realized that I was a fourteen-year-old sobbing into her mother's arms, I grew embarrassed, pushing her away and sitting up tall. "Can I go to the bathroom?" I asked, attempting to regain my composure and dignity. My parents and the nurse once again exchanged that telepathic look, questioning whether it was safe to leave me alone right now. "I'll be fine, Mom," I assured her. So the nurse slowly helped me up, detaching all the cords and wires hooking me up to the machines.

With my IV pole in hand, I shuffled to the bathroom, shutting the door softly behind me. Ignoring everything else in the small room, I headed straight for the mirror. Only one word can sum up the girl I saw in the reflection... lost. Her hair was ratty and knotted in a greasy bun piled on top of her head. Her eyes were rubbed red and raw from constant tears, and her mouth was turned down in a permanent frown. But it was the look in her eyes that scared me the most. She showed only one emotion... disappointment. Even if the redness around her eyes had faded and her hair had been brushed and fixed, the look in her eyes would never be erased. This was a girl who was dying inside, who had no clue who she was or what her purpose was. She looked so weak, like a single blow would turn her to dust. It took me a moment to realize that the girl looking out from the mirror was me.

In the short two minutes I spent staring at myself in the mirror, I made one of the most important promises of my life. I promised myself that I would get better. No matter what it took, no matter how long it took, and no matter how many days I had to spend in rehab, I promised myself that I would overcome the pain I felt inside. I decided I would fix this. I had finally done something that therapists had been trying to push me towards for months.

In a matter of a few hours, I had reached what seemed to be the lowest point in my life. But a few simple actions and words had turned my whole world around. I knew it wouldn't be easy, but that's the beauty of rebuilding your life. You begin with a heart that has been shattered into a million pieces, and though it seems that the parts may never fit back together again, you feel a sense of accomplishment when you come out on top. That's how life is—it hurts, plain and simple, but overcoming the pain always makes you stronger, and in the long run, you will be happy.

~Tracy Sinkhorn

# A Dance with Destiny

*We tend to forget that happiness doesn't come as a result of getting something we don't have, but rather of recognizing and appreciating what we do have.*
~Friedrich Koënig

As a typical fifteen-year-old girl, I thought I could stand to lose a few pounds. The mirror showed me a less then forgiving complexion, and I felt awkward compared to most of the long-haired, porcelain-skinned beauties who walked the halls at school with confidence and grace. I was so shy and intimidated that, when the school dance came around, I couldn't bring myself to move to the music. Rather, I stood timidly against the wall, watching miserably from the sidelines, dwelling on my imperfections.

Then, one Saturday afternoon, things changed dramatically. I was at home when someone broke a glass pitcher in the kitchen.

"Sylvie, can you take this to the garage?" my mom asked, handing me a big, black garbage bag. "But, please, be careful. There's some broken glass inside."

"Sure Mom, no problem." I shuffled my bare feet along the hallway with my arm outstretched, holding the bag away from me as I headed towards the garage door through our laundry room. To this day, I don't know exactly how it happened. I felt an excruciating pain as the bag swung against the doorframe and touched the back of my leg. A small piece of glass protruding from the garbage made contact with the back of my foot and cut me in the heel.

I fell to the ground, shocked, and yelled for help. My mom and little brother came running.

"I don't know what happened," I wailed, clasping my ankle. "My leg..."

My mom slowly removed my hand and examined the damage. I could tell by the look on her face that it was nasty, but didn't have the courage to look myself. "It's a small cut, but you probably need some stitches. I'll get your father to take you to the hospital."

They say that your entire life can change in a second, whether for better or for worse, and that day proved it. Soon, I was off to the hospital to patch up a simple one-inch cut, with no idea of the chain of events that had been set in motion.

I got the stitches that my mom had predicted and was soon back at home, but my leg hurt a lot, and I couldn't find relief from the irritating pain. Strangely, it was sore all the way up to the knee. Days went by and my mom grew tired of watching me limp to favor my wound.

"This doesn't seem right," she said. "How can a small cut still be causing you so much pain? We're going to see your doctor."

Surprisingly, even Dr. Weber, who had been my doctor since birth, was puzzled. Assuming that things had been done properly when I received the stitches, he deduced that I probably just needed more time to heal and sent me home with painkillers.

After ten days the stitches were removed, but I was still limping. The whole leg was sore when I set it down.

So back to the hospital we went, and still we came home with no answer. Frustrated, my mom took me to a different medical clinic. Three weeks and six doctors later, my leg wasn't showing signs of improving. It actually seemed to be getting worse, and the ankle was swollen and a purplish color.

"You must stop favoring your wounded leg and walk on it," was the advise I got from the final physician I visited. It was a glorious summer day, and some friends had invited me to a theme park.

"Do you think I should go?" I asked my mom, adding miserably, "I haven't gone anywhere in weeks, but my leg is bothering me!"

"Well, the doctor did say that you should start walking on it more, so maybe it won't do any harm if you get out for a bit."

I sighed and hugged her, limping to my bedroom to change.

My two girlfriends came to pick me up happily, and my spirits were finally lifted as we drove down the freeway with the breeze from the open windows blowing through my hair, but as soon as we arrived at the theme park, something happened. I put my leg down and felt an intense pain shooting up my body, falling to the ground in anguish. My friends called for help, and the next thing I knew I heard sirens and I was being whisked to a hospital emergency room where Dr. French, an orthopedic specialist, examined me.

"I think I know what might have happened here," he said, "so I am going to admit you to do some tests."

"You mean I can't go home?" I cried, delirious with pain. "I have to sleep here tonight?"

"I'm afraid so."

I spent that evening in the hospital, and then the following. My stay seemed to have no end in sight.

Although my family was with me during the days, the nights were lonely and scary. I remembered my former self, the girl I had been before the accident, and wished that I could go back in time and shake some sense into her. The girl who was always concerned with her appearance when, in reality, she wasn't all that bad. The girl who desperately wanted those five extra pounds to melt away, wished her hair was longer and silkier, and her skin just a bit clearer. How I would have given anything just to be in her shoes again—to be healthy.

My stay in the hospital was extended to three weeks, ending finally with an exploratory surgery that confirmed the specialist's fears: my Achilles tendon had been severed in the small accident and most likely was hanging by a thread until the day I went to the theme park. The brilliant doctor trusted his instincts and operated just in time, for many dangerous blood clots had formed and could have been fatal had I gone on without attention.

Because so much time had passed and no physician had realized that my tendon was cut, a small incident in the laundry room caused a year and a half of havoc. The four-hour surgery to repair the damage to my leg was only the beginning. I spent three months in a cast, another three months on crutches, followed by six months walking with a cane while I underwent physiotherapy.

As I inched though the school hallway, leaning on my cane, I watched as a group of "perfect" girls breezed past me, giggling. When I healed, I decided, not only would I walk, but I would dance... and I wouldn't ever again let fear or insecurity stand in my way.

It took a long time to get there, but I was blessed with a second chance and an eye-opening journey. The moment finally came when I could walk without a cane, and my limp eventually disappeared. All the doctors said that I was lucky, and in my heart I knew that they were right. Maybe I had been silly enough to spend the last school dance hiding, but at the next one, I was the first student to hit the dance floor!

~Sylvia Suriano-Diodati

# Drinking from the Solo Cup of Regret

*We must all suffer from one of two pains: the pain of discipline or the pain of regret. The difference is discipline weighs ounces while regret weighs tons.*

*~Jim Rohn*

"This must be it," Josh said. We were standing in front of a dimly lit stoop. Cigarette butts littered the steps and the air was dense with illegality. This stoop marked the entrance to my first college party. I was a brand new freshman enjoying my freedom.

Josh knocked on the door hesitantly. A minute passed until a boy answered the door holding one of those infamous red Solo cups. "Welcome to the party, guys!" He drunkenly laughed.

Our first college party was in a claustrophobic apartment crowded with drunken people, loud with music and laughter.

The boy tossed us each our own red cup. "Here is the keg if you want beer, and over there is the jungle juice."

I watched as Josh filled his cup with beer, tipping it to the side to reduce the amount of foam, something I would've never known to do. My new friend Mackenzie said something to me but I couldn't hear her over the commotion of the party. She grabbed my wrist and dragged me through the crowd towards the kitchen where there was a huge plastic tub filled with red liquid.

Kenzie handed me a cup and I smelled the concoction, which reeked of fruit punch and alcohol. I took a small sip. It was disgusting.

"Don't worry, Samantha," Kenzie advised me. "The more you drink the less you taste it."

Josh waved us over and introduced us to some people. Meeting new people was always awkward for me but I tried my best to keep my cool. Distracted by the party, I didn't notice that my cup kept getting refilled.

Soon I found myself laughing and yelling with the rest of the crowd. Meeting new people didn't seem so awkward anymore. Josh threw his arm around me and poured some of his drink into my cup.

"Hey Josh, Samantha!" a voice yelled behind us. It was a boy we had just met. "The party is getting so crowded. Do you want to head back to campus and drink in my room?"

"Yeah, sounds good to me," Josh said, as he grabbed my hand and pulled me through the crowd to the door.

We stepped outside to the wet sidewalk. It must have rained while we were inside. I took a step off the stoop and stumbled a bit.

"You okay?" Josh asked as I tried to straighten myself up.

I looked up at him to tell him I was fine when my vision went slightly out of focus. I held my head for a second and sat down on the curb, fending off nausea.

"She doesn't look so great," a voice said to my left. "How much did you drink, Samantha?"

"I'm fine, I'm fine," I said, more trying to convince myself than the strangers around me.

"Let's get her home," another voice said. I think it was Josh.

"Who is this mess? Must be a freshman." An unrecognizable voice laughed.

I stood up to start walking and stumbled. My head pounded. I was confused. I felt so helpless.

"She isn't going to make it home. Someone get a cab. I have..."

I blacked out.

Sometime later, I looked up to see the lights of my dorm shining just around the corner. I had no recollection of how we had gotten there.

"Almost home, Samantha."

Suddenly, a flash of red filled the dark street behind us.

"Stop where you are and step away from the girl," a deep voice barked behind us.

I felt the arms supporting me swiftly release and I found myself standing on the sidewalk alone, swaying slightly. I raised my eyes to find myself face to face with the campus police.

"How much did you have to drink tonight?"

"I'm not sure," I whimpered.

"How old are you?"

"Seventeen," I said. "Please sir, I'm all right. I live right around the corner," I begged, pointing to my building.

The officer just shook his head as he picked up his radio: "Can I have an ambulance outside of Shaw Quad?"

I felt as if someone had punched me in the stomach. I bent over and vomited in front of my new friends and the police officer.

Than I blacked out again.

I woke up sometime later, looking up a tile ceiling.

"Finally awake?" a woman asked. I started to sit up, but my head felt as if someone had taken a hammer to it.

"How's the hangover?" The woman ruthlessly laughed, obviously seeing I was in pain. "Here, drink some juice." I greedily chugged the drink. Never had apple juice tasted so great. Taking it more slowly this time, I pulled myself up and took a look at my surroundings. Men and women in scrubs, stethoscopes, IV bags. I was in the hospital. The pounding inside my head felt stronger as I realized what had happened.

"Don't worry; we didn't have to pump your stomach. All you needed was a little rest." A feeling of relief filled my body. "Still extremely dangerous, my dear. Do you realize what could have happened to you? You are lucky," the nurse scolded. "And we found your college ID card in your pocket so we looked you up and have your parents on the phone."

The feeling of relief instantly drained from my body and my stomach twisted into a knot. "What?"

"We called your parents to let them know you are here and that you are okay." The nurse held out a phone. "Your parents are waiting to talk to you." She shook the phone in front of my face as if I didn't see it the first time.

Slowly, I took the phone with my trembling hand. "Mom?" I croaked.

The silence that followed, although only a few seconds, seemed to last a lifetime. Finally, I heard my mother's quiet voice.

"Samantha."

More silence. I waited for my mother to ream me out. But that was it. My name.

"Mom?" I pleaded through the phone. My mind begged her to yell, scream, lecture me until my ears bled. But nothing.

"Mom I'm sorry, I'm sorry, I messed up, I... I..." I babbled, trying to fill the excruciating silence.

This silence, this empty phone call, was worse than anything my mother could have said. Never had I done something that had left my parents speechless.

"Samantha, why?" My mother's voice was filled with sorrow. More silence. "We'll talk later."

Dial tone.

I dropped the phone into my lap and stared blankly ahead of me.

"Samantha?" A voice snapped me back to reality. It was the nurse. "Samantha, you have been discharged from the hospital. A van is waiting outside to return you to campus."

I blinked a few times, trying to focus my mind on the present. Thanking the nurse, I numbly got up. Mustering all my strength to keep my trembling legs from buckling, I gathered my few belongings and headed towards the exit like a zombie.

"And Samantha," a voice spoke to my back, "I better never see you here again."

I stopped, and turned to face the nurse. Focusing my eyes on her, I replied firmly, "You won't."

The next day my parents and I had a long discussion on the phone, and I was eventually punished for my actions. But the worst part wasn't the fact that my parents grounded me, revoked my car, and almost withdrew me from college. It wasn't the $200 fine I had to pay my school, or the 1,000-word essay, or the alcohol classes I was required to attend, or even being on probation for my entire first semester. The memory of that night still haunts me. I made a terrible first impression on my new friends, that image of me stumbling and vomiting on the street. I learned the hard way that you can't undo your past.

But without a doubt the worst part was the worry and humiliation I caused my parents. I severely damaged the trust they had in me, something that takes years to build up but only one second to tear down. I still have a vivid memory of the silence on the phone that morning. I let them down, and I will never forget it.

~Sam Capagna

# 97

# Get Off the Bleachers

*Turn your wounds into wisdom.*
*~Oprah Winfrey*

I was soaring. Final cuts for the junior varsity basketball team at Fountain Valley High School were over and I was still around. I had a false sense of security when I strolled into practice on Monday.

My teammates and I were spread out on the court, doing our stretches. It was routine. I didn't realize how much I loved the feel of that gym floor. There was something magical in it. Maybe it's how an artist feels when his brush meets canvas.

My coach beckoned me over. He walked me to the baseline of the center court where the varsity team was practicing. He then spoke the dreaded words: "Steve, I've been thinking about it. It's hard enough to play twelve guys, so we aren't going to need a thirteenth. You can finish out today's practice if you want."

The whole varsity team had stopped practice and they were staring at me as if they could see through my veneer of toughness to the fragile boy inside who had just been crushed. "That's okay, Coach," I said, and walked out of the gym into the locker room.

I was sixteen years old and I had never felt more worthless. I was alone in the locker room. Usually it was a place of hustle and bustle, loud noises, and bad smells. Now it was empty. I stood and stared at my locker. Twenty minutes earlier I stood in the exact same place, but I was a completely different person then. If I had known it would be the last time I would get dressed for a basketball practice, I would have savored it. I would have taken forever; slowly slipping that jersey on and letting the mesh slide over my skin.

Suddenly I realized my bag was still in the gym. I didn't have the courage to go back in there, so I walked out to the track and up to the top of the bleachers. There was an hour and a half left before practice was over. I sat up there and waited it out.

When five o'clock came, I walked back to the gym. My former team was out front with a big birthday cake celebrating my former teammate's birthday. I snuck in the back door, grabbed my bag, and ran back out like a kid who knew he was somewhere he didn't belong.

As worried as I was about avoiding my former teammates, I was petrified of having to face my father. I got into the car and he asked, "How was practice?" I said, "fine," and took refuge in silence the rest of the ride home.

For the remainder of that week, I walked up to the top of those bleachers every day after school, and sat there for two hours thinking about what a loser I was. At five o'clock, I got in my dad's car, pretending I had just finished practice.

On Friday, after sitting up there for twenty minutes, I decided to get off the bleachers. I walked home, called my dad, and owned up to my failure. After all those hours sitting up there, just me and my thoughts, I decided I wasn't going to buy into someone else's narrative. I wouldn't let that coach or anyone define my worth or write my story.

I became the author of my own life and started working out every day and reading books on basketball. The next year I started coaching my younger brother's youth basketball team.

After I graduated from Fountain Valley High School, my old coach retired, and I came back as the freshman basketball coach. The next year, I was hired as the head junior varsity basketball coach. In three years, I had gone from being cut from the JV team to becoming its head coach.

When I was sixteen I had to sneak in the back door to get my bag, and now at nineteen I had the keys to the whole gym. This never would have happened if I had not decided to get off those bleachers. What I've learned is that too many people remain seated when life knocks them down. They spend the rest of their lives as spectators instead of participants. They feel safer in the crowd than on the court.

Instead of adopting a "poor me" attitude, I took on the "I'll show you" mindset. Although at the time I could not understand it, all that pain I went though prepared me to have the compassion to help others find their strength.

After a few years of coaching the JV team, I had to cut some players for the first time. Before this, I had been able to keep everyone who wanted to play, but this year we had more people who wanted to play than we had uniforms. I had to cut four people.

I tried to approach them with dignity. I let them know how much I appreciated their efforts. I informed them we were not able to offer them a jersey but they could remain part of the team as managers. Three of them declined, but one said he would accept on one condition: He wanted to be able to do all the drills every day at practice because his goal was to make the varsity team the next year.

His name is Peter Boutros. I accepted his offer and he made the varsity team his senior year. His story has inspired many people and you can read about it in *Chicken Soup for the Soul: Inside Basketball*. When the book was published, I took my basketball team up to the top of those very same bleachers, where I once sat as a distraught sixteen-year-old. As a published author and accomplished coach, I read them the story I wrote.

I am now an English teacher at FVHS and JV basketball coach at one of the top basketball programs in Orange County—Los Alamitos High School. A few years back, FVHS tore out the old gym floor and got a new one. The section of the floor where I was cut from the team now rests on the wall in my classroom. What was once the location of my defeat is now my symbol of triumph.

~Steve Schultz

# 98

# The Sport that Saved My Life

*Rowers do more before 8:00 a.m. than most people do all day.*
*~Rowing Shirt Logo*

**M**y first year of high school was rough. Everything started out fine, but by the time winter came rolling through, freezing and cloudy, I was pessimistic, moody, and sick of staring up at the gray sheet of clouds covering the sky every day.

The bullies at school also became more of a problem. It seemed like there was a new person to pick on me in every class. The worst, by far, was my math class. There was a group of at least eight girls who terrorized me every day, and the teacher let them. It got to the point where I was asking myself why I should even bother getting out of bed in the morning.

By March, it was still freezing and ugly, the bullies were still in full force, and I had a terminally ill friend in the hospital. I felt like life had lost all meaning—I had no hope for the future. I had begun to think about suicide. Over the weeks, the thoughts became stronger. I had even developed a plan for how I was going to do it, what I would say in my goodbye letter to everyone, and when I would do it. I had a timeline, and by mid-March, I only had a few weeks left. I would be done with the bullies and the stress, done with the problems of living.

One day, out of nowhere, the school's TV news team made an announcement in homeroom. I never really watched the announcements, but this one got my attention. The crew team was looking for new members. For some reason, I was intrigued. Maybe it would be fun. I kept the idea in the back of my mind until I got home that night. When I told my mom about it, she was pretty shocked. "Crew? Why would you want to do that?" she asked. I looked at the team's website. You had to pass a swim test to be on the team, and it was only a week away.

I really, really wanted to try out. However, there was one thing in the way: the cost. The price to be on the team was really expensive. But I begged and begged, and my mom agreed to let me try out. Then I realized I had another problem. How was I going to get in shape in time? It had been nearly a year since I dropped out of my dance classes, and I hadn't done a workout or anything since!

There was no time to lose. I managed to develop my own little workout plan. Every night I did push-ups and sit-ups on my bedroom floor, adding more each day as the week went on. I also started watching what I ate. I packed my lunch all week instead of just eating a bag of cookies from school. I knew it wasn't much, but I felt like it was at least something. I was determined to keep at it and make the team.

That Monday, a rainy St. Patrick's Day, I tried out for the crew team. For the swim test, you had to swim six lengths of the pool without touching the bottom, and tread water for five minutes. I remember walking out to the pool and thinking my life was going to change forever, hopefully for the better.

Somehow, even though I felt like I couldn't walk afterwards, I managed to pass the swim test. And, even better, I made the crew team! I was ecstatic. On Thursday, we boarded a bus to the murky Hudson River for our first day of practice. I had already met some people, and discovered that one of the girls from my French class was on the team also.

To be honest, my first day of practice was pretty scary. I was put into a skinny little boat and I had no idea what I was doing, not to mention it was thirty degrees out and we weren't allowed to wear gloves because we had to grip the oars. But after about two hours, I finally got the hang of it—and I loved it! From then on, my entire outlook on life changed. I made a ton of new friends, and I became much more physically fit. I went from sitting inside, bored and depressed, to being outside, enjoying myself every day of the week. I jumped out of bed every morning, knowing crew was coming after school. Most importantly, I no longer wanted to end my life. I was a new person—self-confident and happy.

After that first season, I made the varsity crew team. To this day, I think about when I heard that announcement about try-outs. If I hadn't, I might not be where I am—and who I am—today.

~Jess Forte

# 99

# Dying to Fit in

*If you don't control your mind, someone else will.*
*~John Allston*

**G**rade ten math. Somehow, between my psycho babbling teacher and trigonometry, I began to dread going to my fourth period class. Aiden was the only thing between 12:30 and 1:45 that kept me sane. He wasn't my boyfriend or anything—I didn't even think he was all that attractive to be quite frank—but he was funny. For an entire semester we bonded over music, chatted about his girlfriend Christina, and laughed every time the teacher tried to explain the concept of "independent" studying to get us to stop talking.

Aiden wasn't perfect though. He was nice, funny, and even volunteered once a week with me, but he was also a casual drug user. He was in a band and he told me once that it just came with the scene—something he did to fit in.

One particular Monday, Aiden strolled into class in a disoriented haze. As the period progressed, his stomach began to hurt, his brow began to sweat, and he started slurring his words. He explained to my teacher that he had the stomach flu that was going around my school at the time. I was the only person close enough to him to see that his pupils were dilated and his eyes were burning red. Before I left class I told Aiden he needed to go home and rest. I should have done more but I figured that this wasn't anything he hadn't done before. When I left my final class I found Christina, Aiden's girlfriend, crying against her locker. I quickly ran to embrace her and asked her what was wrong.

"Aiden was just taken to the hospital on a stretcher," she wept. "He overdosed." She exhaled the rest of the story through her sobs, explaining that Aiden had taken a drug used as a surgery sedative. He and his friends had planned to do it together, but at the last minute they decided to use Aiden as a guinea pig. Comforting Christina in the hallway that day, I made a silent oath never to take drugs. I swore to myself I would never put myself, or the people that I loved, at risk for something as juvenile as social status.

Aiden was released from the hospital a week later, and he's been sober ever since. Christina told me that if he had stayed at school for even an hour more he never would have recovered.

Aiden almost lost his life to fit in with people he thought were his friends. But to fit in with me, all he had to do was be himself.

~Kaity D'Agostino

# A Change for the Better

*People are always blaming their circumstances for what they are.*
*I don't believe in circumstances.*
*The people who get on in this world are the people who get up*
*and look for the circumstances they want,*
*and, if they can't find them, make them.*
*~George Bernard Shaw*

From an early age, I was told not to make the same mistakes as my mother. She hadn't had an easy life since getting pregnant with me at seventeen, and she always blamed me for her failures. Unable to care for me, my grandparents took me in at six weeks of age and raised me as their daughter. I excelled in school and took pleasure in being on the track team, part of Camp Fire and attending ballet classes. I had a great relationship with my grandparents. Then, in eighth grade, I discovered that staying out late with my friends was more fun than going home.

Losing interest in my activities and school, I skipped a lot of class with a group of friends. My grades started to suffer, and I was suspended for truancy and being disrespectful to the teachers. I became addicted to drugs and constantly ran away to attend parties. I dressed all in black and had a horrible attitude. I began to spiral out of control.

My lowest point came when I was at a friend's house one after-noon. They brought out a shotgun and told me to get up. I laughed and told them to shoot me. They pulled the trigger—miraculously, it wasn't loaded. I shrugged it off and went home. After a few months of this destructive behavior, my grandparents just couldn't watch me destroy myself anymore. My life was going nowhere good, and the worst part was that I didn't care at all.

After fourteen years of avoiding responsibility, my mother decided to swoop in and "cure me." She saw me becoming like her, and couldn't watch me go down that path any longer. She brought me to a rehabilitation center to be detoxed. The hospital was scary and I didn't like it there. I tried to run away, but the doors were locked and I got caught. The staff mistook the cuts on my arms as suicide attempts and put me on medication that made me crazy. I cried every night, and wondered how I had gotten to this place. I felt guilty about hurting my grandparents and I desperately wanted to go home to them.

After about a month, I met with a therapist who ran a treatment center for girls. She said I was a good candidate for their program, but I had to prove to them that I would follow their rules. I wrote a letter promising I would do everything they told me—at that point, any place would have been better than the rehab center! I thought it was going to be a place where I could manipulate everyone and get sent home quickly, but I would soon be proved wrong.

I was transferred to the treatment center in the middle of a nice suburban neighborhood. There were counselors on staff to help you change your self-destructive behavior, and we were asked to go to school and perform community service. It was not what I was expecting.

My therapist had said that the center was not like the hospital. The doors were not locked, and I was free to leave at any time, but if I did, I would not be welcome back. She said that the counselors were there to help me, but it was up to me to make the final decision to change. I realized I didn't like what I saw in the mirror anymore, and I knew I needed to stop letting my family down. So I decided to change.

I began to focus on my schoolwork again and really take part in my therapy sessions. I started to thrive, and even joined the track team again. I developed good relationships with the other girls who lived there. We did a lot of fun activities and field trips and I learned to enjoy myself again without substances. During my stay there, I even began to restore my relationship with my mother and grandparents. A lot of this was because of my therapist. She was an amazing woman, and she helped me figure out a lot of my issues and heal some of the hurt I had inflicted on my family and myself. She showed me that if I really wanted to succeed, I could.

After graduating the program, I moved in with my mother. This was not good for either of us. We were very similar in both good and bad ways, and we argued over everything. Our relationship hadn't fully healed, and her continued drug use didn't help matters. She was emotionally and verbally abusive, and continued to blame me for ruining her life. I didn't want to stay there and become depressed, so I packed my duffel bag and ran away. After two months of hiding at friends' houses, my mother threatened to have my grandparents arrested for kidnapping. Since I cared about my grandparents and knew it wasn't true, I turned myself in and was put in a juvenile detention facility. The social workers decided where to place me, and I was very adamant that I would not go back to my mother. She missed two court dates, and I was released to my grandparents until I turned eighteen, as long as I didn't skip school or resort to drug use. I stayed out of trouble and did well in school again. I received an award for "Turnaround Student of the Year." I became a person they could count on again.

Graduating high school, I decided to attend veterinary nursing school. I married young, to the love of my life, and purchased a house—all before I turned twenty-five. I was able to accomplish all of the things that my mother had dreamed of for herself and for me. She was proud of me, even though our relationship still wasn't great. In fact, she started to turn her life around too, and even began a job she really loved. Unfortunately, she died before she turned forty—her demons finally got the best of her.

When my mother died, I was angry with her. She had worked so hard to make me turn my life around, but she hadn't saved herself. Over time, I realized that I am grateful to her for putting me in that treatment center, because I might have met the same fate as her—or worse—one day. If she were alive today, instead of being angry, I would thank her for saving my life.

I know that there are many teenagers out there in similar or worse situations than I was in. If I could tell them one thing, it would be that if you believe in yourself, you can succeed. You can always change for the better. I'm proof that it can be done.

~Megan Waterman-Fouch

# Someone's Watching Over Me

*Nothing is a waste of time if you use the experience wisely.*
~Auguste Rodin

I've always been a 110 percent, full out, go big or go home kind of guy. In high school, I was the leader of my little clique, and we mostly did what I wanted—which happened to be partying most of the time. I'd do just about anything to get a buzz.

I was pretty into drugs for a while. Alcohol was always a staple, amplified by strong alcoholism on my biological father's side, and traces of the disease on my mom's. My first issues with alcohol came the first month of ninth grade. I chugged a twenty-ounce bottle of vodka during my first time drinking. I passed out, and my cousin called my mom, who was looking for me because I wasn't answering my phone. She found me, not breathing and a pale shade of blue. She said a simple "Please God..." and I rolled over and puked.

You'd think that would have caught my attention, but I'm much more hardheaded than that.

My first year out of high school, I was headed to a party on a Friday night in June. My mind was heavy and foggy because I didn't want to go to college, and I didn't know how to tell my parents I wanted to join the Marines because I felt like I was out of options. Instead, my friends and I were throwing an open house party at some kid's house whose parents were out of town. After winning who knows how many games of beer pong, with another beer in hand and a lot of drugs in my system, I blacked out around 2 a.m. According to my friends, all that liquid courage made me want to go home and talk to my parents about joining the Marines. No matter what they did, they couldn't stop me from getting in my car and driving off.

Halfway home, I wrecked. I was thrown through the sunroof because I thought seatbelts were highly overrated, and I was nineteen and invincible anyway. I landed on my head after being ejected, cracking my occipital bone, which happens to be the body's hardest. My Ford Escape — ironic, right? — flipped six times and stopped, no joke, eight inches from my body. One more flip and I would have been under it. Here's where you have to start thinking that someone was looking out for me for some reason bigger than I could understand.

I crashed in front of a gas station, the only place open on that street for two or three miles either way. An EMT who had just finished her shift and was on her way home saw my wreck from the opposite lane. She got out to take care of me while the gas station cashier called 911 and prayed until the ambulance arrived. I was responsive, sort of, until I arrived at the hospital, where I fell into a coma. They ran tests and told my parents that with the damage I had, including intense cranial pressure from my brain bleeding, I'd be extremely lucky to make it through the night. And if I did, I'd need months of rehab because the brunt of my brain trauma affected the parts of my brain that controlled my inhibitions, motor skills, short-term memory, and my sight.

With seemingly every machine in the hospital hooked up to me, including two catheters (one to my brain, the other the normal kind), I looked like my life was done — game over, man. When I woke up for the first time, after three days in a coma, I had no vision. I still don't remember this part, but I'm told I freaked out when I realized I couldn't see, and I was forcibly put back into a coma. The next day, I woke up without sight and was put back to sleep, but in the evening

I woke up, looked at my mom, and told her she was wearing a blue shirt before passing out again. I could see.

The catheter in my head was eventually removed, along with the neck brace, but I was still in bad shape. I tried to feed myself on day five, my first very foggy memory after the wreck, but unless my mouth was on the side of my head, that idea was out. Yeah—say goodbye, motor skills. On day six I regained my motor skills enough that I could shovel Jell-O into my mouth, but that was about it, and the doctors still didn't think I'd regain everything.

Early morning day seven, around 4 a.m., I woke up, looked at my mom who was asleep on the couch in my room, and told her I was hungry. I grabbed my tree of my IVs, tubes, and catheter bag, and set off to the cafeteria like nothing had happened. I hadn't been able to keep any food down the past six days, and I needed food right then.

I don't think I need to say that my doctors and mom were in awe. I seemed like nothing had ever happened. After some final cleanup of the glass and asphalt in my back (there's still some in there), I walked out on my own the afternoon of the seventh day. Even the doctors said it had to be a "God thing."

After all that, I walked out of the hospital with some scars, a new hole in my head, some ADD, and a new respect and belief that there is something bigger out there. I figure that's a decent trade-off, and an important lesson learned. In the passenger seat on the way home from the hospital, the first words I said were, "I think I had alone time with God. I had to make a choice between myself, and believing and following Him." Do I need to tell you what my decision was?

Three months after being discharged, I ran my first 5K, took third in my age group, and have been hooked ever since. That love, and healthy addiction, led to competing in triathlons. A little over three years from the wreck, I've raced in sixteen triathlons, numerous running events, and I've bagged ten podium finishes. Only two years after that first 5K, I competed in a full iron distance triathlon in North Carolina.

I've used this new ability as a way to share my story of His glory and power. I've learned a lot since then, but most importantly that God kept me here for something more than myself. I'm not invincible. I've learned to be humble, and that not many people are as lucky and blessed as I have been.

~Joshua Stephens

# Meet Our
# Contributors

**Brianna Abbott** is a happy-go-lucky girl who loves her friends and family with all her heart. She plans to continue writing for the rest of her life.

**Latira Anderson** was sixteen when she met Kevin. Now nineteen, she plans to become a child-life specialist so she may help other families live with medical conditions. Latira sings, dances, and plays the harp. She wants to say thanks to all who have stuck by her when life got hard. E-mail her at latiraanderson@gmail.com.

**Bailey Baer** is a teenager who spends most of her time with her nose in a book. She loves to write and this is her first published story. E-mail her at Baileyspazztic@yahoo.com.

**Jessica Ball** is a senior in high school. She loves to write, as well as play tennis, race soap box derby, and read. She plans to one day be an animator at Disney and a published author. E-mail her at ballmj@live.com.

**Jill Barry** attended UC Santa Cruz and Université Stendhal in Grenoble France. She taught English to adults in France and now works for the magazine *Zoptrope: All-Story*. Jill writes screenplays and short stories and would like to visit every country in the world. E-mail her at sjillbarry@gmail.com.

**Angela Bell** is a home-school graduate, living in South Texas. She is a member of the American Christian Fiction Writers and was a 2010 Genesis Finalist. Angela's passion is fiction writing, and she is pursuing the publication of her novels. Please check out her blog for teens at www.chosen129.blogspot.com.

**Valerie D. Benko** is a freelance writer who resides in western Pennsylvania. She attended Slippery Rock University where she minored in creative writing and obtained a bachelor's degree in communications. She is a frequent contributor to Chicken Soup for the Soul and other anthologies. Visit her online at http://valeriebenko. weebly.com.

**Kierra Burda's** hobbies include cheerleading, reading, and camping. Kierra loves spending time with her friends and found poetry as a way to express her emotions after the death of her friend, Dakota. She hopes to become a teacher when she grows up.

**Laura Campbell** received her bachelor of arts degree from Shepherd University this past December with a major in psychology and a minor in English. In her free time Laura enjoys exercising and freelance writing. E-mail her at Lcampb05@shepherd.edu.

**Sam Capagna** is a sophomore at Northeastern University majoring in international business. She enjoys writing in her free time.

**Shellique Carby** was born in Durban, South Africa. She earned a BA in journalism and anthropology from Rhodes University. She does freelance editing and talks about autism for teachers. Her interests include language, politics, religion, singing, dancing, modeling, conservation, the outdoors, exercise, photography, and working with animals or children.

**Megan Carey** is currently a sophomore in high school. She hopes to attend Penn State to study either pre-med or pre-law. Megan spends most of her time swimming and playing soccer with her friends. She hopes to keep Jamie's spirit alive by continuing to help others through the foundation established in his name.

**Sarah Catherine** will graduate high school in 2014. She plans to attend college and major in psychology. Sarah enjoys playing softball, acting, writing, and being with friends. E-mail her at scatherine96@gmail.com.

**Christine Catlin** is a teenager. Besides being a triplet, she has survived hypothermia and recovered from an eating disorder, and has also traveled to countries around the world. When not writing she plays sports, reads, and enjoys all life has to offer. E-mail her at thompson1news@yahoo.com.

**Rebecca Cattaneo-Harris** has since moved to Florida to restart her life, in a place where no one knows her past. She is happily married, has a loving family, and continues to miss her brother every day.

**Saige Falyn Cavayero** is a graphic design major in the S.I. Newhouse School of Public Communications at Syracuse University. Saige also serves as the youngest board member for the Vascular Birthmarks Foundation as their student representative. E-mail her at sfcavaye@gmail.com.

**Aaron Chan**, born and raised in Vancouver, realized he was a true artist at heart when he began taking piano lessons at the age of five-ish. A graduate of Vancouver Film School, Aaron is a writer, musician, and filmmaker. He also likes cats and cheesecake. E-mail Aaron at evil_ice_dragon@hotmail.com.

**May Nou Chang** is a Hmong-American writer and a mom of three girls.

Both she and her husband are educators. E-mail her at maynouchang@hotmail.com or visit her blog at http://reallifemusings.blogspot.com.

**Jennifer Lynn Clay**, twenty-two, has been published over eighty times in national and international magazines and in several world-wide-distributed books including *House Blessings* and *Forever in Love*. Her work has appeared in six other *Chicken Soup for the Soul* anthologies. Three of her young-adult novels are under publishers' consideration.

**Alexandra Cooper's** biggest passion in life is animal rights. She works for a non-profit organization called Last Chance for Animals, which helps put an end to animal abuse in all different forms. She dedicates her story to Laura, France, Susan, Samantha, Boyd, Aram and Chris DeRose.

**Emma Copeland** is a high school student. Her interests include books, animals, and art. In the future, she plans to attend college and possibly major in English.

**Josephine Cruz** is a student at Mount Royal University working towards a bachelor of arts degree in English. She enjoys reading, writing, music and spending time with her family, husband and cats. She would like to thank her instructor Karen and classmates in ENGL 2207 for their support and encouragement.

**Kharmisha Cummings** is a potential-filled teenage high school student with ambition to be a lawyer and psychologist. She spends her free time reading, writing, and with her son. She plans to write many more stories in the future.

**Kaity D'Agostino** is currently studying the dramatic arts at Cawthra Park and hopes to pursue a career in journalism or acting. She has a passion for dance, music, and literature. As a member of Me to We youth mobilizers, Kaity is an active volunteer devoted to bettering her global and local community.

**Denise A. Dewald** has been writing for the Christian market for over twenty-five years. She enjoys interacting with her family, camping, needlework, traveling and reading. She has written one young-adult novel and a book of her memoirs. E-mail her at denise_a_dewald@ yahoo.com.

**Ann Dolensky** is a wife, mom and volunteer. She's currently attempting to write her first teen novel.

**Nayantara Dutta** is currently a junior in high school. She loves to sing, write, read, watch movies and listen to music. E-mail her at nayantaradutta@hotmail.com.

**Kate Edwin** is currently working towards her PhD in anthropology. She lectures part-time and spends her free time as a volunteer dog walker at a nearby animal shelter.

**Kristen Elias** is a senior in high school. She actively participates in her school's newspaper as a reporter and photographer while maintaining an "A" average. She is also a member of many clubs and organizations. Kristen plans to attend college in the fall and major in journalism. E-mail her atjjsea12@yahoo.com.

**Makaila Fenwick** lives in the little town of Willis in the big state of Texas where she and her husband Chris are raising their two-year-old daughter. Makaila volunteers in youth ministry at their church and loves it.

**Kirstin Fitzgerald** is a nursing student at NEMCC and plans on continuing her education at the University of Southern Mississippi. She plans to become a flight nurse. She enjoys color guard, spending time with her son, and being with friends and family. E-mail her at kfitzge109@tigers.nemcc.edu.

**Jess Forte** is a high school student who has enjoyed writing since she was seven years old. She hopes to become an author who will leave an impact on the world. Her greatest writing interests are poetry and science fiction. Jess also enjoys spending time with her friends and family.

**Jessie M. Garneau** is a high school junior who enjoys writing and music. She spends most of her time dancing and with friends. Through ups and downs, Jessie's friends have been her inspiration for most of her writing pieces. She hopes to continue a writing career throughout high school and the remainder of her life.

**AC Gaughen** is the author of *Scarlet*, her debut young-adult novel coming out February 14, 2012, from Bloomsbury/Walker. You can find her on the web at www.acgaughen.com and on Twitter as @acgaughen.

**Kristin Goffman** earned her bachelor of arts degree in psychology in 1996, while also being a young mother. She works as a consultant in national drowning prevention work. As a singer/songwriter, the majority of work she writes is set to music. E-mail her at kristin.goffman@roadrunner.com.

**Christi Grewohl** is a student in California who loves to read and write. She aspires to become a teacher and one day publish a collection of her own short stories. Christi enjoys going to church, being with friends, and going to concerts. E-mail Christi at clgrewohl@adelphia.net.

**Alyssa Guthrie** received her degree in education from Sam Houston State University, where she graduated summa cum laude in 2009. She teaches fifth grade science in southeast Texas and loves spending time with her family and friends. Alyssa's interests include reading, drawing, and shopping. E-mail her at awg003@gmail.com.

**Janessa Harris-Boom** is sixteen years old and involved in community theatre and drama club. She plans on attending an art conservatory and then starting her career as an actor, writer, director and owner of a production company. She wants to open an art high school. She wishes to thank her wonderful family and friends for all their support!

**Laura Hemphill** is a young recovering cutter who lives in the greater DC area. Martial arts is her passion and she currently teaches karate at her local karate school. E-mail her at laura.hemphill@yahoo.com.

**Paula Perkins Hoffman** is currently working on her bachelor's degree in secondary language arts education at Anderson University. She has been an Army wife for almost eight months now, but she feels like it's been longer. She hopes to one day pursue a master's degree in educational psychology.

**Ava Hope** is a high school student who loves to travel and have fun with her friends. She's inspired by writing, and hopes to someday become a child psychologist.

**Brianna J.** began writing short stories when she was six years old. She loves to read, write, and listen to music in her spare time.

**Kate Jackson** is a high school student. When Kate isn't with friends or studying, she enjoys sewing, writing, photography, swimming, baking and acting. She hopes to pursue a career in history or film after school.

**Delayne Jo** will graduate in 2012. Aside from her family, music inspires her to do many things in life. She also loves to sing. She plans to touch as many hearts as she can, and share the story of kindness and love.

**Louise Johnstone** received a bachelor of education degree in 1995 and a post-graduate diploma of arts degree in creative writing in 2011. She is a freelance writer from Adelaide, Australia who loves traveling and adventures. She desires to write children's books and biographies.

**Kendyl Kearly** is seventeen years old. She is editor-in-chief of her high school newspaper and plans to study journalism and creative writing in college. E-mail her at kendylkearly@gmail.com.

**Matthew Lang** writes behind a desk, on trams and sometimes backstage at amateur theatre productions. Matthew is suspected of frequenting libraries and loitering in bookstores: his therapists believe he may be plotting literature. Learn more at www.matthew-lang.com and on twitter @mattlangwrites.

**Ali Lauro** is a fifteen-year-old high school sophomore. She has previously been published in *Chicken Soup for the Soul: Just for Preteens.* She loves writing, reading, knitting, and doing artwork. She wants to continue writing for the rest of her life and one day hopes to publish a book.

**Hannah Leadley** is looking forward to starting the English Literature and Creative Writing program at the University of Windsor. She has aspirations to become a successful author, and anticipates a career in writing. She spends her free time running cross-country, working out, and writing poetry. E-mail her at hannah.leadley@hotmail.com.

**Eve Legato** somehow managed to get through high school relatively unscathed. She studied writing and storytelling in college and now works for a children's publishing house.

**Dylan Liebhart** has struggled with depression, addiction, self-injury and suicide, although he has now recovered. He enjoys writing, producing movies and video production/editing. He is currently a film student. To Write Love On Her Arms (www.twloha.com) is a non-profit organization dedicated to helping people fight depression, addiction, self-injury and suicide.

**Emily Ann Marasco** is a graduate student in electrical engineering at the University of Calgary. In her time outside of the lab, she enjoys playing her oboe, reading, and belly dancing. This is her second Chicken Soup for the Soul publication, and she is working on a novel. Visit her website at emilyannmarasco.wordpress.com.

**Kristen Marrs** is currently a student at the University of Maryland, and self-proclaimed geek. She loves science fiction and fantasy and aspires to have her own series published in the near future. E-mail her at Semisilver@gmail.com—even if you just want to talk about awesome science fiction stuff!

**Anna Martin** is a high school student. She enjoys writing as a way to express her thoughts and feelings. In addition to writing, Anna is very active as a member of the swim team and National Honor Society. Anna appreciates the support of her loving family.

**Jordan Mata** lives in Youngstown, OH. Her niece and nephew inspired her to become a kindergarten teacher. Her friends describe her as always bubbly and happy-go-lucky. Jordan enjoys reading, writing and playing with her niece and nephew.

**Jessica McCallum** is currently studying for her bachelor of arts degree in graphic design at Vancouver Island University. She is an artist and enjoys spending time with family and friends. Jessica plans to continue writing both fiction and nonfiction throughout her schooling. E-mail her at dark whispers_244@hotmail.com.

**Gina McGalliard** is a freelance journalist based in San Diego, CA. She graduated from the University of California, San Diego in 2008 with a degree in political science/international relations and a minor in literature/writing. Her work has appeared in numerous national, online and local publications.

Considering herself a thirty-year-old know-it-nothing, **Ryan Rae McLean** has spent every single day of her life learning and absorbing light and love from those around her. A car accident created an unforeseen alternate future nearly half of her life ago. To learn more about Ryan's journey, please visit www.ryanistryin.blogspot.com.

**Lisa Meadows** is a social worker and outdoor education instructor in Pennsylvania. She enjoys hiking, biking, and spending time with her wonderful husband and dogs. She enjoys writing short stories and keeping a nature journal. E-mail her at laddiethecollie@gmail.com.

**Lisa Millar** is currently a freshman. Lisa enjoys writing, singing, and spending time with her family. She plans to continue on to college and finish a novel.

**Amy F. Miller** received her BA and BSEd degree in English from Missouri Western State University, and is currently completing her MSEd degree in literacy at the University of Missouri. Amy teaches high school English in Northwest Missouri, where she lives with her husband and three children. E-mail her at afmiller4451@gmail.com.

**Gabrielle Miller** graduated from high school in 2010, and spends most of her time with her horse, friends, working, reading or writing. She hopes to soon attend school to become a psychologist, nurse or interior designer.

**Jonah Miller** was born with the name Liza and is a transgender youth.

Jonah is just like any other teenager—enjoying using the computer, hanging out with friends, and listening to music.

**C.G. Morelli's** work has appeared or is forthcoming in *Philadelphia Stories*, *Highlights for Children*, *Chicken Soup for the Soul* books, *Monkey Puzzle* magazine, *Jersey Devil Press*, *The Ranfurly Review*, *House of Horror* and *Ghostlight* magazine. He is the author of a short story collection titled *In the Pen* (2007).

**Abby Moriarty** is a high school student. She understands the effects of sexual assault and would like to encourage others to get help. She enjoys fencing and horseback riding and would like to study international business. E-mail her at nttratswen@gmail.com.

**Schuyler Newberg** is a sophomore in college. She loves yoga, traveling, and writing. She hopes to be an inspirational speaker one day.

**Rachel Nolan** is pursuing a bachelor of arts degree in photography at Taylor University. Above all else, she loves her family, her friends and her wonderful boyfriend. In her free time she enjoys reading juvenile fiction, writing in her journal and playing Chopin on the piano.

**Allyson O'Donnell** is a student at Indiana University. She enjoys writing, reading, cooking and blogging. She owes all her strength and inspiration to her wonderful family and friends.

**Stephanie Pabst** is thankful to have the opportunity to share this moment of her life with the world. She began writing in seventh grade and is now enrolled in college, majoring in creative writing. This is her first published piece, and she hopes to be a known author someday.

**Monica Petruzzelli** is a junior in high school. She plans to pursue a liberal arts degree and to join the Peace Corps after college. Check out her guitar performances at www.youtube.com/monicapetruzzelli.

**Isaac Preiss** is a high school student. He has identified as transgender for four years. He enjoys filmmaking and watching documentaries. He is an avid transgender rights activist, advocating for transgender teens through video-blogs on his YouTube channel, GLBTQcommunity. He hopes to study philosophy, and become a bioethicist.

**Katherine Randall-Mallinson** graduated from high school in 2011. Writing is her passion and she took the opportunity to share that with Chicken Soup for the Soul readers as well as trying to pass along a very important message. She plans to publish her own book in the future.

**Alandra Kent Rasheed** served in the United States Army Reserve for nine years. She lives in Bremen, GA, with her husband Karim and son Karim Jr. In her spare time she enjoys reading, writing, cooking, listening to music, dancing, and watching movies. E-mail her at alandrakent@yahoo.com.

**Giselle Renarde** is a queer Canadian, avid volunteer, and donut devourer. She is a prolific author of fiction for adults and holds an honours degree from the University of Toronto. Giselle loves a geek girl and lives across from a park with two bilingual cats that sleep on her head.

**Jamie Rinehart** is married and has two amazing children, a boy and a girl. She received her bachelor's degree from the University of North Texas. Jamie loves teaching English at Aledo High School. In addition, she enjoys reading, writing, traveling and spending time with her family. She aspires to write a novel someday.

**Amy Rolfs** is forty-two years old and lives in Bloomington, IL. She is a graphic artist and works at St. Patrick Church of Merna. Amy enjoys spending time with her two Labs: Shanti and Payton. She enjoys writing short stories about the many people who have touched her life. E-mail her at tkcareofu@comcast.net.

**Courtney Rusk** is an English teacher in Central Louisiana. She is married with two children. She loves traveling, reading, and spending time with family and friends. She is a firm believer in her faith. She plans to write youth fiction one day. E-mail her at courtleerusk@yahoo.com.

**Janine Russell** is currently a business student at the University of Manitoba. She loves music, especially playing piano and saxophone. She also enjoys soccer, running, and playing sports. E-mail her at janine.russell@hotmail.com.

**Sarah Sawicki** is a student at Taylor University studying professional writing. She has written for *Guideposts* books, *Church Libraries Magazine*, and the *Christian Communicator*. Her hobbies include music, horseback riding, and traveling. She aims to write memoirs and theological/philosophical exhortations of modern issues.

**Steve Schultz** teaches English at Fountain Valley High School and is the head JV men's basketball coach at Los Alamitos High School. Steve had two stories published in *Chicken Soup for the Soul: Inside Basketball* and writes a monthly column for *Fountain Valley Living* magazine. E-mail him at personalbest22@gmail.com.

**Meaghan D. Scott** received her bachelor of science degree in elementary education at Ball State University of Indiana in 2010. She is considering a master's degree in school counseling. She plans to publish a book of poems she has written over the years.

**Alessandra Shurina** graduated from high school in 2011. She now attends Florida State University and is pursuing a degree in legal studies. Alessandra is an enthusiastic vegetarian and feminist who hopes to go on to improve the rights of both women and animals.

**Tracy Sinkhorn** is a high school student and will graduate in 2012. She hopes to attend business school following graduation. She enjoys volleyball, swimming, spending time with her friends, cooking and traveling.

**Carissa Smith** is a high school junior. She loves music, art, and writing. She is learning to play guitar and she writes lyrics. Her major interests are listening to heavy metal music and improving her photography skills. In the future she would like to be a journalist.

**Jordan Solomon** is a junior in high school. She would like to pursue a career in medicine, and is hoping to be accepted to an Ivy League school. She enjoys writing, traveling, music, and spending time with close friends and family.

**SS's** main passions could best be described as: reading, writing, travel, and Jack Kerouac. She would like to express her eternal gratitude to her parents, family, friends, and also to her grade twelve Writer's Craft class for supporting (and proofreading!) her various writing endeavours.

**Diane Stark** is a wife, mother of five, and freelance writer. She loves to write about the important things in life: her family and her faith. E-mail her at DianeStark19@yahoo.com.

**Rae Starr** is a homeschool student. Her passions are God, children, rescue animals, the outdoors/wildlife, and writing. She hopes to work with rescue animals (especially horses), children in need, and write full-time. She often says, "I may be the writer, but God is the author." E-mail her at notesofhope@live.com.

**Joshua Stephens** is a college student, writer, endurance coach, and triathlete working toward racing professionally. Joshua was born and raised in Atlanta, GA. He is currently taking advantage of the second chance God has given him by sharing his story, and living without regret. E-mail him at joshuastephens88@me.com.

**Allison Sulouff** is a freshman at Illinois State University and is studying bilingual elementary education.

**Sylvia Suriano-Diodati** is a piano instructor, composer and writer in Toronto. She enjoys pursuing creativity and spending time with her husband and energetic two-year-old daughter and loving every second of her journey! Sylvia believes in destiny and is spiritually driven. E-mail her at Sylvia__Suriano@Sympatico.ca.

**Lauren Thoma** is a student at the College of Saint Benedict, working towards a degree in English and eventually wants to teach high school English. Her interest in writing fiction and poetry has been spurred by periodic publishing. Lauren is grateful to have such wonderful support in all she does.

**Diana Torres** is a high school student. Her goal is to someday become a movie producer and write one of the greatest scripts. She enjoys writing, drawing, playing her violin and taking long walks. One of her greatest achievements is knowing that her parents are proud of her. She plans to attend a four-year university.

**Rachel Vachon** is a professional writing major at Taylor University, where she is on staff for her campus newspaper *The Echo*. Her freelance articles have appeared in such publications as *The Aboite Independent*, *Church Libraries*, and *Christian Book Previews*. She also writes for *Vista*, a publication of Wesleyan Publishing House.

**Julia Valentine** grew up in the south Seattle area. She has always had a passion for writing. She lives and works in south Seattle where she attends Seattle Central Community College and studies dance.

**Melanie Vandenbark** currently studies nursing and Spanish as a student at Brigham Young University. She enjoys traveling, reading, playing music, spending summer afternoons by the pool and being with her family. E-mail her at melvandenbark@gmail.com.

**Rachel Walters** is a high school student. She loves writing and hopes to use it in the future. She also enjoys being a part of her school's color guard, singing, orchestra and reading.

**Megan Waterman-Fouch** has always been inspired to be an author. She has written many short stories as a hobby. The *Chicken Soup for the Soul* series has always been a comfort to her during her youth, and it is a great honor to see her work in this publication.

**Chelsey Wright** was born and raised in Florida and moved to Alabama at the age of thirteen with her family. For a long time, they lived in the valley but didn't know the people whom they now love. It is the best community/family they have ever been a part of. The one good thing that came out of the storm was bringing them closer together.

**Amanda Yancey** endured two major spinal surgeries while in high school, yet still managed to graduate with a 3.64 GPA. She is a sophomore in college majoring in creative writing and is currently working on getting her young-adult novel published. E-mail her at amanda.c.yancey@gmail.com.

# Meet Our
# Authors

**Jack Canfield** is the co-creator of the *Chicken Soup for the Soul* series, which *Time* magazine has called "the publishing phenomenon of the decade." Jack is also the co-author of many other bestselling books.

Jack is the CEO of the Canfield Training Group in Santa Barbara, California, and founder of the Foundation for Self-Esteem in Culver City, California. He has conducted intensive personal and professional development seminars on the principles of success for more than a million people in twenty-three countries, has spoken to hundreds of thousands of people at more than 1,000 corporations, universities, professional conferences and conventions, and has been seen by millions more on national television shows.

Jack has received many awards and honors, including three honorary doctorates and a Guinness World Records Certificate for having seven books from the *Chicken Soup for the Soul* series appearing on the New York Times bestseller list on May 24, 1998.

You can reach Jack at www.jackcanfield.com.

**Mark Victor Hansen** is the co-founder of Chicken Soup for the Soul, along with Jack Canfield. He is a sought-after keynote speaker, bestselling author, and marketing maven. Mark's powerful messages of possibility, opportunity, and action have created powerful change in thousands of organizations and millions of individuals worldwide.

Mark is a prolific writer with many bestselling books in addition to the *Chicken Soup for the Soul* series. Mark has had a profound influence in the field of human potential through his library of audios, videos, and articles in the areas of big thinking, sales achievement, wealth building, publishing success, and personal and professional development. He is also the founder of the MEGA Seminar Series.

Mark has received numerous awards that honor his entrepreneurial spirit, philanthropic heart, and business acumen. He is a lifetime member of the Horatio Alger Association of Distinguished Americans.

You can reach Mark at www.markvictorhansen.com.

**Amy Newmark** is Chicken Soup for the Soul's publisher and editor-in-chief, after a thirty-year career as a writer, speaker, financial analyst, and business executive in the worlds of finance and telecommunications. Amy is a *magna cum laude* graduate of Harvard College, where she majored in Portuguese, minored in French, and traveled extensively. She and her husband have four grown children.

After a long career writing books on telecommunications, voluminous financial reports, business plans, and corporate press releases, Chicken Soup for the Soul is a breath of fresh air for Amy. She has fallen in love with Chicken Soup for the Soul and its life-changing books, and really enjoys putting these books together for Chicken Soup's wonderful readers. She has co-authored more than three dozen *Chicken Soup for the Soul* books and has edited another three dozen.

You can reach Amy with any questions or comments through the webmaster@chickensoupforthesoul.com.

And meet editor **Madeline Clapps**, who lives in Brooklyn, NY, and is a writer, editor, and proofreader for Chicken Soup for the Soul. She has worked on many books, but most recently she was an editor for *Chicken Soup for the Soul: Just for Preteens*, *Chicken Soup for the Soul: Just for Teenagers* and this book, *Chicken Soup for the Soul: Tough Times for Teens*. Madeline also designs *The Inner Circle*, the Chicken Soup for the Soul communiqué for contributors.

She graduated from NYU in 2010 with a double major in vocal performance and journalism, and is now pursuing a career as an actor and singer. She is a founding member of Libra Theater Company, where she also serves as Communications Director. Madeline spends her free time exploring Brooklyn, playing *Scrabble*, exercising, and eating good food. She loves being a part of the Chicken Soup for the Soul family!

You can reach Madeline with any questions or comments through the webmaster@chickensoupforthesoul.com.

# Thank You

**W**e owe huge thanks to all of our contributors. We know that you poured your hearts and souls into the thousands of stories and poems that you shared with us, and ultimately with each other. We appreciate your willingness to open up your lives to other Chicken Soup for the Soul readers and share your own experiences as teens, which we know is both an exciting and a challenging time in your life. We loved your stories and they brought back our own memories of those years.

We could only publish a small percentage of the stories that were submitted, but we read every single one and even the ones that do not appear in the book had an influence on us and on the final manuscript. Our editor Madeline Clapps, who was a teen herself just a few years ago, read every submission to this book and put together the manuscript with great care and a real understanding of the kinds of stories that would be most helpful and inspirational for our readers. Our assistant publisher, D'ette Corona, worked with all the contributors and their parents as kindly and competently as always, obtaining their approvals for our edits and the quotations we carefully chose to begin each story. Senior editor Barbara LoMonaco and editor Kristiana Glavin performed their normal masterful proofreading and made sure the book went to the printer on time.

We also owe a very special thanks to our creative director and book producer, Brian Taylor at Pneuma Books, for his brilliant vision for our covers and interiors.

# Improving Your
# Life Every Day

**R**eal people sharing real stories—for eighteen years. Now, Chicken Soup for the Soul has gone beyond the bookstore to become a world leader in life improvement. Through books, movies, DVDs, online resources and other partnerships, we bring hope, courage, inspiration and love to hundreds of millions of people around the world. Chicken Soup for the Soul's writers and readers belong to a one-of-a-kind global community, sharing advice, support, guidance, comfort, and knowledge.

Chicken Soup for the Soul stories have been translated into more than forty languages and can be found in more than one hundred countries. Every day, millions of people experience a Chicken Soup for the Soul story in a book, magazine, newspaper or online. As we share our life experiences through these stories, we offer hope, comfort and inspiration to one another. The stories travel from person to person, and from country to country, helping to improve lives everywhere.

# Share with Us

We all have had Chicken Soup for the Soul moments in our lives. If you would like to share your story or poem with millions of people around the world, go to chickensoup.com and click on "Submit Your Story." You may be able to help another reader, and become a published author at the same time. Some of our past contributors have launched writing and speaking careers from the publication of their stories in our books!

Our submission volume has been increasing steadily—the quality and quantity of your submissions has been fabulous. We only accept story submissions via our website. They are no longer accepted via mail or fax.

To contact us regarding other matters, please send us an e-mail through webmaster@chickensoupforthesoul.com, or fax or write us at:

Chicken Soup for the Soul
P.O. Box 700
Cos Cob, CT 06807-0700
Fax: 203-861-7194

One more note from your friends at Chicken Soup for the Soul: Occasionally, we receive an unsolicited book manuscript from one of our readers, and we would like to respectfully inform you that we do not accept unsolicited manuscripts and we must discard the ones that appear.

Teenage years are tough, but this book will help teens as they journey through the ups and downs of adolescence. *Chicken Soup for the Soul: Just for Teenagers* provides support and inspiration for teenagers as they grow up, reminding them they are not alone, as they read stories from teens just like themselves about the problems and issues they face every day. The stories in this book serve as a guide on topics from the daily pressures of life and school to love, friendships, parents, and much more. This collection will encourage, inspire, and amuse teens, showing that, as tough as things can get, they are not alone!

978-1-935096-72-6

# More for Teens

Chicken Soup for the Soul

www.chickensoup.com

*ML · 2-12*